UNGOD

UNGOD

HUMANITY'S GLORIOUS STRUGGLE
WITH HELL OVER THE IMAGE OF GOD

Barry W. Mahler

EQUIP PRESS

Colorado Springs

First Edition: 2022
Ungod: Humanity's Glorious Struggle with Hell Over the Image of God / Barry W. Mahler
Paperback ISBN: 978-1-951304-98-0
eBook ISBN: 978-1-951304-99-7

DEFEND THIS IMAGE!

Barry

In the beginning God created man in His image.
Ever since then, the Enemy has been trying to remake us
in his own.

PROLOGUE

Darkness is on the march and is moving virtually unhindered across the face of Earth. If not thwarted, this Darkness will soon envelope our fair planet, and our generation may very well have the sad distinction of being the generation that lost Earth to the tentacles of Hell.

There is but one way to defeat Darkness, and that is to battle it with the timeless truths of God's Word, since every good, every great and every beneficial idea for humanity has its genesis in the principles of Scripture. Ignoring such principles is something we therefore do to our peril, and embracing such principles is something we do to our blessing. It is time to embrace them without hesitation or apology.

And so the book that is before you has been written with two primary purposes in mind. The first is that of exposing the hideousness and reality of the Darkness so prevalent upon Earth. Secondly, it has been written so that we may know how to defeat this Darkness on all levels by championing the ideas of Scripture in our lives, families, societies, cultures and nations.

However, I must warn that what follows is not for the faint of heart, for it is war we are contemplating here. Darkness believes in its cause, is playing for keeps and does not second-guess itself. It is therefore serious business to challenge Hell, and I would have you know that it's not without cost to enter the fray, for Darkness does not give ground without bloodletting.

I nevertheless give a hearty welcome to every brave Image Bearer (Genesis 1:26,27) who will join the ranks of Light in order to challenge the dominance of Evil in our world. There may yet come a day when all that is good and noble and fair will become extinct upon Earth, but we who are born of Heaven's seed (1 John 3:9) must see to it that it is not this day.

May God richly bless, reward and protect you as you embark on this journey.

Barry Mahler

TABLE OF CONTENTS

THE IMAGE WAR: HUMAN GOVERNMENT 227

V-DAY 291

BOOT CAMP

Boot Camp

A CALL TO ARMS

A long time ago in a galaxy far, far away (at least it seems so now), I was teaching a Bible study when an interesting phrase escaped my lips:

In the beginning God created man in His image.
Ever since then, the Enemy has been trying to remake us in his own.

The study I was teaching had me in the midst of lamenting the tremendous and rapid decline of the northern Kingdom of Israel in the Book of First Kings, since that nation had gone from being a lighthouse nation for Heaven to one plunged into near total pagan darkness in the span of a generation, and it had seemed to happen more rapidly than was possible.

I thought it was a simple enough phrase when I spoke it, but it soon grabbed my attention like no other ever had, burrowing its way into my soul so that I couldn't escape it no matter how hard I tried. And as I began contemplating the idea of this phrase, a clearer description of the battle between good and evil than I had thought possible began to emerge, leading me on a years-long journey of discovery through Scripture. This journey ultimately resulted in the following chapters of this book, which detail the great clash between Heaven and Hell over the issue of humanity, and is what I define as the *Image War*.

But before we proceed to the battle lines, we must go through Basic Training, which for us is simply the definition of three ideas that will enable us to arrive in hostile territory equipped for the fight. These ideas are the *image of God*, the *genesis of evil*, and the *sinful human nature*, each of which we shall now briefly study. But please don't be afraid of such scary-sounding theological terms, for they are simple ideas that are easy to understand and which will most naturally define themselves more fully as the chapters unfold.

The Image of God

An image is a representation of an original, and a photograph is an excellent example of this. Apart from my memories of her, for several years now I have had only photographs to remind me of Sasha, my first dog. In these photographs I can see images of her, and seeing her image reminds me of her and tells me about her. But the real test is what the images in the photographs would tell a stranger about her.

A stranger would see that she was large and wolf-like in appearance, and that her thick, nearly white coat would keep her warm in even the coldest conditions. It would be noted that she was strong and deep-chested – suited more to feats of strength than to speed. Her eyes would seem intelligent, quiet and calm, and her close proximity to her master would speak of her sense of loyalty and protection. After such a study of my photographs, the stranger would have a fairly accurate understanding of my beloved former pet.

In this same way humanity is a reflection of God – what I refer to as the Divine Image or the Divine Reflection – and a deep study of the human being will therefore tell us marvelous and wonderful things about our Creator (and vice versa). For nowhere is the image of God as focused, as concentrated and as glorious as it is in humanity (Genesis 1:26,27), effectively making us an advertisement for the very nature of God. It is the glory of this concept in humanity that we shall have the privilege of studying in the following pages.

The Genesis of Evil

At the end of the second chapter of Genesis, evil did not exist. By the beginning of the third chapter of Genesis, however, we see evidence that evil did exist, from which we learn two important things. The first is that evil is real, and the second is that it had a beginning. From a comparison of Genesis 3, Isaiah 14:12-15, Ezekiel 28:12-17 and Revelation 12:9 we are able to surmise that evil was represented in Eden through a powerful yet fallen angelic being inhabiting the body of a beautiful serpent, and that humanity had its first contact with evil there.

This fallen angelic being (a mighty former cherub) was originally good, but became evil through the choice of his willing arrogance. Once known as Lucifer (meaning Morning Star – perhaps due to his brilliance and beauty), he led a rebellion against Heaven in which he was followed by fully one-third of his angelic comrades. These rebels were defeated and then cast down to Earth, where to this day they have existed as fallen angels, demons or unclean spirits (depending upon your preference of terms).

What precisely started the change in Lucifer we aren't told, but the timing of the introduction of evil between the second and third chapters of Genesis (coinciding with the creation of humanity) seems to me most telling, and so I will now offer my thoughts as to how it may have unfolded, for it seems a reasonable enough explanation to me.

We know that angels are created beings whom God brought into existence very early during the week of Creation, since they shouted for joy at the later formation of Earth (Job 38:7). We also know that all angels are ministering spirits sent to serve those who inherit salvation (Hebrews 1:14), which means that though created prior to humanity, the angels were meant to be the servants of humanity. After some thought, Lucifer the Beautiful and Magnificent apparently decided that he wouldn't serve what he considered to be lesser beings, and so changed from good to evil.

All of Creation was originally proclaimed by God to be very good (Genesis 1:31), and since Lucifer was part of Creation, this means that he was originally good. When he became evil (Ezekiel 28:15; Isaiah 14:13,14), it therefore represented a wholesale change to his nature, for good was no longer found in him. This gives us the best and most important definition of evil available – it is simply the absence of good. Evil is not the opposite of good, and good and evil are not co-equal and co-eternal competitors. Instead, just as darkness is technically the absence of light, and cold is technically the absence of heat, so evil is the absence of good.

This also tells us that evil originally only had the potential to exist, and that this potential existed within beings that were capable of choice. These beings were capable of choice because they were beings capable of love, and love requires a choice in order to be valid. For instance, if humanity had no choice but to love God, God could simply pull a string and we would say *I love You, God*. As funny as this thought is, we understand that such a state of affairs would be considered nothing more than computer programming, and in no way would resemble anything approaching the idea of love as we know it.

For the angels, this ability to love was summarized in their ability to choose to obey God by serving humanity, or to choose to disobey God by refusing to serve humanity. To willingly disobey God – who is good – therefore meant divorcing themselves completely from Him, and so from all that is good. Since nature abhors a vacuum, evil fills the void left by the absence of good, and in this way evil was born into a universe where it had once only been a potential that existed in holy created beings (angels) who were capable of love.

Regarding the nature of evil, just as it did at its birth (Ezekiel 14:13,14), it must forever war until all that is of God (all that is good) ceases to exist in the universe. For although it is true that it is not the opposite of good, evil is still the absolute enemy of it, and the Apostle Paul described evil as yeast that would work its way through the entire batch of dough (1 Corinthians 5:6; Galatians 5:9). This means that evil will not (and cannot) rest until all that is good ceases to exist, and it will never tire or capitulate until this is accomplished. And where evil is successful in replacing or polluting the Divine Image in humanity, it will give rise to Hell's counter-image in us, which is the Dark Image.

But before we move on, I must take the time to introduce the reader to my personal term of reference to the fallen Lucifer, who is referred to in Scripture by many names, including Satan (the Accuser) and the Devil. Since evil is the absence of good (or the "un" of good), and God is good, I find it helpful to refer to our ancient enemy as the "un" of God, or simply as the ungod, for I believe it accurately represents him and his mission of evil – whose embodiment he is and always will be.

THE SINFUL HUMAN NATURE

Prior to the Fall (where the first human beings fell from perfection in the Garden of Eden), Adam and Eve were still perfect and good. As the embodiment of evil, the ungod therefore had to set himself about the process of their corruption, and his success is detailed for us in the third chapter of Genesis. What is remarkable about the Fall, though, is that the change in humanity when it fell was apparently not as severe or potentially final as the angelic fall had been, for the fall from perfection had left the fallen angels entirely evil, whereas the fall from perfection left humanity only infected by evil (though greatly changed by it).

Unfortunately, however, the change it brought was one of death and decay. God had told Adam that on the day that he disobeyed God he would surely die (Genesis 2:17), yet after the eating of the forbidden fruit Adam lived to see nine hundred and thirty years (Genesis 5:5). Since God neither does nor cannot lie, this means that the death that Adam and Eve experienced on that day was not immediate physical death, but was rather an immediate internal death, or spiritual death. Since God is life – and death is the absence of life – this meant that the First Couple (Adam and Eve) experienced complete spiritual separation from God, the outward significance of which was demonstrated by their consequent expulsion from Eden, an act that represented physical separation from the presence of God.

This internal death is referred to in the New Testament as the sinful nature or the flesh (Romans 7-8), and is also commonly referred to as the fallen nature or simply as human nature. However it is phrased, though, it is born of the nature of the ungod and is corrupted and evil, and is the unfortunate birthright of all of Adam's descendants (Romans 5:12), making a proper understanding of it essential to reasonable human existence upon Earth.

Whereas humanity was originally only capable of holy conduct, it now became natural for the absence of holy conduct (which is sinful conduct) to be the norm for humanity under the new ownership of the sinful nature. This new norm is horribly indicted by God in Genesis 6:5, where we are told that the LORD saw how great man's wickedness on the earth had become, and that every inclination of the thoughts of his heart was only evil all the time. And lest we fall into the trap of thinking that humanity is perfectible, a similar indictment was delivered thousands of years later, and may be found in Romans 1:18-32. I highly recommend taking a look.

Regarding how best to understand this issue, I prefer to think of it through the idea of language. Humanity's original native language was that of holiness; its native language had now become that of wickedness, and everything humanity would do and touch from that point on would naturally tend toward the corruption of evil. Much as with a native tongue, humanity would now instinctively think with the language of wickedness as though it were as natural as breathing (for in fact it had become precisely that).

This doesn't mean that we're incapable of good; it simply means that doing good is no longer natural for us. As most of us know, this is most clearly demonstrated through the great task of parenthood, for all children are essentially born as sociopaths requiring to be forced into learning appropriate behavior. To do good – or to exert holy conduct – is something that is unnatural to the human being, but it is possible. And it remains possible because although we are greatly tainted by evil, the flame of the image of God still burns in our breasts and is not fully overcome. This makes us beings who are still capable of speaking the language of holiness, despite the opposition to do so from our now-native language of sin.

Additionally, this remaining imprint of the Divine Image means that all is not lost for us, and that we are redeemable by Heaven. In light of this wonderful truth, the great story of Redemption begins in the Fall's immediate aftermath (Genesis 3:15), is carried to its height at the Cross and the empty Grave, and is finished in Revelation 21:1.

That's the good news. The bad news is that humanity's sinful nature will never stop or sleep until we are destroyed or all that was once good in the universe is overcome. Apart from the sovereign and overruling hand of Heaven (which we are not promised until the twentieth chapter of

Revelation), the only hope for staying the hegemony of evil upon Earth is therefore the intentional human pursuit of the image of God, to which we now turn ourselves in earnest.

* * * * * *

Now that our terms are well enough understood to frame participation in the great Clash of Ages, let us gird ourselves for war, as the battle is already afoot. Turn this page solemnly and resolutely, for it is the portal to the Image War, where the Dark Image of Hell vies through all things toward the elimination of the Divine Image in humanity, and the shores there already run red with blood. You may fire at will.

THE IMAGE WAR:
THE INDIVIDUAL

BATTLEFIELD: GREATNESS

Great is the LORD and most worthy of praise;
his greatness no one can fathom
Psalm 145:3

When considering the infinite attributes of the image of God, it is a daunting thing to know where to begin a study of them. Bearing this in mind, I have chosen to begin with a study of the idea of *greatness*, for God's greatness is an idea as simple as it is majestic, and lends itself perfectly to the foundation of understanding the Image War. Since greatness is intrinsic to the nature of God, no study of God would be true or appropriate without it, and therefore neither would be any study of those who have the privilege of bearing His magnificent image. So let us join the fray by turning to the Scriptures and to our ability to reason.

THE ORIGINAL IMAGE

God is great. His excellence and His majesty in all things are not just the themes of Scripture, of our hymns and songs of worship, or of our prayers, but they are the themes which drive our very understanding of God. By definition, God is (and must be) great in His person (Psalm 145:3) and great in all of His works (Job 38-41). Creation was a thing of greatness; humanity a thing of greatness; the establishment of Israel and the Law a thing of greatness; and Redemption a thing of greatness. God can do nothing apart from greatness, for it is His very fingerprint.

Creation was stamped with this amazing and Divine fingerprint, and humanity was Creation's masterpiece and crowning achievement. As evidence of this I offer the testimony of Scripture, which tells us that the angels were created to serve humanity (Hebrews 1:14); the universe was created to mark seasons and days and years upon the earth (Genesis 1:14), to give light on the earth (Genesis 1:14-18) and to teach humanity

---

(Psalm 19:1); and the earth was created as a home to humanity and was subject to human rule and stewardship (Genesis 1:26-28).

As this masterpiece and crowning achievement, humanity bore the Divine stamp of greatness like no other component of Creation ever could or would (including the angels), for humanity uniquely bore the image of God (Genesis 1:26,27). Greatness was therefore the natural birthright of Adam and Eve, and they would have intrinsically known greatness in relationship with God, greatness in physical form and beauty, greatness in thought, greatness in language and speech, greatness in love and relationship, greatness in marriage and family, and greatness in their stewardship of Earth. In all things would greatness have been as natural to them as breathing.

THE IMAGE UNDONE

To the undoing of this greatness the ungod had to naturally employ his energies, for Evil cannot rest until all that is Good has been eliminated. And here we come to a point of such tremendous importance that the Image War cannot be understood apart from it: As the ungod is the absence of all that is God, and as Evil is the absence of all that is Good, so too is the Dark Image (the ungod's image in humanity) the absence of the image of God. The Dark Image is not the *opposite* of the Divine Image; it is its *complete absence*. While it is true that these ideas do oppose one another in the Image War, they are not opposites, for all that is of the Light has eternally existed within the nature of God, while all that is of Darkness began at a specific point in time (Ezekiel 28:15) and represents merely the undoing of what previously existed.

It is in light of this understanding that we shall take up study of the Dark Image's answer to the facet of greatness within the Divine Image, for its reply shall be the absence of greatness, which is *mediocrity*. Our first field of battle, where the Divine and Dark Images trade blow after severe blow with one another, is therefore the battle between the greatness of the Divine Image and the mediocrity of the Dark Image. And since mediocrity was originally foreign to the First Couple, to make mediocrity even possible for humanity the ungod needed to engineer the Fall, which severed humanity from God and introduced humanity to its new native language of wicked conduct. Once accomplished, the Dark Image had arrived in principle; it would now advance degree by degree.

CAN'T BE BOTHERED

The ungod's greatest weapon in the struggle to mold humanity into the mediocrity of the Dark Image is the sinful nature's natural bent toward apathy and laziness, which are things foreign to God. If one does not care at all for something, or is not driven with purpose regarding something, or cannot be bothered with something, it is impossible to accomplish anything of note or merit regarding that something. And since it takes focused and caring effort to accomplish something of note or merit, apathy and laziness will result in the accomplishment of nothing of note or merit. This is mediocrity in its purest form.

When apathy and laziness are limited to a small portion of one's life, they result in mediocrity in that portion of one's life, such as David's apparent nonchalance in the raising of his children (2 Samuel 13:1-13; 15:1-6). When apathy and laziness are systemic to one's life, an entire life can be relegated to complete meaninglessness (Proverbs 24:30-34; Isaiah 22:13), which is the natural end result of pure mediocrity. Though it is doubtful that there are many people who actually aspire to living truly mediocre lives, the sad truth is that a great many lives are indeed noted for mediocrity, as it is the path of least resistance for the sinful nature.

One need not look hard or long to find lives devoid of greatness, or devoid even of the pursuit or attempt at greatness. Such individuals are mired in apathy and are mediocre workers, mediocre spouses, mediocre parents, mediocre thinkers, mediocre friends, mediocre neighbors, or mediocre sons and daughters. Such people seem resigned to live bland, purposeless lives, with their only claim to greatness being their ability to handle the television remote or to surf the internet. Yet the majority of such people would undoubtedly recoil at the thought of the following epitaph on their tombstone:

Here Lies John Doe
Mediocre Husband, Father, Friend, Worker and Human Being
He Cared For Nothing

Why then are so many lives mired in mediocrity? It is simply because the natural apathy and laziness of the fallen nature are easily influenced into dominance by the ungod, thereby advancing his Dark Image in humanity.

I DID IT MY WAY

Try as he might, though, the ungod cannot extinguish the spark of greatness within humanity, for the Divine Image in us is not removed but only stained, and this spark is a spark of ferocious strength. Wherever we look we therefore still see evidence of the Divine fingerprint: great parents, great children, great teachers, great athletes, great warriors, great leaders, great architecture and great feats of engineering and technology, to name but a few. And where these pursuits of greatness are driven by a purpose fueled with Scriptural thought, the Divine Image is advanced, lifting the human condition out of the cesspool created by Hell's Dark Image.

Such an advance of the Divine Image is simply unacceptable to the Enemy, and so with such non-apathetic people he must use a different approach than that used with those previously discussed, and that new approach is to pollute the very motivation for greatness. Initially, all the greatness intrinsic to humanity was in lockstep with the idea of holiness, and holiness springs from purity of motivation in the same way that wickedness springs from impurity of motivation (Matthew 15:18-20). By staining the motivation for greatness in a person, the ungod is thereby able to render the act of greatness itself stained, and since greatness stained by Evil is great no longer, the ungod has succeeded in turning greatness into mediocrity. What is Good cannot be established by the pursuit of Evil.

For example, an athlete may spend decades training in his sport to achieve greatness. If he does so merely for fame or money or personal glory, though he may climb to his sport's highest pinnacle of greatness, he has succeeded only in achieving mediocrity. It is a fantastic mediocrity, to be sure, but it is mediocrity nonetheless. However, should he achieve the same heights out of a motivation to bring glory to the Creator of the human body's ability and magnificence, he will then indeed have found true greatness.

This stained greatness, so often sought and achieved for seemingly noble human reasons, is the most prevalent form of mediocrity upon Earth. Here the Image Bearer unwittingly clothes himself in the ungod's dark mantle, for he has allowed his motivation to be stained. When purpose and effort are not directed Heavenward they are directed Hell-ward, for that is the only other direction possible. And Hell-ward purpose, no matter the outcome, results in the advance of the Dark Image. *He who is not with me is against me* (Matthew 12:30).

EXCELLENT SIN

Finally, we must discuss the idea of achieving greatness in wicked pursuits, for it represents the fullness of the mediocrity of the Dark Image. There are among us those who excel at things dark and evil; some excel at running drug cartels, some excel at heading gangs or criminal enterprises, some excel at aborting babies, some excel at fomenting terror, and some excel at producing and marketing pornography.

This is Sodom and Gomorrah revisited, and such apparent greatness represents the blackness of Hell itself, for it is excelling at overtly sinful behavior. All those who dedicate themselves to such pursuits are (despite their success) avowed and open enemies of Heaven and of the Divine Image. They are thus Hell's disciples – dutiful foot soldiers who openly and willingly follow their Dark Master in his quest to extinguish the Light. It also represents the ungod's perfect idea of greatness, for it is human purpose and effort bent solely upon wicked enterprise.

THE BELIEVER'S OFFENSIVE

I have until now left the idea of greatness somewhat vaguely defined, for I wanted us to see God's definition of it in its proper place, and here is the best place to do so. At the baptism of Jesus, a voice from heaven said to Him: *You are my Son, whom I love; with you I am well pleased* (Mark 1:11). And later in His ministry, when three of the disciples were with Jesus on the Mount of Transfiguration, Jesus was transformed before them into a greater display of His rightful glory there, with Moses and Elijah appearing with Him.

When the disciples (especially Peter) seemed overawed at the presence of the Lawgiver and the Prophet, the Father appropriately redirected their awe when He spoke from the cloud: *This is my Son, whom I love; with him I am well pleased. Listen to him!* (Matthew 17:5). Now, we must give Moses and Elijah their due, for they were both remarkable (even great) men in service of the Living God. But they literally and figuratively paled in the presence of Jesus. God – who is greatness personified – is pleased with greatness; He was (and is) pleased only with His Son.

Jesus, as God in human form (Hebrews 1:3; Colossians 2:9), is also greatness in human form and, from the Father's perspective, the only form of greatness possible for us. The Father (who does not change) was pleased then only with the Son, and He is now pleased only with the Son. His being pleased with us is therefore solely dependent upon our being like His Son. Our greatness, then, can only be in the form of our being transformed into Christ's likeness, something done only through our submission to the work and power of the Holy Spirit in us.

There is an unmatched beauty and greatness to the person, nature and character of Jesus, and our call to greatness is therefore summarized in the mirroring of His glorious image (2 Corinthians 3:18). We are to work steadfastly and obediently with the Holy Spirit in this transformation of our characters and lives into those bearing the image of Christ. We must love Him and pursue Him more passionately and doggedly than anything else in life, and we must never relent or give ground. For as we pursue Him and as His image is molded in us, His greatness in us will become the internal spring from which all human pursuit (both the inward and the outward) will be nobly and beautifully enabled, elevating the human condition toward all that is dignified and excellent, and the fingerprint of God will be seen upon Earth as possibly never before.

But to be like Christ carries with it the need to understand Him, and He (as the Living Word of John 1:1) is defined fully only in the pages of the written Word of God. He is far more than this world understands or defines Him to be, and so we must no longer allow this fallen world to define Him and His image. Let Scripture alone be our guide, and not the shifting and whimsical thinking of fallen humanity.

BATTLEFIELD: THE HUMAN BODY

Do you not know that your body is a temple of the Holy Spirit,
who is in you...therefore honor God with your body
1 Corinthians 6:19a, 20b

From the idea and study of greatness we now move quite naturally into a study of the human body, for it is the finest and greatest and most magnificent thing in all of Creation. Here the Divine Image finds its apex in the physical universe, and nowhere else will we see or find such an obvious advertisement of the existence and nature of God, for it is the expression of God in physical form.

God is spirit, of course, and therefore has no physical form (John 4:24). But had He physical form, that form would be naturally and wonderfully human, since He created the human body to represent His attributes in the physical universe (Genesis 1:26,27). A largely overlooked lesson of the Incarnation and Resurrection is that not only is the Son at home in human form, but He will bear human form for all of eternity (Hebrews 8:1,2; Acts 1:11; 7:56). It is unlikely that God would willingly dwell forever in a form that was not conducive to the expression of His nature.

THE ORIGINAL IMAGE

In all of Creation there is nothing more beautiful, able, expressive, graceful, lordly and wonderful than is the human form. The human body is capable of greater athletic endeavor by far than any animal, and is able to walk, skip, leap, swim, catch, throw, kick, slide and run with singular beauty. The human hand alone is unmatched for its ability and dexterity, and in artistry the human body knows no equal in its ability to sing and to dance. No vocal chords can match the human ability for language and sound, and no form is as capable of expression as is the human face and body.

The human form is lordly and noble in that it stands and walks upright in its natural state, making it unique in bearing, dignity and beauty. The human body is naturally upright because the Being in whose image it was formed is upright and holy in His character. It is noble in appearance because He is noble in nature, and it is expressive because He is an expressive and emotional Being. To all who would see, the human form would forever speak of the attributes of the Living God.

THE IMAGE UNDONE

Of course, one of those who would see is the ungod, and he could not and would not let such a constant reminder of his hated Creator go unchecked. Toward the remaking of the human body into a form that reflected his dark nature he would therefore set himself with a vengeance until all that was noble, dignified and beautiful in its appearance was gone.

The most obvious answer to what from Hell's perspective would be considered a plague of advertisement for the nature of God would be the physical extermination of the human form (complete destruction of human life upon Earth). As a former cherub, the ungod is undoubtedly a being powerful enough to accomplish such a feat, but we are shown in the first two chapters of the Book of Job that he and his minions are kept on a short leash in this regard by the Almighty.

This short leash effectively means that Satan is not allowed to overpower humanity, but is instead relegated largely to suggestion, coercion and temptation when dealing with us – something at which he has proven only too adept. And while the above passage in Job indicates that the ungod has some rather formidable abilities regarding nature, it should be borne in mind that he has no actual creative ability, for true creation occurs when something is brought into existence from nothing – an act solely reserved for God. But the ungod does have the capacity to remake or reform what has already been created, and it is only natural for him to turn these energies loose upon the much-hated human form.

DECADENT

It is regarding the laws of physics that we shall begin our discussion of Hell's movement of the human form toward the Dark Image. All of Creation originally existed in a state of perpetual perfection, for it was *very good* (Genesis 1:31). Now, however, Creation exists under the bondage of decay (Romans 8:21), which in the field of physics is known as the Laws of Thermodynamics, or simply as the Decay Laws or the Entropy Laws. Though the titles may sound a bit disconcerting, the idea is a simple one that everyone inherently understands: *Everything gets worse with time.*

The intervening event between the perpetual perfection of original Creation and the current state of decaying affairs was the Fall. Adam and Eve were lords of Creation, and all of it was subject to them, reaching from Eden to the ends of the universe. When they fell from perfection, so too did the universe created for them, thus beginning the inevitable slide from perfect order to absolute chaos.

These new Laws therefore represent the absence of the Law of Perpetual Perfection (which was God's), and so belong heart and soul to our great Enemy, who is their author and originator. Under these dark Laws all of Creation decays toward complete chaos and death, where all order and life shall eventually be lost. Not a single ounce of further effort by the ungod will ever be required to bring this decay to fruition, for decay is now a process on autopilot – the yeast is working its way through the whole batch of dough. It can be stopped now only by the sovereign and overruling hand of God.

As a part of physical Creation, the human genome is no exception to these Laws, and several millennia and scores of generations now find us but a sickly, weak, diseased, homely, small and short-lived facsimile of that once physically perfect, glorious and most noble First Couple, and we grow sadly weaker with every succeeding generation. The greatness that once was physical humanity is no longer even a memory, but something about which we may only ponder with a sense of gravity and loss.

Yet this slow, inevitable and passive decay of time is not nearly enough for the ungod. He must also by his very nature hasten the decline of the noble human form by all *active* means possible. By him, therefore, no manner of remaking or reforming is overlooked, and no manner of remaking or reforming is not pursued relentlessly. He will not and cannot stop until he sees humanity physically bear his image in its fullness.

FASHIONABLE GENES

It is quite likely that one of the ungod's favorite methods of actively hastening the decline of the human form is through genetic tinkering, by which he is able to further destroy the ideal of perfect health that humanity knew in the Garden. Not only had humanity been genetically perfect then, but they had also been perfect in health, for there is no lack or weakness within the nature of God, in whose image they had been created. Good and robust health, then, is a thing hated by the Enemy, and something which he must see replaced by its absence, which is *illness*. While the Decay Laws themselves will eventually nullify all good health, we cannot expect the ungod to simply sit on the sidelines and watch time take its inevitable course, for his hatred runs too deeply for that. Always expect your enemy to act like your enemy.

Since we know that the ungod is able to affect nature (Job 1), we should not be surprised that he has the ability to affect genetics apart from (and in addition to) the natural workings of the Decay Laws, for genetics are part of nature. While I want to be careful in how I present this argument, it seems obvious from Scripture that just such a thing has happened in humanity's past, and is in no way out of keeping with the nature of our Enemy. In Genesis 6:4 we are introduced to the *Nephilim*, which were a race of extremely violent giants described as the offspring of human women and the *sons of God* (fallen angels). While the mechanics of how it may have occurred are admittedly difficult, the fact of their existence is recorded in Scripture both prior to the Flood and afterward all the way until the time of David (Goliath and his kinsmen).

If we are today mapping the human genome and making great strides in the field of genomics, it should not at all surprise us that our extremely brilliant, powerful and malicious Foe has long ago beat us to the punch.

And while those fallen angels guilty of the crime have long been locked away (Jude 6), there is no reason to think that the ungod has ever tired of work in this field, or that he is not personally behind the corruption of human genetics in order to weaken or deface our physical form, as the sheer hideousness of what befalls some of humanity can only be of Hellish origin and thought.

Additionally, it is not unthinkable to believe that the same thing has occurred with the microorganisms of our planet, all of which were once beneficial. Many viruses and bacteria have today become troublesome, dangerous or even remarkably deadly to humanity, and I cannot but think that the ungod (with his inherent powers and brilliantly malicious mind) has had a hand in this work. His ultimate goal in this would be to see humanity bowed and disfigured under the weight of sickness, disease and deformity, with the evidence of God's hated image of health and wholeness completely absent.

WANT FRIES WITH THAT?

Apart from the work of the ungod through the Decay Laws and his probable genetic tinkering, people are still largely responsible for their own health. Sadly, it is here that the ungod finds so many willing accomplices in the pursuit of his image of illness. Simply stated, the human body is a magnificently designed biological machine that needs to be treated with great care and respect in order to bear what it can of God's image – that of health. Unfortunately, though, people often put more care and respect into their automobiles and lawns than they put into their own bodies.

Good nutrition and a healthful lifestyle are the two major ingredients to good human health. Through the poverty that covers much of the Third World, the ungod has managed to mire much of humanity in poor (or nonexistent) nutrition and in lifestyles that are in no manner healthful. The physical calamity that has become humanity in these parts of the world is as catastrophic as it is heart-rending, and marks a spectacular victory for the ungod and his image.

But we in the prosperous world are not so far behind our Third World cousins as we might like to think. Whereas their poor nutrition is due to dire poverty and lack, ours is due to poor decision-making and expedience at a time when we know more about nutrition and health than at probably any time in human history. The modern diet of civilized man – replete with fast food, frozen food, microwavable food, junk food, soda and mass-produced foodstuffs so devoid of healthful ingredients that they have shelf lives likely to remain intact through the Millennial Kingdom – can only be an idea spawned in the heart of Hell. This diet is so devoid of anything even remotely beneficial to our bodies, and so full of that which is actually harmful to us, that the fact that we still live and breathe is an astonishing testament to the magnificent design of our bodies by our Creator. Yet this slow poisoning and embalming of our bodies is not without effect, as modern man is now experiencing an epidemic of new sicknesses and diseases even as the old maladies of humanity grow worse.

When to this modern diet we add the apathetic, sedentary, fast-paced and stress-filled modern lifestyle, we are practically begging to host a cornucopia of illnesses and are openly inviting the destruction of our bodies. We are excessive in our laziness, excessive in our eating, excessive in our use of chemical stimulants and alcohol, and dangerous in our use of mind-altering drugs. When all of this leads (as it inevitably will) to the breakdown of our bodies, we run immediately to our physicians and pursue either over-the-counter or off-the-shelf pharmaceutical help, usually exacerbating the problem. Our bodies simply don't stand a chance. But the Dark Image certainly does.

From Noble to Savage

Among all living physical forms, there is none so noble in appearance and bearing as is the human form. This is because God is all that is meant in the truest sense of the word *noble*, and His nobility in us – though dimmed – is still inherent in the design, bearing and appearance of our bodies. That we alone of all Creation should stand and walk upright with heads held high, gazing upon a world over which we were meant to be masters and stewards, is a continual slap to the face of the ungod, and by nature he must marshal his forces against such human nobility.

If we will allow it to do so, the inherent posture of humanity is all that is needed to describe for us that nobility for which we were created. We can stand sturdily upon two legs, and when we do so it is with natural grace and dignity. We can walk and run upon those same two legs, and this also is done with natural, unmatched grace and dignity. We are upright creatures, and we are meant for upright character. Our bodies naturally bear our heads toward Him in whose upright image we have been formed, for the body does not so much support the head as it is crowned by it, exalting the center of reason and thought above all else.

God is upright in all His ways, and we have been formed upright in our carriage to spur us toward upright lives and upright ideals. Our posture naturally leads us to wisdom, learning, courage, justice, love, strength, compassion, beauty, fidelity, truth, righteousness and all that is fair. This is what it means to be truly noble, and therefore what is captured in the highest ideals of being *civilized*.

Because the human form is so inherently noble as to embody the uprightness of God, the ungod must naturally seek to supplant such nobility. This supplanting is done by replacing the noble with the ignoble, and civility with savagery. For if he can change the noble form (which naturally leads mankind God-ward) into the savage form, then the human form will naturally lead mankind toward the ungod and his savage (uncivilized) ideals.

To this end, the ungod takes great delight in overtly deforming humanity, which is why such things were a part of the pagan worship in and around the Promised Land (Leviticus 19:28). It is already understood that he is bent upon deforming the human genome; what I am speaking of here is literally the outward mutilation of the human body. As the West slides further from Biblical thought, it is absolutely no coincidence that we are becoming a people obsessed with mutilating our bodies – only we now call it *body art*. Body-piercing, tattooing and willing disfigurement are enjoying an astonishing rise in popularity in Western culture, and are becoming widely accepted and celebrated phenomena.

I am quite aware that many Believers make their livelihoods in this arena, and that multitudes more have willingly participated in what I have just deemed bodily mutilation and to which I have attributed the underlying purposes of the Devil himself. Some like to think of what they do as art (and I cannot deny their great talent), while others like to use their body as a canvas with which to advertise Scripture or Scriptural themes. But this thinking misses the point entirely, which is that our bodies *are* the art of Heaven – our bodies are themselves the advertisement.

Consider, for a few moments, the First Couple in the Garden of Eden. Can we even remotely picture them as tattooed, pierced or disfigured? We instinctively understand that they were not, and the reason is simple: the human form needed no such additives to physically portray the image of God, which was its purpose. Exactly how many tattoos and piercings do we think that Jesus had on His body? He now bears stripes and is pierced, it is true; but I think that these are of a highly different nature.

The ungod is passionately bent upon marring the singular beauty and nobility of the human form, seeking to replace it with an image both savage and bestial. While we might like to think that we may be dealing in an art form, the Enemy surely thinks otherwise, and we have only to look at his end game among many of the savage peoples to see the truth of it, for that is where we're headed.

Television now brings into our homes what National Geographic, travelers, historians and missionaries have long reported: how savage peoples, long bereft of the knowledge of the Living God, have sunk to levels of human disfigurement unimaginable. By these peoples the face is the most often and most horrifyingly corrupted, with ears and lips impossibly distorted and distended; bones, wood and metal pierce the nose, cheeks, chin and brow in horrific manners; and teeth are filed to look most fearsome. Bodies are ritually cut, burned and otherwise scarred and tattooed until they are mutilated shells of what once was. To the truly civilized mind it is utter madness and depravity.

Some will argue that this is simply a cultural issue, for who is to say that one culture is superior to another? Such thinking is as shallow as it is pathetic, and shall be dealt with in later pages, but for now let it be sufficient to say that it is a cowardly thing to hide behind the skirts of cultural relativity. It would be interesting to hold a worldwide tattoo competition, and to then bring the top ten artists to Florence, Italy, where they would each be given the opportunity to do their best work on Michelangelo's *David*. I would assume that 9 out of the 10 (and probably all ten) would recoil in horror at the thought of making any permanent change to such a masterpiece and known work of art. And that's my point – the human body *is the masterpiece*, and tattooing is merely graffiti on the artwork. It may be incredibly artistic graffiti in some cases, but it's graffiti nonetheless. Let us tread cautiously and with respect.

Finally, and on a softer note, let us reflect that after millennia of decay we are little more than homely copies of that noble First Couple, and there are things we can do to try and reasonably bridge that gap of lost physical nobility and beauty that have come in the long years since the Fall. But let us tread carefully here, for all should be done with respect to restoring or enhancing the nobility of the human form, and not of degrading it.

FROM GLORY TO SHAME

Yet try as he might, the ungod is still not successful in coercing everyone to poisonously mistreat, neglect or disfigure their bodies, for there are always those who have too much respect for their bodies or who take pleasure in robust health and physical fitness. People such as this actually put forth great effort toward nurturing excellent health, maintaining a nice physique or simply delighting in athletic endeavor and so maintain their bodies in optimal condition. With these individuals the ungod must take a very different approach in remaking them into his image than with those previously discussed.

The physical human form is meant to mirror the invisible qualities of God, who is spirit (John 4:24). As such, the human body is meant to constantly remind us of Him in whose image we were created, and therefore to point us toward worship of Him. The human form, then, is meant to be both the cause of human worship of its Creator, and the vehicle through which that worship is rendered. It is *not* meant to be the *object* of worship. When understood in its proper context – that of pointing humanity toward loving worship of God – the human body is the glory of humanity. When the human form itself is worshipped, it then becomes the shame of humanity, and since shame is the absence of glory, it is therefore the image of the ungod upon us.

The human form is perhaps worshipped more today than at any time in history. Cosmetics, cosmetic surgery, fashion, dieting, nutritional supplements and physical fitness are all billion-dollar industries, and show no signs of letting up. Yet rarely (if ever) do I hear a word from these industries concerning the glory of humanity being the image of God, and rarely (if ever) do I hear a word concerning the worship of God from them. How often do any of the innumerable fashion, fitness, diet or supplement magazines ever tease us with such a storyline upon their covers? It simply doesn't happen, for Darkness and Light have nothing in common (2 Corinthians 6:14), and the Enemy will not share his space. Here, all is about the body and only the body; the Creator being reflected in the body is an idea that is cast aside.

It is likely a form of bodily worship to sit for hours in front of a mirror, concerned only with thoughts of appearance and not of the God in whose image we appear. It is likely a form of bodily worship to work relentlessly on the shape of one's body, giving no thought to the God of whom our shape is to remind us. It is likely a form of bodily worship to condition ourselves toward athletic excellence apart from understanding that such abilities shadow those of a God who is strong, enduring, agile and graceful in nature. It is likely a form of bodily worship to pay meticulous attention to a healthful diet, and to religiously exercise in order to maintain optimal health, giving little to no regard to Him who endures forever perfect and whole. All of this is shameful, and the glory has departed. The Dark Image is the victor.

The Believer's Offensive

It is probably by now evident that I have a great appreciation of the human form, and I admit to it readily enough. I sincerely believe that the human form is (and must by definition be) the most wonderful and impressive thing ever to grace the physical universe. It is simply without peer, fallen though it be.

How marvelous, how sublime are its features, movements and abilities! Consider what expressive ability has the body, face and voice; what beauty of movement is brought to us by dance and sport; what agility is presented to us in the hands of a skilled surgeon or musician! It is not difficult to see how we could be less than we are, but difficult to see how we could be more than we are, and this is not without reason – our bodies have the distinct privilege of reflecting the image of One who is infinitely capable and amazing. As Believers, should we not, then, highly honor our bodies for the image they bear?

The Christian needs to be cautious of thinking of the body as merely a *jar of clay* or an *earthen vessel* (2 Corinthians 4:7). Biblical terms these are, it is true, but we can all too easily be lured by them into thinking that our bodies must somehow be irrelevant or worse – objects of disdain and disgust. The Bible does not teach that our bodies are evil, for Scripture teaches that our bodies are the temple of the Holy Spirit (1 Corinthians 6:19). Could or would He inhabit what is evil? The sinful nature is what is evil – not the body – and this distinction must be clear in both doctrine and thought.

Furthermore, we must bear in mind that we will always have physical bodies, for that is part of what is meant by being human. Truly we yearn for those promised resurrection bodies (which according to 1 Corinthians 15:42 will no longer be subject to sin, decay and death), but we must remember that they will nonetheless be real, physical bodies. In His resurrection body, Jesus walked, talked, touched, breathed and ate, and so shall we. Let us not, then, look askance at our bodies, as if physical form were some type of curse; let us rather look upon it as the greatest of honors, for there are two very good reasons to do so. The first reason is that though fallen, we still bear the Divine Image. The second reason is that the Eternal Son took on human form and became a man, and so shall He ever remain, thus hallowing the very idea of the human body.

The Believer should (and so should all people, though they know it not) be filled with honor at having the privilege of physically bearing God's image, and with that honor also a great sense of stewardship over the body bearing that image. We should make every reasonable effort to eat and live healthfully, prolonging as long as possible that good health and physique which best reflect His image and therefore bring Him glory. Likewise, we should do all that we can to ensure the nobility and fairness of our appearance, utterly forsaking all things savage, bestial and degrading.

Every beautiful, amazing movement and facet of the human body tells us something of the Person of God, and we should therefore always be moved by it into remembrance of – and reflection upon – Him whose matchless image we bear. But the human body (whether yours, mine or someone else's) should never be worshipped. Worship the Creator; honor the reflection.

BATTLEFIELD: HUMAN SEXUALITY

Let my lover come into his garden and taste its choice fruits
Song of Songs 4:16c

Though we have until now spoken of the human body in general terms, any even momentary glance at humanity will highlight the fact that it is divided into the different genders of male and female. From the differences between these genders arises the idea of human sexuality, mandating that we include human sexuality in our study of the Divine Image, and we shall do so now.

The amazing facets of the genders of humanity and what they teach us about God and His image will be more thoroughly explored when we delve into the issue of the family in later Battlefields. For now we must satisfy ourselves with dealing generally with the topic of human sexuality itself, and of its relationship to the nature of God.

THE ORIGINAL IMAGE

As we follow the Creation account in the first chapter of Genesis, we find that an interesting pattern appears. From Day One through much of Day Six, God simply announces His creative intent with a phrase beginning with the words *Let there...* or *Let the...* But with the creation of humanity a tremendous shift takes place, for God begins this creative process with the phrase *Let us...* This is of deep significance, for the *us* implies a relationship (and by extension an intimacy) that was nowhere else in the process of Creation made evident.

There are two things of great importance to learn here. The first is that the idea of intimacy is fundamental to what we call *the Godhead* (God the Father, God the Son and God the Holy Spirit), and is therefore part of God's image. The second is that the idea of intimacy was first

---

introduced in Scripture during the creation of the Image Bearers. While all of Creation was undoubtedly a concerted and intimate work for all Members of the Godhead, the introduction of the idea of intimacy during the creation of humanity points to the significance of the idea within humanity's very nature.

Another Divine attribute associated with human sexuality is *life-giving*, and the vehicle by which humanity reflects this part of God's image is through the procreative act between a man and a woman. For us, then, life-giving is most naturally and wonderfully accomplished (modern science and technology aside) through the intimacy of sexual intercourse. In fact, when Cain was conceived in Genesis 4:1, the King James Version classifies the sexual intercourse as Adam *knowing* his wife, and it is such an intimate act that the Scriptures describe it as becoming *one flesh* (Genesis 2:24; Matthew 19:5). This ultimately links intimacy with life-giving, which is precisely what we see taking place within the Godhead in the creation of humanity.

Finally, there is pleasure. There really is no way to dance around the issue, so I will simply state it clearly: sexual pleasure is the greatest physical pleasure in existence. And we must give credit where credit is due – God created this pleasure for us, and He has never apologized for it.

Of note regarding the idea of pleasure is that when we find pleasure in something it signifies that this something has become a source of delight or joy to us. Since God experiences delight (Isaiah 42:1), it means He is therefore capable of experiencing pleasure. As those who bear His reflection, we have thus been granted this ability; in fact, the literal translation of Eden is *delight*, making the Garden of Eden the literal Garden of Delight.

Our sexuality therefore encapsulates three facets of God's wondrous image: intimacy, life-giving and pleasure. However, it is my belief that we would be doing both ourselves and God a disservice if we too easily think of them as separate issues, rather than as one. God's intimacy and life-giving brought humanity (bearing His image) into existence, and He declared that this was *very good*. In other words, He was *very pleased*.

THE IMAGE UNDONE

Except for the possibility of the trait of human freedom (especially as it relates to notions of human government) nowhere today do I see more evidence of the work of the ungod than in the arena of human sexuality. We are a world awash in sexual deviance, awash in unbridled sexual activity, awash in sexual imagery, awash in pornography and awash in misguided notions of human sexuality.

This is not without good reason. The human population of Earth began with just two people, and was meant to eventually fill the entire planet (Genesis 1:28). The mechanism by which this would be accomplished was through human sexuality, making human sexuality the gateway through which all of human life could be corrupted by the ungod.

No Boundaries

God created human sexuality, and as its Creator and Author, He has the right to set the boundaries by which it is to be used. Scripturally, the boundaries that He has set are both simple and clear: sexual activity is to take place only between one man and one woman who are husband and wife. All other sexual activity is sinful and wrong. There are many who chafe against such boundaries, but this does not (nor can it) change what God has created and decreed. It is the potter who sets the rules, not the clay (Isaiah 45:9).

In fact, in the Law of Moses all sexual activity outside of marriage resulted in capital punishment for the offenders (Leviticus 18). This is indeed a stern thing, but a brief look at the results of sinful sexuality will explain the stern response. If human sexuality is polluted, the idea of marriage will be polluted. If marriage is polluted, the idea of family will be polluted. If family is polluted, the idea of society will be polluted. If society is polluted, the ideas of culture and human government will become polluted, leaving all of Earth stained by the Dark Image. Human sexuality is the very spring of human life; if the Enemy can pollute this spring, he wins the war.

As fallen beings we naturally disdain rules and boundaries, and may tend to want to shake our fists at the divine Potter who sets them in place. Yet as fallen as I am, I wouldn't dare to venture out in my truck if there were no Vehicle Code to maintain safe conduct upon the roads, for it would be sheer madness to do so. While I may be bothered by the restriction of a speed limit or the length of a red light, I instinctively recognize the value of such boundaries, for they keep me safe.

And so it is with God's boundaries concerning our sexuality, as they are meant to safeguard the dignity of human existence. A great deal of human pain, suffering, sickness and disease would disappear if humanity would simply abide by God's ordained boundaries of human sexuality. But we have largely shunned Heaven's sexual boundaries, and we are paying a hefty price in the damage this has caused and continues to cause among us.

Apart from safety, there is another blessing of boundaries, for they give purpose (and therefore beauty) to that which lies within them. A good example of this may be taken from soccer, my favorite sport. Let us for a moment pretend that we are standing before a large, rectangular, immaculately manicured and grassy green field. In this pretend world of ours soccer does not exist, there is no FIFA (the governing body of world soccer) and no FIFA rules. The field is unlined and unremarkable, perhaps best suited to the grazing of livestock more than anything else.

But now let soccer, FIFA and its rules magically exist, and behold the transformation! Lines, goals and corner flags appear, and upon this field now is played a game of such skill and beauty that it has captured the imagination of billions of people, and is a showcase for the amazing human body. In like manner, what FIFA does for that field, God's boundaries do for the sexuality with which He has gifted us – they bring purpose and beauty.

It is therefore a high priority for the ungod to influence our understanding of human sexuality away from where the image of God flourishes through it to a place where the unholy image will flourish through it, and that place is outside of God's boundaries. Once there, all safety, purpose and beauty are lost, while intimacy, life-giving and pleasure are redone in Hell's image. Outside of those boundaries (though marketed with exquisite skill to the contrary by the ungod) lie only sin, heartache, sickness, disease, ugliness, devastation, despair and death. But such realities barely slow the sinful nature's headlong pursuit of inappropriate human sexuality.

Loss of Control

One of the greatest lies ever perpetrated by the ungod upon a gullible humanity is the idea of the *sex drive*. It is a Darwinian and Evolutionary idea that has unfortunately found its way into mainstream thought, including that of many Believers. Since Evolution postulates that we are nothing more than highly-evolved animals, and animals do have a sex drive, it naturally follows that we must have one as well. And since it is a drive that must be consummated, it is something beyond our control, and we are therefore slaves to it.

It is of vital importance that we understand that we are *not* members of the animal kingdom. While it is true that we share things in common with the animal kingdom (for we have a common Designer), we are beings of a much higher order (Genesis 1:26,27). Animals are unthinking beasts, mere creatures of instinct (2 Peter 2:12). We, on the other hand, are inherently noble, upright beings capable of coherent thought and higher reasoning (Isaiah 1:18), and are the very antithesis of brute beasts needing instinct in order to survive. Because we bear God's image – which includes the idea of freedom – we are not under bondage to instinct, as are the lower creatures.

In humanity, sexual expression is subject to self-control (Acts 24:25; 1 Corinthians 7:5) and is therefore a matter of the exercise of human decision, being tied to our thoughts, desires, emotions and will. It is not an inexorable and uncontrollable drive powered by an instinct that masters us, but is rather nothing more than a potential action subject to human decision. For instance, I can at almost any time break into a sprint if I so choose, but I generally choose to limit my sprinting to times when I'm exercising, playing soccer or running for my life. Sprinting is a potential that I always possess, but I choose to exercise that potential judiciously.

The when, where, how and with whom of our sexual expression is therefore entirely within our control, for it is something we do by an act of free will. This is a far cry from the Darwinist's idea of the sex drive, which controls us and to which we must be blindly obedient. But such is the plan of the ungod, who would have us crawling on all fours in the dirt as if we were but brute beasts, and not acting as the noble and reasoned choice-makers who were meant to rule over them (Genesis 1:26).

There are many who no doubt find this to be a rather alarming position to take, but this is only because we have been conditioned by the sinful nature to naturally accept the explanation that leads us into moral degradation. Let us consider that Jesus lived his entire earthly life with no sexual expression. You may argue that He was fully God, but I would counter by pointing out that He was also fully human (John 1:14; Philippians 2:7,8), and so quite capable of sexual expression. Jesus is our High Priest (Hebrews 7-8), and any man with damaged testicles was forbidden from the Priesthood in Leviticus 21:20. He was also the fulfillment of the Burnt Offering (Hebrews 10), for which no animal with damaged or nonfunctioning testicles could be offered (Leviticus 22:24).

I don't point to these issues to be unnecessarily graphic, but rather to underline the fact that Jesus lived as a fully functioning human male upon Earth. He gave Himself no advantage over us in His earthly experience, but was tempted in all ways just as we are (Hebrews 4:15). This *all ways* would naturally have included sexual temptation, but yet He was without sin in this regard as well (also 4:15). Had the idea of the sex drive been true, He would have had to consummate it. But He didn't, because the sex drive is a lie, and He exerted self-control exactly as we're expected to do. Sexual desire and expression are subject to the exercise of our free will.

If we must learn a lesson from nature, I have a better example in mind – the remarkable idea of *dormancy*. In the uncultivated hills of Southern California there grows a low, spreading vine with lily-like white flowers. After the late winter rains (which are inevitably followed by our gloriously warm springs), this plant will shoot forth from the soil, and will spread and blossom.

It will share with us its beauty for but a few brief months, after which it will succumb to the inevitably long, dry and hot months of summer and fall, not to be seen again until the following year. This wild plant is (as are its more cultivated cousins) a wonderful picture of the workings of human sexuality. Its source of life is a bulb firmly entrenched some inches below the surface, and during much of the year in our rather harsh desert atmosphere, it lays dormant. Not *dead*, we must understand, but *dormant*, for it awaits those awakening signals bidding it to grow.

And the bulb is so awakened by the deep-reaching winter rains that are followed with the warming of the soil produced by the springtime's strengthening sun. When these conditions occur, the bulb puts forth its shoots, which break the surface, spread forth and blossom into beauty. The bulb is always ready and capable for this to occur, but it requires the appropriate conditions to be realized.

The Song of Solomon is a book dedicated to the celebration of sexual attraction and sexual intimacy of marriage. When it speaks of love, it is speaking of sexual love. Three times in this book the Beloved gives the Daughters of Jerusalem this interesting charge: *Do not arouse or awaken love until it so desires* (2:7; 3:5; 8:4). In other words, *let sexual love remain asleep, or dormant, until its appointed time.* In Ecclesiastes we are told that there is a time to embrace and a time to refrain. *Marriage* is the time for embracing; *marriage* is that deep rain and warming sun meant to bring our dormant sexuality beautifully (and appropriately) to life.

The Enemy's great triumph in this regard has been to convince humanity – against the evidence – that our sexual desires and expression are literally beyond our control, and we have bought his lie hook, line and sinker. His is the Darwinian idea of the uncontrollable and bestial sex drive, and so we are quickly becoming a planet devoid of any degree of sexual control, and will soon find that we will be looking toward Sodom and Gomorrah as pillars of sexual virtue.

PLEASURE WORSHIP

As mentioned earlier, the sheer physical delight engineered by God into the act of sexual expression is without equal. This delight (or pleasure) is a reflection of the God who created us, and who took great pleasure both in this act of creation and in the intimacy shared among the Godhead as it was done. This supreme pleasure, very much like the form and function of the human body, is therefore meant to remind us of God and cause us to render worship unto Him. But the ungod will have none of this and, much as it has happened with the human body, he will influence human thought and action toward the open and unceasing worship of sexual pleasure.

If it feels good, do it has become the mantra of our modern, secular society. There is very little restraint left, and soon there will be no form of sexual gratification that is off-limits. Here, pleasure is god, and pleasure is all that matters. Having an affair? Great! If it feels good, do it. Sleeping around? Great! If it feels good, do it. Homosexual relationship? Great! If it feels good, do it. Got a thing for kids? Great! If it feels good, do it. Thinking about raping that woman? Great! If it feels good, do it. On and on the list could go, but the picture should by now be clear. The rulebook is gone, and the field has gone fallow, bereft now of all beauty and purpose.

ON DISPLAY

With the exception of that strange brand of human being known as the nudist, most right-thinking individuals intuitively understand that a certain degree of modesty is appropriate when it comes to our bodies, especially as it relates to the parts of our bodies that are inherently sexual. After the Fall, Adam and Eve's first action was to cover their nakedness (outward sexuality) with fig leaves sewn together (Genesis 3:7), and God later slaughtered at least one animal to make that covering more appropriate and lasting (Genesis 3:21). Their bodies and sexuality were now corrupted by the sinful nature inhabiting them, and it seemed right – *both to them and to God* – to cover that which was fallen. Hence, modesty was born.

If God approves of modesty as it relates to human sexuality, then it is automatically understood that the ungod would rather have human sexuality on public display, which introduces to us the idea of sexual immodesty. Rampant sexual immodesty virtually makes sexual dormancy impossible, as it constantly awakens that which is not meant to be awakened. Furthermore, sexuality in a constant state of wakefulness is nearly impossible to control, and will inevitably lead to every kind of sexual expression outside of the God-ordained boundaries.

New Testament Believers (especially women) were therefore encouraged and admonished to dress modestly, as was becoming of God's people (1 Corinthians 12:23; 1 Timothy 2:9), and the idea behind this modesty was that of not being overtly sexual in one's attire or lack of it. Today, we would better understand this admonition as not trying to be *sexy*. *Sexy* is for the privacy of husband and wife, and is meant for no one and nowhere else. It is a fine and a good thing to possess physical beauty, and there can and should be no admonition against it. But it must always be borne in mind that physical beauty should be used to reflect the beauty and nobility of Him who is all that is fair and noble, and not to exalt itself or become the object of lust.

That which now passes for civilization is fast becoming the most sexually indecent and immodest culture perhaps ever seen. Everywhere we look, listen or read we are bombarded by the issue of open sexuality. All sense of decency, all sense of modesty and all sense of propriety have now nearly been lost. We are so gorged on sexuality that, like the Exodus Israelites of old and their meal of quail, we are literally vomiting over the excess of it (Numbers 11). Hardly a movie is made without it, and rarely a television show. Modern music and its attendant lyrics, videos and dance moves are awash in it, and our kids unthinkingly drink it in as if it were the very Fountain of Life.

Pornography, now ubiquitous on the Internet, is more popular than ever and continues to grow exponentially. Women, girls and even some men parade virtually naked across our beaches and around our pools, while those in the fashion industry race against one another to see who can be more successful at overly sexualizing humanity's sense of style.

And behind it all lurk the slowly blinking eyes of the Serpent, who watches with perverse delight as hated humanity lustily bears more and more of his Dark Image.

INTIMACY LOST

The net result of a people or culture who have forsaken all God-ordained sexual boundaries, and who put their sexuality on constant display while worshipping sexual pleasure as though they were no more than glorified animals is something devastating to the image of God. This is true not just of humanity in general, but also of the individual, and the greatest devastation to the Divine Image in the individual is wrought upon the facet of intimacy.

The human capacity for intimacy is both wonderful and dangerous. That it is a wonderful thing needs no further comment; that it is a dangerous thing does. Intimacy by its very nature implies that it is a deep, personal and emotional thing, and therefore hinges upon love and trust. Trusting always opens the door to betrayal, and few things can hurt or scar as deeply as betrayal does (Psalm 41:9). What is unfortunately not admitted to in this out-of-control sexual culture of ours is that sexual activity is a form of intimacy, but is deemed instead to be nothing more than a sport or the pursuit of another fleshly pleasure, like eating your favorite ice cream.

This is most dangerous and damaging, as the Bible is clear that sexual intercourse is the highest form of human intimacy possible, for only of sexual intimacy does the Scripture describe two people as *becoming one flesh* (Genesis 2:24). Because it is such an intimate thing, it is designed to be a thing shielded by love, trust and loyalty, and only in marriage is that shield to be found. Sexual activity outside of the God-ordained boundaries of marriage therefore involves intimacy apart from love, trust and loyalty, and thus by definition involves a form or degree of betrayal.

Betrayal hurts and scars deeply, and by its very nature the betrayal of sexual intimacy can hurt and scar most deeply of all. We must also remember that we are finite beings, and that we therefore do not possess an unlimited capacity for pain. Our minds and hearts must deal with the pain of betrayal, and they do so by building a protective layer of scar tissue that shields them from further intimacy. Those who wantonly share sexual intimacy with others (or who have it forced upon them) will thus eventually lose the ability to have meaningful personal relationships and be relegated to mere shells of humanity.

It should therefore be no surprise that the Enemy throws so much into his effort of robbing humanity of sexual boundaries and beauty. He encourages children to become sexually active in elementary school, long before they understand the capacity for intimacy; he gets boys and men hooked on pornography; he gets girls to go wild; he gets schools to encourage sexual activity and to hand out condoms; he encourages people to have multiple sexual partners; he delights in rape, incest, pedophilia, polygamy, adultery, homosexuality and bestiality; and he gets girls and women to put on a never-ending sexual display through the clothing that they do (and do not) wear.

All of this should be seen for exactly what it is – a frontal assault by our Enemy upon God's wondrous trait of intimacy reflected in us. The ungod knows no intimacy, and he will not rest until we are all as he is.

Womb of Death

In a no-holds-barred and sexually out-of-control culture, the Divine facet of intimacy is not the only casualty to the Divine Image; also affected is the attribute of life-giving. In a world where sexual pursuit is based largely upon pleasure, there will be a great deal of human conception taking place outside of marriage. For those who worship pleasure, being pregnant or having a child will greatly interfere with the pursuit of their chosen deity. It becomes necessary, then, to find a way to offer the child now conceived to this god.

The sexually immoral Ammonites of Old Testament fame, lacking our modern medical and technical expertise, created an interesting way of dealing with this problem of unwanted children. They would simply sacrifice their offspring to their god Molech by burning them to death (2 Kings 23:10), something we today find murderous and callous.

But we are a people no better than they, for we are just as murderous and callous – if not more so. To be sure, we no longer call it *child sacrifice*, but have instead simply relabeled it as *abortion*. Labeling aside, Scripture is quite clear that human life begins at conception (Psalm 139:13; Jeremiah 1:5; Luke 1:39-44), meaning that any form of the taking of a life in the womb is considered homicide (Exodus 21:22-25). And purposeful homicide is murder.

Whether we use the Morning After Pill or medically induce a miscarriage, it is still murder. Whether we burn the baby alive in the womb with a saline solution, hack her to pieces bit-by-bit in the uterus or bring him to the point of delivery only to crack open his skull and suck out his brains, it is still murder. And let there be no mistake that this is an idea that comes from one whom Jesus described as the original Murderer (John 8:44), despite how Planned Parenthood may try to frame the issue. This Murderer still takes a special, perverted pleasure in seeing the life-giving facet of the image of the Living God turned into the bringer of death.

UNNATURAL CELIBACY

Finally, the ungod must deal with those for whom – whether through decency of character or religious teaching – the wanton pleasures of sexual promiscuity hold very little or no attraction. These the ungod influences toward lifelong abstinence of sexual expression, something typically accomplished through pious or religious form. By both decree (Genesis 2:18) and by the act of creating one man for one woman, God has shown that it is normal and expected that each person should have a spouse with whom to enjoy the beauties of human sexuality and the Divine Image that it promotes. If that expression of human sexuality cannot be corrupted by the ungod, he will then naturally see to it that the sexuality and its expression be denied. Perversion and corruption of sexuality is preferred of course, but denial of sexuality will do in a pinch.

Before we finish this section, though, allow me to take some time to put celibacy into Biblical perspective. Celibacy is *expected* of anyone who is not married. We are to remain celibate until we are actually married, and to return to celibacy when no longer so. Celibacy is simply a Biblical mandate for all who are unmarried; it is *not* a calling or a gift. By citing First Corinthians 7:7, some may argue that the Apostle Paul had the gift of celibacy, but nowhere in Scripture is the *gift of celibacy* mentioned as such, and so we must tread carefully in how we use such terms.

As one who lived long as an unmarried man, I believe that the gift of which Paul spoke is better understood along the lines of a *gift of singlehood*. He simply did not – for the sake of his call and of the Gospel – desire to be married. Paul is perhaps best described in this regard by Jesus in Mathew 19 as one who has (figuratively) made himself a eunuch for the sake of the Kingdom of Heaven. Such a thing should be as rare as the Apostle Paul himself, and should be done only through great care, prayer and advice. It should never be *imposed* upon an entire set of people (such as with Catholic priests and nuns or Buddhist priests) nor should it ever be done at the expense of denigrating human sexuality or marriage, or be done with ideas of spiritual superiority. It must be remembered that it was God Himself who decreed that it was not good for the man to be alone (Genesis 2:18). It is not wise to pit yourself against God.

THE BELIEVER'S OFFENSIVE

It is difficult to fathom a more wondrous and personal reflection of the image of God in humanity than human sexuality, and so upon all of Earth there should be none who appreciate it more than those who love and know Him of whom it is such an amazing and evident reminder.

Our sexuality adds to life a beauty, depth and magnificence that may not otherwise be known, and so should generate constant praise and thanksgiving toward its heavenly Author. It is He who has inspired it, He who has engineered it, and He who has designed the boundaries that give its expression beauty and purpose. As redeemed people of the Word, then, it is we who should honor those boundaries in our thoughts, in our intentions, in our words and in our deeds.

Furthermore, we must understand that since sexuality is the wellspring of human life, it is the object of a special hatred by the Enemy, who would change it into the source of poison for all of humanity. It is therefore incumbent that we lift high and untiring the lamp of Truth into the Darkness of sexual misunderstanding, sexual deviance, and sexual depravity. Finally, let us seek through the love of Christ, through the example of the beauty of right conduct, and through the superiority of ideology to rescue those in whom all things beautiful and intimate are being stolen, killed and destroyed (John 10:10).

BATTLEFIELD: THE HUMAN MIND

"Come now, let us reason together," says the LORD
Isaiah 1:18a

We move now from consideration of the outward form of humanity to consideration of its inner form and workings, leading us first and most naturally to the workings of the human mind. Here the physical universe finds its champion in thought and reason, for though it may rightly be said that humanity is bested by members of the animal kingdom in things specifically physical, the great chasm existing between human and animal intellect is simply an unbridgeable thing. Marvelous indeed is the human mind.

THE ORIGINAL IMAGE

Here, again, the human intellect owes its superiority to the Divine Image, for we are meant to reflect and know Him who created the universe with mere thought and speech (Genesis 1:3,6, etc.). God is a thinking Being (Isaiah 55:8,9), a reasoning Being (Isaiah 1:18) and an emotional Being (Genesis 6:6). As beings designed to reflect His image, we are likewise thinking, reasoning and emotional beings.

Since this capacity of ours does not exist in a vacuum, but rather is designed to (among other things) allow a meaningful relationship between human beings and their Creator (Genesis 3:8; Isaiah 1:18; John 1:12), His is the Heavenly Mind after which our minds have necessarily been designed and created. That which constitutes the human intellect, then, while finite and limited in us, must necessarily be of tremendous magnitude if we are to be beings that relate to Him on a personal level.

As such, the whole purpose of the incredible and gifted human mind was to center humanity upon thoughts of God. And since all facets

---

of human existence pass through the halls of the human mind, it is necessarily the wellspring and cornerstone of humanity's reflection of the Divine Image, for all else depends upon it.

When such intellect was paired with the purity and innocence of the First Couple before the Fall, the result would have been a beauty of fellowship with God literally undreamed-of today, and would have shrouded all of life in the noble mantle of God-centered thought (which is greatness of thought). This greatness of thought would have naturally moved the human intellect toward all things beautiful, noble and majestic – reflective of (and bringing glory to) the One with whose image it was so intricately woven. Human thought would naturally trend toward Heavenly thought, resulting in a planet that in all measurable ways would grow to resemble Heaven itself.

THE IMAGE UNDONE

Because the human mind is so fundamental to the reflection and spread of the Divine Image in humanity, it is key for the ungod to wage relentless war upon it and the thoughts coming from it. And since the designed purpose of the human mind was to point all thought God-ward, the ungod must simply redirect thought away from God in order to be successful. It matters not where, as long as thought is not God-ward, and through pollution of this wellspring he is able to remake every aspect of the image of God in us into that which reflects the image of Hell.

THE FALL OF TRUTH

Inherent to the ungod's assault upon the human intellect is the constant assault upon Truth, for God and Truth are one and the same, making an understanding of Truth imperative to understanding the Image War. When I was younger I was bothered at the lack of response by Jesus to the question of Pontius Pilate in John 18:38: *What is truth?* How I wished that Jesus had answered Pilate's question, thereby answering my own. What I had then failed to realize was that He had already answered the question the evening prior when He told the disciples *I am the Way, the Truth and the Life.*

Jesus, who is God Incarnate, *is the Truth.* I like to think of the Bible as having two great statements of Truth (although I'm sure this is something of an understatement). The second of these statements we have just discussed, and is found in John 14:6. The first of these statements famously opens the Scriptures: *In the beginning God...* In these two great statements, humanity is given all that is needed to *embark* upon the road of Truth.

Here is Truth: God is, and God is personified fully in the Person of Jesus Christ. Any believed moral, ethical, philosophical or spiritual truth not founded upon (or which deviates from) this Truth is a lie. It is *the Lie*, originating from the great Liar who, when he lies, is speaking his native tongue (John 8:44). And in order for the great Liar to pollute human thought, it is imperative that he supplant the Truth with Lie. The Truth sets humanity free (John 8:32); the Lie holds it in bondage. The Lie would seek to teach humanity that God is not, or (if that will not be believed) that He is other than He has clearly revealed Himself to be.

Evolution teaches that God is not. It is part of the Lie. Theistic Evolution teaches that God is other than He has clearly revealed Himself to be. It is part of the Lie. The Allah of Islam is other than the Jehovah of Scripture. It is part of the Lie. The God of the Book of Mormon is other than the God of Scripture. It is part of the Lie. The teaching that the universe is God is part of the Lie, as is the teaching that we can become God.

For these or any other facets of the Lie to take hold in the minds or philosophies of humanity, it is obviously necessary to suppress humanity's exposure to (or acceptance of) Truth, which is embodied in the Scriptures (John 17:17). Hence, human history has, since that first seed of Hellish doubt was sown in Genesis 3:1, always run concurrent with a ceaseless and vicious war against God's Word and those who would honor it – from Abel to the Israelites to the Church.

The Lie is dangerous and enslaves, while the Truth is beneficial and brings freedom, and a great example of this has played out in the rise of modern science. Though the secularists would deny it, modern science (with its attendant blessings) arose largely out of the Protestant Reformation, when Bible-believing, intellectually-gifted individuals took the Biblical mandate of Genesis to rule over the earth as an imperative to understand Nature. They believed (correctly) that the God of Creation, while transcendent, was nevertheless the God of order, and not of chaos. Surmising from this that there must be order in Nature, they set about to discover those Laws that must exist for Nature to be orderly.

Contrast this with the scientific achievement of Islam during this same period. As the West rose to prominence on the crest of Biblical science, the Islamic Near East remained mired largely at the scientific level of the first millennium. Even today there are no great Islamic schools of science, medicine, engineering or technology, and parents in the Islamic world must send their children to schools and universities in the West for excellence in such forms of education.

The most prominent reason for this is the Islamic belief that because Allah is capricious, he is inconsistent and ultimately unknowable (unlike the consistent and knowable Jehovah of the Bible), and would not therefore create Nature as consistent or knowable. Hence, to the Muslim mind, it was absurd (not to mention heretical) to pursue such lines of study. One can only imagine how much more blessed the world would be had so much intellectual prowess as has existed in the Islamic world for the past fourteen hundred years been allowed to flower in the direction of the pursuit of Truth.

Since the Lie enslaves, it is no wonder that the ungod has put forth so many facets of it, or that he guards the Lie with such murderous jealousy as he does. *Did God really...* was the beginning of the Lie (Genesis 3:1), and it sadly has not had to change much to be as readily received today as it was so long ago. *Does God really exist?* or *Is God really like...?* are only slight permutations of that first hellish hiss, but are every bit (or even more so) effective today among the descendants of those who first fell.

Keep Your Head Down

Aside from the great Lie, the ungod must take great care lest even the thoughts of everyday life (or the mundane) stir humanity into consideration of God. As stated earlier, the sinless disposition and intellect of Eden's inhabitants would have caused those ordinary things we tend to find so uninspiring to actually inspire their thoughts God-ward. In some way, therefore, all of life would have been a wonderful reminder of Him whose image they reflected, resulting in inspired thought and worship of the Giver of All Good Things (James 1:17).

A recurrence of such thought and worship is always a possibility for humanity today, for God has set eternity in the hearts of men (Ecclesiastes 3:11), and so great diligence is required of the ungod. This diligence does not require the great sophistication of the Lie, but rather the attention to detail necessary to turn humanity away from God in the lesser things of life. The primary sense lifted God-ward concerning what we now consider the everyday – food, drink, health, family, jobs, friendship, safety, etc. – is naturally that of gratitude or (if due to lack) that of supplication. Such God-ward gratitude or supplication must therefore be undone.

This undoing comes primarily in three forms, each relatively simple. The first is quite obviously thanklessness toward God, or *ingratitude*. It is the form truest to the nature of the ungod, who is its progenitor (for he was the first to lack gratitude), and is therefore the most preferred by him. The second is that of apathy, which is simply not caring or giving thought to God concerning such things. The third form is that of misplaced gratitude or supplication, consisting usually of being thankful to oneself or another person or agency as the ultimate provider. Supplication in this third form is most typically directed toward a governmental agency, as it is the natural tendency of government to supplant God. All of these fulfill the design of the ungod, for any turning of thought away from God-ward is a turning ungod-ward.

BESIDE TROUBLED WATERS

The human intellect is capable of great thought, great ideals and great philosophy, but must be focused in order to do so, for all things of greatness require tremendous focus and dedication in order to be accomplished. The greatest possible exploit of the human mind is to accomplish a Biblical view on all matters of life, and such a Biblical worldview is possible were a person to focus deliberately, deeply and long upon the Truth as revealed in Scripture. Since the ungod so fears such a capacity and what might happen should this great thinking occur, he must by all means necessary keep humanity from such focus.

Most all people (with very few exceptions) are capable of such penetrating thought, but great focus upon the matter of Truth must be attained and held in order for this to be accomplished. This is what is meant by the Biblical idea of *meditation* – it is a deep, inward, spiritual and intellectually intensive musing upon Truth and Lie that seeks to apply the principles of Scripture to all of life. Such Biblical, focused meditation requires a certain degree of quietness, or a *stillness*. This is why God exhorts us to *be still, and know that I am God* in Psalm 46:10.

Here we come to a most important point, especially in these days of overpowering mental stimuli: Only the mind that is stilled can know God, who is Truth. God is calm, and not chaotic. We therefore cannot learn of Him and Truth through chaos of mind. God is also complex, and the complex cannot be learned through simplicity, but only through discipline and training. Stillness of the mind, therefore, is warred against most strenuously by the ungod, lest such stillness lead to great thought, whose natural outcome leads one toward God. And he likewise seeks to keep us simpleminded and undisciplined of thought, for it makes great thoughts and ideas out of reach for us.

Simplicity is the absence of complexity, and the ungod achieves this facet of his image through human simplemindedness, which is the inability to think deeply or in a complex manner. I must point out that such a state is unnatural to the human condition, and must be trained into us. This training is accomplished by having emotion rule over the thinking process, rather than having the thinking process being ruled by logic, reason and revealed Truth. It is also accomplished by the purposeful shortening of the mental attention span, which the ungod pursues with great success today.

Emotion-based reasoning is the death knell to profound thought, for emotion has the great effect of short-circuiting reasoning, and reason leads to depth of thinking. Emotion is *passion,* and in our fallen state passion wields tremendous destructive power over our ability to think clearly. Since God is an emotional Being, we must understand that passion is not an inherently evil thing, but passion not aligned with Truth *is* inherently dangerous. Emotion-based reasoning is essentially aligning one's thoughts according to what one *feels,* and not what is necessarily true. This is little better than the instinctive reasoning of beasts, and precisely the goal for humanity set by the ungod.

Departing now from simplemindedness, we move on to intellectual chaos, which is the lack of the order and serenity found in the Heavenly Mind. The ungod simply will not let our minds be still enough to know God or the richer things of Him, and at no time has this effort been more apparent than now, for we have become a people dangerously addicted to a mental onslaught of chaotic input. From the moment when we first awaken to the moment when we lay ourselves down for a night's rest we allow ourselves to be barraged with audio and visual input from every direction, and many are so addicted to this noise that they can't sleep unless the television or music is playing in the background. Stillness is positively shattered in our lives.

And let us understand that this is not without sinister design. With such lives, and with such minds, it is impossible to know God as He desires to be known. The human intellect thus enslaved to simplicity and chaos has lost all semblances to its Divine model, and will soon be enslaved by a complete loss of Truth, as many now experience. The image of the ungod is in this way rapidly gaining ground among us, for many have already become simpleminded slaves to stimuli – human drones hardly better at thinking than the pets of our households.

DESTRUCTION

It should finally be noted that in his battle against the mind, the ungod has at his disposal the ability to attack the brain itself. As the complex physical organ that houses the intellect, the fully-functioning brain delivers to the mind the ability to function at its highest levels. If the ungod is therefore able to physically destroy all or part of the brain (or even to diminish its ability or capacity) he has succeeded in destroying or diminishing a person's ability to reflect the image of God through his or her intellect. And where there is the absence of the Divine Image, by definition we then have the image of the ungod.

Among his arsenal of weapons in this assault upon the brain itself are, of course, the Decay Laws with their inevitable corruption of the human genome. This corruption may result in the arrested development of the brain, the undesired rewiring of the brain or the chemical unbalancing of the brain, all of which have the desired effect to one degree or another. Death or injury to all or part of the brain via physical damage or stroke are also part of the Hellish arsenal, and although they are primarily the result of human action, the ungod must still be seen as their ultimate author, for catastrophe did not originate in the mind or plan of God (Psalm 91:12).

Another mode of attack upon the brain is through chemical substance use and abuse, which at its least is an attack on clear-mindedness, and at its worst is a full assault upon sobriety. Clear-mindedness and sobriety are hated by the ungod, for through them the human intellect might rise to the heights for which God intended it. The ungod assaults them, then, at every turn.

The most successful salvos fired by the Enemy in this arena are those of mind-altering drugs and of alcohol abuse. The ungod positively loves an altered brain, and has enslaved people by the millions in this form of darkness. A mind dependent upon such an altered brain simply cannot know God, since function and reason are obliterated. The only god that may be known is the God of the Altered State, and his name is by now pretty well known.

THE BELIEVER'S OFFENSIVE

The human intellect is, by definition, our greatest facet of the Divine Image, and we must defend this facet of the Divine Image as strenuously as the Enemy wars against it. All things human filter through the intellect, and therefore all aspects of our reflection of the Divine hinge upon our health, strength and purpose in this arena. Believers must therefore disrobe themselves of Lie, putting off all falsehood, and return to being the people of Truth. Every good, every great and every beneficial idea for humanity has its genesis in the principles of Scripture, and we must set ourselves to the task of thinking in accordance with these principles.

The Lie is not for us, and must not only be rejected, but must be intellectually crushed wherever it is encountered. Crush the Lie and its facets; grind them into dust, for they are the enslavers of humanity. It is for freedom that Christ Jesus has set us free (Galatians 5:1); let us then be free. We must wholly align our intellect with Truth, for it is the noblest purpose for which intellect was created. We simply must become people whose minds are utterly transformed by the Word of God, for it is the wellspring of all of life.

Not only should we (and must we) be the people of Truth, but we should be those whose thoughts are Heaven-bent in all things. This does not mean that we must be thinking of God at all times, for that is neither called for nor possible. What we should be doing, however, is allowing everything to turn our thoughts God-ward in the proper course of time. We should not be found guilty of thinking that God is concerned only with the great and ponderous issues of our lives, for He is equally concerned with the seemingly inconsequential. Has He not given to us the beauties of the rose and of the sunset to enjoy? Does He not know the joy of a fresh breeze on a warm day, or the beauty of a child's laugh? Does He not understand the pleasure of using one's taste buds or the pleasure of a full stomach? Would not He who created man to work not take delight in being part of such an experience? Does not He who allows trying and difficult circumstances into our lives, for the purpose of molding in us the character of Jesus, desire to share these experiences with us?

There is nothing in our lives meant to exist apart from Him; we must, therefore, train our minds to connect all of life with Him. From the ordinary to the extraordinary, all things should send our thinking God-ward, for there is nothing in our lives that is mundane or uninteresting to God.

Yet we must understand that God-ward thinking and an intellect deeply guided by Truth are not things that happen by accident or good fortune, for they happen by deep and regular study of Scripture with stilled and disciplined minds. We must actively shut out the noise of stimuli that would keep us from deep, disciplined thought, though this may be painful to us and to our families. We need to quiet our lives.

Likewise, as we quiet our lives and bring our thinking into line with Scriptural principles, so too must we subject our emotions to those same principles. If our feelings or emotions disagree with Scripture, our emotions or feelings are wrong, for Scripture is never wrong (Romans 3:4). Too many Believers live as slaves to emotion instead of as free citizens of Truth.

Finally, let us always treat our brains with respect, maintaining that sobriety and alertness befitting followers of Christ (Ephesians 5:18).

BATTLEFIELD: SPEECH AND LANGUAGE

In the beginning was the Word, and the Word was with God,
and the Word was God
John 1:1

As marvelous and peerless as the human mind may be, it is obvious that without its ability to function through the complexities of language we would be reduced to little more than an animalistic existence. It is language that enables and elevates great thinking (and thereby elevates all aspects of life), and it is the sharing of this thinking with others that we call *communication*.

Words – whether written, spoken, sung or signed – are what we use to communicate to others that which dwells within us. Whether our thoughts are deep or shallow, they remain our own until they are communicated to another. Our thoughts essentially form who and what we are, and when we share our thoughts with others, we are therefore sharing of ourselves with others, for we are letting them know some of who and what we are. This makes the ability to communicate as well as we do something both deeply personal and decidedly powerful.

The Original Image

God speaks almost immediately in the Bible (Genesis 1:3). Since God speaks, it means that He communicates. He communicates because He is a relational Being, and to be a relational being one must have the ability to communicate with another relational being.

As beings created in God's image, we likewise are relational beings with the ability to communicate. And this ability to communicate must by definition be quite expansive, for we are not only meant to communicate with one another, but also with Him (Genesis 1:28). The human ability to communicate is therefore one of the more remarkable

---

ways in which humanity reflects the Divine Image.

Much as it was with the human mind (which was meant to focus all thought God-ward) communication was likewise meant to bend all human relationships God-ward, as well as to be the conduit for each person's relationship with God. Prior to the Fall, all communication between Adam and Eve would have been centered upon God, for nothing of the Lie or Darkness was then known to them. The mouth speaks out of the abundance of the heart (Matthew 12:34), and theirs were then without blemish. The same was meant to be true of their relationships with their children, and as the population of Earth grew there would have been a wonderful lifting of communication Heaven-ward in corporate human worship of its Creator, shrouding human existence in profound dignity and wisdom.

THE IMAGE UNDONE

What the ungod must do with this facet of the Divine Image in humanity is not at all hard to fathom: he must turn all human communication away from God-ward. As has been previously discussed, any such turning is a turning away from Heaven, and so bears the Hellish image. His success at this is, yet again, as remarkable as it is widespread.

FALSE WITNESS

The human mind and emotions were meant to function according to Truth, and the tongue controlled by them was meant to communicate Truth. Truth-based communication would therefore have been always God-ward, God-centered and God-glorifying. For the Evil One, then, it is imperative that the emotions and minds of humanity be caused to function according to Lie, that they might continually communicate Lie to one another.

The Lie can have as many facets as there are differing minds, but all of these facets ultimately accomplish the same goal: causing people either to believe that God does not exist or to believe that He is other than He has revealed Himself to be. Yet what is held of the Lie in one individual cannot generally be held by another unless it is first communicated to them, for the Lie only affects a single person until it is passed on, at which time the Darkness of the ungod (or a greater degree of it) spreads to another. Communication, then, as something created by God that we might more fully bear His image, when tainted with the Lie easily becomes an instrument of the ungod to remake humanity in his. We must remember that the very nature of Evil requires that it spread until all that is Good is gone; what we see in this Battlefield is that human communication is the primary means by which this is done.

It is for this reason that he who controls the bastions of mass communications will see their standard most often win the day in the battles of the Image War, and is why the Enemy so jealously and murderously guards his control of such media where he has it.

DIVERSION

Apart from being the vehicle by which the Lie is spread, another tactic used by the Enemy is to simply have humanity keep God absent from their communication. In this regard the particular topic is of little importance, for any topic of conversation will do, as long as it is used to keep God away from communication and from being considered in thought. This is simply known as *diversion*, and is an attempt by the ungod to keep communication from its intended purposes.

Humanity's obsession with celebrities is an excellent example of the diversion. Has any Hollywood icon or gifted athlete (as incredible as they may be) ever done for humanity a fraction of what the Savior has done? Why then is so much communication devoted to them? The answer is simple: diversion.

It is an incredible testament to the ungod's abilities that he has managed to so isolate God from the communication He authored. God and Truth inhabit so little a percentage of human communication that it would be laughable were it not so wrong and dangerous. Of course, we cannot at all times and in all ways speak of God, but that does not explain the near-absolute dearth of God and Truth in human communication.

Only the existence and purpose of the ungod do so.

DEVALUED

When I spend time in the Gospels, I must confess to a certain envy concerning Jesus, for He had such an economy of words. He could say more with fewer words than anyone who has ever walked the planet before or since, and I do so admire that ability. His words had behind them such great thought, such great wisdom and such great inspiration, and never was a word wasted or was one more word needed. He was – and is – simply the greatest communicator of all time.

Communication today could scarcely be more different if it tried, and one of the most remarkable differences is in the multiplication of words. While it is also true of writing, it is far more impacting to simply state it in terms of human speech: PEOPLE TALK TOO MUCH!

Words (or communication) are how the inner being of one person is shared with another. As such, it is a form of intimacy and must therefore be used with a measured degree of caution and respect. Intimacy too often shared is robbed of its glory, and words too often shared are robbed of theirs. In some ways, words too often shared empty a person of intimacy, and for this reason many who are incessant talkers are those most unable to obtain true intimacy with others. Conversation is much like any commodity – the less there is of it, the higher its value. Our words should be few (Ecclesiastes 5:2).

If the ungod can train humanity to be constantly conversing, he then has had the effect of devaluing communication to nearly zero. Much as a currency is devalued when more of the currency is printed, so communication is devalued when it is unnecessarily multiplied in a person's life. This is the inflation of communication, and inflation always lessens value.

Furthermore, when we are speaking, we are giving out rather than taking in, and so are not learning anything. Since the ungod fears the mind that learns (especially at the foot of Truth), he convinces many of us to speak far more than we listen.

Because I happen to appreciate symmetry, I'm quite glad that God gave us two ears. I think it just looks good this way. However, I doubt that symmetry was the overriding concern in the matter, but rather I see a great deal of truth in the old adage, which says that *God gave us two ears but only one mouth, that we might listen twice as much as we speak.*

DOWNSIZING

We pastors have a saying that goes something like this: *If you want to read something truly well-written and insightful, go and read from the works of the Old Dead Guys.* This may sound a bit disrespectful, but in fact is meant with deepest respect. For instance, when I read the theological works of some of the Puritan writers, I am shamed both by their insight and by the beauty and eloquence with which they use the English language. And I do not for an instant believe that the coupling of insight and great language is a coincidence, for it is a logical thing that deep understanding and communicating great insight requires a commensurate greatness of language use.

As a former and longtime youth pastor, I am amazed at the literary achievements of many teenagers of a century or two ago, especially when compared with the literary abilities of the average teenager of today. Of old, the level of thought was deeper, as was their ability to communicate that level of thought. And whether young or old, when we compare ourselves with them, we find that it is we who are lacking, and not they. Instead of improving, we have regressed, and today find ourselves speaking a lesser form of the English language (as I suspect now do most all speakers of any language).

This regression of language is by Hellish design, for understanding requires language and is therefore functionally limited by it. Great thinking needs great language in order to occur. A student in the first year of elementary school cannot too deeply ponder the works of ancient Greek philosophers, for the thinking is above the student's literary and linguistic ability. The Enemy, therefore, has a vested interest in the regression of any language, which is precisely why we find ourselves so far behind those of years long past. Poor spelling, poor grammar, low vocabulary and the inability to craft meaningful sentences are markedly on the rise in Western civilization, despite the effort and astronomical funding applied to the educational process.

Those who follow such trends call this the *dumbing down* of a culture, but are often at a loss as to explain why such a thing is occurring. For instance, we Americans find ourselves spending more years in the educational system than generations previous, but with far less knowledge and intellectual ability to show for it than they. The reason is simple: the ungod is the ideological master of our educational system, and he is working through it with ever greater success to keep our minds mired at the grammar school level (or lower), unable to lift our intellect into the realm of great thought.

CESSPOOL AND SLANDER

Marching lockstep with the regression of once-beautiful language is the rise of the filthy vernacular seeking to rob communication of all dignity. This, too, must be seen for what it is: language rolling ever on toward the image of the ungod.

Aided by technology, the ungod is presiding over the most widespread and rapid decline of the beauty and dignity of human speech probably ever seen. Mirroring his design to change the human form from noble to bestial and savage, the Enemy is likewise robbing language of its order, civility and nobility, and in so doing is reducing us to wallowing in the linguistic gutter of savagery and filth. Once taboo, obscenity is now *celebrated* in public and private discourse, and all of speech is becoming as base, lowly, coarse, undignified and vulgar as are the people and events upon which they dwell.

Much of this vulgarity is naturally aimed at humanity itself, for few things bring the ungod greater pleasure than to have speech and communication used to denigrate those who, though fallen, bear the Divine Image. The ungod has therefore turned one facet of the Image upon another, and done so quite successfully. How many terms have we now to describe one another in an undignified manner? Terms such as *loser, idiot, retard* and *jerk* are so common in our speech that it is stunning, but yet are merely the tip of the iceberg. I will not here repeat such terms as are now common when referring to girls and women (especially among certain genres of music), nor can I bring myself to pen the horrendous and never-ending stream of racist epithets stemming from Hell's dark mind.

We are quickly becoming a planet of Hellish speech: vicious, debauched, degraded, base and foul. All loftiness and dignity of language and communication are disappearing at an alarming rate, and fallen humanity is only too comfortable with wallowing in such foul and wreaking mire. Very little now remains of that Edenic manner of speech once so magnificent, noble and dignified, and the ungod's image has not long to come into its fullness.

Funny Bone

With not a little joy I now have opportunity to momentarily depart from discussing things serious and move to things jovial, for no treatment of speech and language would be complete without discussing humor. Our wonderful sense of humor comes to us as part and parcel of that wonderful Heavenly image bestowed upon us (much as it may come as a surprise to those who tend to view God as a celestial ogre playing whack-a-mole with anyone who dares lift their head out of the hole of misery and solemnity), for in the Psalms alone (2:4, 37:13, 59:8) He is three times portrayed as One who laughs. That this is laughter at the expense of those who practice evil makes no difference to the point at hand, which is that God has a sense of humor and comedy.

The Bible is by and large a very serious Book, for the Fall and Redemption are tragedy in the deepest sense. In like manner the Gospels do not showcase the humor of Jesus, for His work and mission were serious beyond description, and He was the Man of Sorrows that we might not have to be. But there is comedy hidden cleverly there for the astute observer (such as when He renamed the brothers John and James as the *Sons of Thunder*), and it is not hard to understand how great a sense of humor was needed to last three years with the Twelve at His side. And then there is the undeniable fact that the common people loved to be with Him, which tells us He was quick with a smile and good humor, for no one wants to be around a sourpuss.

God is the Author of laughter, and so by extension is also the Author of humor, mirth, enjoyment, fun, the party and the festival. In fact, with the exception of the deeply solemn Yom Kippur, the Israelite Festivals instituted by God were times of festive joy, laughter, dancing and merrymaking for the Chosen People. As Eden originally showed us, life was meant to be saturated with delight.

The ungod would, of course, disown God of these characteristics and claim them as his own, and in his usurpation would paint himself as the Great Reveler, while painting their true Author as the terrible Cosmic Killjoy. The Enemy has therefore brought all the arsenal already mentioned in this Battlefield to bear upon laughter and its natural extensions, lowering them to the level of his lewd and filthy sewer of crudeness, debauchery and moral stench. In the end, however, it shall be God who has the last laugh.

THE BELIEVER'S OFFENSIVE

As the passage of Scripture used to open this Battlefield indicates, *the Word* is one of the titles ascribed to Jesus in the Bible (John 1:1). Since *word* is what we use to communicate that which is inside of us (or who and what we are) to others, this then means that Jesus is the fullness of God's communication to humanity of who and what God is. This hallows – or makes holy – the very idea of communication. As people redeemed by this Living Word, then, Believers should be people of holy speech.

Our speech must primarily be speech dedicated to Truth, and not to Lie, for it is inappropriate that the Lie pass either our lips or our pens. Since we know that we speak out of the abundance of the inner being (Matthew 12:34), it therefore becomes requisite that we put forth all effort into being people of the Biblical worldview and of Christ-likeness, for these things bring inner beauty.

Once guided by an inward foundation of Truth, our communication will be far more precious to us, and so become something both of greater focus and of less use. The greater focus will result in (like God-wardness of thought) a turning of all communication Heavenward in due and appropriate time. We must bear constantly in mind that the pinnacle of purpose for speech is Truth and Him who is Truth. Our speech, even in ordinary things, should therefore never be far nor long from Him. Likewise, as we acknowledge that we are people redeemed by the Living Word, and are molded into His image by the guiding work of the Holy Spirit, we should more and more begin to mirror His use of language. Our words should become less even while their impact grows. This means that we should reflect His economy with words, moving ever further away from the meaningless chattering and blabbering that so plagues fallen human speech.

Such Christ-centered appreciation of speech will necessarily produce a profound change both upon our working vocabulary and how we direct our conversation concerning our fellow human beings. The low, base, defiled and meaningless topics of communication will be replaced by ideas noble and dignified, and a fairness and beauty will season that which passes our lips and pens. Likewise, this more Heavenly attitude will allow us to see our fellow Image Bearers in the light of Truth, compelling us to change our thoughts, vocabulary and speech about (and toward) others. The same mouth that praises God has no place cursing or degrading those who have been made in God's likeness (James 3:9,10).

Finally, I must end this Battlefield with a frank discussion upon the understanding of language. As stated earlier, the working of the human mind is functionally linked to (and therefore limited by) the mind's understanding of the working of language. The human intellect is capable of profound thought, but this thought must occur within the boundaries of language, for words must be put to the idea for it to be both understood and communicated. An understanding of language, therefore, may either hinder or enhance thought. Where understanding of language is limited, depth of thought is limited; where understanding of language is deep, depth of thought is enabled.

We are today hobbits of thought and language when compared to our forefathers in the faith of but two and three centuries ago, and the reason is not hard to surmise: such thought and language arose from people whose lives and culture were centered upon Truth. Truth *elevates* language, and elevated language elevates thought. Elevated thought allows for greater understanding of God (who is infinite Truth), which is why the ungod has such a vested interest in miring our understanding of language at the lowest level possible. Such a miring hobbles our ability to understand that which the human mind was meant to understand: truth in ever-increasing proportion.

Believers must, therefore, make every effort to be masters of language. We must know how it operates; we must know well its rules; we should know of its syntax and punctuation; we should be able to write it and speak it with equal fluency; we should strive to find a comfort and personal style with it; and we should strive to master its lexicon. We must return to being students of language, for the very quality of that which is truly Life depends upon it.

BATTLEFIELD: LOVE

This is how we know what love is:
Jesus Christ laid down his life for us
I John 3:16a

God is known for few things (if any at all) more than He is known for love, and so to this wonderful idea we now turn, for it is humanity's deep and distinct privilege to reflect such a far-reaching and nearly indescribably wonderful Divine attribute.

The Original Image

As discussed in this book's opening chapter, love is a most dangerous thing, for to exist it requires choice, and choice requires the exercise of free will. Adam and Eve were created as beings capable of such love, and the ultimate object of that love was God Himself (Deuteronomy 6:5). For them to love God therefore required that they be able to *choose* God, which meant that they likewise be able *not* to choose Him. This is why the Tree of the Knowledge of Good and Evil had to be part of the floral arrangement in the Garden of Eden – it represented choice for them. In their supreme innocence (which is a far cry from our current fallen nature), loving God would exist through their continuing choice to abstain from the fruit of that Tree.

Regarding love's capacity, it would have been much the same with love as it was with the mind: God is infinite love, and so to maintain a loving relationship with Him, the human capacity for love must be (though finite) quite substantial in scope, for one must assume that a loving, personal God would derive pleasure from such a relationship, and thus would have designed and infused humanity with a tremendous capacity for love. For the unfallen First Couple, this would have naturally centered the idea of love upon love's Author in its outlet and expression,

---

and from there it would have turned beautifully toward their fellow human beings, bathing human relationships in great richness and beauty.

But we must now turn away from the Garden (even before the discussion usually held in *The Image Undone*) in order that we might more fully define love, for it is rare among the facets of the Image in that it is better defined *because of* the Fall, rather than before it. Now there are many human definitions of love (ranging from the absurd to the truly noble), but love is properly defined *only* by the act of the Cross, for it is God who reserves the right to define Himself in this regard, and He does so quite clearly in the epistle of First John.

In 1 John 4:16 we are told that *God is love*. In 1 John 3:16 we find this statement: *This is how we know what love is: Jesus Christ laid down his life for us*. Since we know that Jesus laid down His life for us upon the Cross, we're able to understand that the Cross therefore defines love as it exists in the nature of God. In effect, regarding His characteristic of love, God says *I am the Cross*.

Upon the Cross, Jesus (who is God) gave up everything for us who had nothing. He lost all; we gained all. He considered Himself unimportant; us as important. He who was sinless became our hated sin that we might be holy. His wrists and feet took the nails that by right should have been ours, and He experienced the despair of the separation from God (Matthew 27:46; Mark 15:34) that was our rightful inheritance for all eternity. It was the unshakeable, unconditional and willing commitment to serve another despite the cost of doing so. True, Biblical, God-centered love is therefore an absolutely unselfish giving to the one loved, thinking nothing of oneself. This is our God, and this love that defines Him is the most powerful thing in existence.

THE IMAGE UNDONE

Since this God-defined – or *true* – love is such a powerful thing, the ungod must at all costs bring about its undoing in humanity. And we must remember that the Devil is in this regard both peerless specialist and author, for it was he who first used the choice inherent in his own capacity for love to usher Evil into existence. That he could then likewise turn a third of the hosts of Heaven to his cause speaks to his rather remarkable persuasive ability in this arena, and we must begrudge the ungod the respect he is therefore due. To not do so would be both unwise and dangerous, for we must know our Enemy.

Regarding the undoing of Good among the rebellious angels, it seems to have been as complete as it was final. It may be due to their nature as pure spirit, but whether they chose Good or Evil in the Rebellion, love the choice of each angel appears to have been set for all eternity once the fateful decision was reached: those who chose Good are now forever good and loving, while those who chose Evil are now forever evil and unloving. As for the fallen angels, each was now as fully ungod as their leader, although apparently without his level of power or pedigree. When the Rebellion was later quelled and the fallen angels captured, they were then sent to their prison (the pristine planet Earth), where the ungod would naturally marshal his efforts against the human lords of it, for Evil must at all times spread until all that is Good is removed from existence.

Having had such personal and coercive success at turning the capacity for love into Evil in the heavenly realm, the ungod then set his sights upon the same achievement with the unfallen First Couple, something at which he was again successful (as the third chapter of Genesis ably describes). Yet even though the Enemy was indeed successful in separating humanity from its Creator via the introduction of the fallen sinful nature, his success with humanity was not as thorough as it was with the fallen angels, for in humanity the Divine Image was not fully exchanged, but merely corrupted.

The existence of the human conscience (the ability to be aware of sin and repent of it) apparently caused the Fall and the exchange of the Image in humanity to be greatly tempered when compared to that of the angels, for Adam and Eve were ashamed and sorrowful over their choice and actions – something not seen among the fallen heavenly host. Whether the ungod was surprised by this we shall never know in this life, but I have no doubt that he was deeply angered by the failure of eradicating the Divine Image from humanity. And when humanity retained its ability to love as their Creator loved (something no longer possible for the Evil One), the eradication or pollution of that love became a top priority of the ungod.

UNLOVELY

The primary tactic used by the ungod would necessarily be that of turning love away from its Source. True and Divine love is *outward* by necessity, for it must be directed toward another to be valid. And just as we were meant to be recipients of God's love, He was meant to be the primary recipient of ours, for we are called to love the Lord our God with all our heart, soul and strength (Deuteronomy 6:5), making love a God-ward thing in its first and most natural expression.

Using God's own definition of love, we are therefore called to put all of who and what we are into willingly, unconditionally and selflessly serving Him, which will translate into doing all for His glory. To bring God glory simply means to see that He is the object of honor, praise and distinction, a calling which is the highest purpose of human existence. This God-ward love from humanity is the summary of what is meant by *worship*, for it implies an understanding by the created both of their Creator and of the rightful position between the two: the finite before the Infinite, the small before the Great, the weak before the Mighty, and the mortal before the Eternal. As such, it is an utter selflessness before God, and a turning of humanity from such love is therefore an imperative for the ungod, who is the sworn enemy of selflessness.

To accomplish this, love must first be redirected away from God by the ungod, and then redefined until its original definition is forgotten either through lack of use, ignorance or outright pollution. When the human capacity for love then becomes other than or less than it was intended to be, the *other than* or *less than* component of what once was love now becomes that which might truly be known as love's absence, or *lovelessness*. Any departure from love in its purest and God-defined state (however slight in degree) is therefore an entering into a degree of lovelessness, and advances the standard of Evil upon Earth.

While the term *lovelessness* may seem a bit cumbersome to use (especially when we have the term *hatred* available to us), I am disinclined to use hatred to describe the absence of love, as hatred is not a thing foreign to God (Amos 5:21; Zechariah 8:17; Malachi 2:16). We must realize that since He is a perfectly holy Being, God must by definition hate all that is Evil (for He cannot do otherwise), thereby making hatred (of Evil only) a Divine attribute, however strange that may sound to us.

SELF LOVE

It is through the fallen human nature that the Enemy finds his softest target in convincing people to be lovers of themselves (also known as *selfishness* or *self-centeredness*). True love is always outward – first toward God, then toward others – for it is never concerned with itself. Turning one's love upon oneself, then, is the true absence of love and therefore the purest form of lovelessness. It is also the truest reflection of the image and character of the ungod (who embodies selfishness and self-centeredness), and it provided the impetus for both the Rebellion and the Fall. Ever since then it has been the driving force for most all human calamity, for where it thrives everyone is living strictly in order to serve themselves, thereby depleting humanity of the Divine Image and making decent society a virtual impossibility.

And so these thousands of years later we are now nearly consumed with *self*, and as the ungod exerts his ever-increasing hold over communication and education, it will only grow worse. Self-image, self-esteem, self-help and self-love have become terms so commonplace that we never think to question their validity or their ultimate Hellish source, even as they destroy nearly all that is of Heavenly inspiration. Sadly, even now that final bastion of God's image of love in humanity – the unconditional love of parent for child – is teetering under the onslaught of this lovelessness, as parents are conditioned at an ever-increasing rate toward abandoning the raising and loving of their children in pursuit of selfish gain and pleasure. Children raised without knowing love will not then know how to give it, and so we are as a culture perhaps two generations from being absolutely enveloped by lovelessness if this trend is not interrupted.

Humanity is truly hastening its own end.

Such a loving of self obviously replaces the rightful loving of God (which is worship), and so is little more than self-worship, through which a person pursues all things for the glory of him- or herself. Here the self is what matters most – whether it be pleasure for self, money for self, power for self or fame for self – and is the human complement to the attitude of Lucifer in the Isaiah 14:13,14: *I will ascend to heaven; I will raise my throne above the stars of God; I will sit enthroned on the mount of assembly, on the utmost heights of the sacred mountain. I will ascend above the tops of the clouds; I will make myself like the Most High.*

CAUSE AND EFFECT

Yet despite the Enemy's monumental success in the realm of love, there are those among humanity with whom rampant selfishness and self-centeredness just do not sit well, and so self-worship with them is not a sound tactic for the ungod to pursue. To keep such people from turning love's capacity God-ward, the Enemy must divert love downward and yet at the same time away from self. This he does by coercing people to subscribe to the idea of a *cause*, into which they pour forth love's selflessness. When we discuss such causes, we must remember that any diversion from love's God-ward direction is a diversion ungod-ward, and therefore *any* cause will do, whether noble or ignoble. Let us remember that the directing of love God-ward is worship, and since all people possess this aptitude, all people are naturally worshippers. The only difference between people in this respect is the object of their worship: God, self or cause.

The cause-worshippers of today subscribe to a dizzying array of causes, many of which are seemingly quite noble. But none are noble when in a person's life they are used to divert one's love away from God (the direction of worship) toward things earthly, whatever they may be. Some people will spend weeks or months perched atop a majestic oak or redwood tree to save it from the saw, but will never deign to set foot in a church where the Word of God is clearly taught. And how many across our world give their lives in the cause of human freedom while never stopping to consider that the foundation of the human heart's cry for it is a reflection of the image of Him who is completely free?

Worship of the cause is done in the absence of worship of the Creator, and so is in fact worship of the ungod (as is worship of self). Yet for all the success that the Dark One has achieved here, these modern causes of ours have merely scratched the surface of all that the Enemy has accomplished in this arena of the Image War, for he has wrought far greater-reaching havoc upon the facet of love and worship through the seemingly innocuous instrument of attempting to worship God – that of false religion.

THE SANTA CAUSE

If we consider that the purpose of the cause is to divert human love away from God, it will become immediately evident that there can be no more ingenious and deceptive cause than that of coercing humanity into the realm of false religious worship. Every form of human religious worship done apart from the perfect confines of God's perfect Word is a form of worship of this type of cause, and therefore has the ungod as its author and the one to whom the worship is therefore ultimately (though indirectly) given. Every Hindu, albeit indirectly, worships the Prince of Darkness, as does each Muslim, each Buddhist, each Sikh, each Druze, each Latter Day Saint, each Jehovah's Witness, each New Ager, each cultist, each occultist, each pagan, each animist, each follower of Messiah-rejecting Judaism, each follower of works-based or aberrant Christianity, and each and every follower of any other Darkness-inspired form of human worship.

I do not mean to be unnecessarily harsh with this description, for I know well enough that there are many wonderful and sincere people included in the list above. But we must remember that sincerity does not make something true. One may be the most wonderful person alive and believe with all sincerity that two plus two equals five, but he or she will still fail their math test. When we consider that all religions ultimately claim to be the true path to God or Enlightenment, it likewise means that they are all mutually exclusive. This in turn dictates that there are only two possible conclusions at which we can arrive: either they are all wrong, or only one is correct. By rising from the dead to eternal life, Jesus proved Himself to be the One who is True, and also validated the Bible as God's revealed Word to humanity. Worship of God through the confines of that Word is therefore the *only* form of worship deemed unacceptable to the ungod, for he is the author of all others.

LOVEY DOVEY

As we move from the God-ward aspect of love, we encounter that which was meant to be the greatest of blessings in the earthly realm – that of God-defined love between human beings (Leviticus 19:18). Since this love and its attendant blessings are such a hated reminder of the Divine Image, the ungod must do all that he can to see them completely extinguished from humanity and replaced with the curse of his image. As we have already seen, much of the human ability to express selflessness toward their fellows has been dealt a great setback through the worship of self and cause by means of his dark influence. But since this has not resulted in seeing love fully extinguished among us, the ungod must make yet further assaults upon the idea of love, and he does this by redefining and demeaning the human understanding of it.

From Hell's perspective, God's definition of love must not be allowed to reign over the human understanding of the concept, and so the ungod has proffered to us some ingenious replacements. Chief among them is the idea that love is something into and out of which we can fall, and so we routinely find ourselves using phrases such as *falling in love* and *falling out of love*. In so doing, we have reduced the concept of love to no more than a mushy, warm-and-fuzzy emotion – a far cry from that which was so painfully exhibited upon Calvary's Tree.

A further redefining of love comes by way of the idea that love is something that we make; hence couples retire to the bedroom to *make love* or for *lovemaking*. This denigrates the very concept of love (as the ungod knows full well), for love is not something that can be made, but is, rather, evidenced in the unconditional commitment to another. Through thinking and language such as being *in love* and *making love*, the

Enemy has managed to disrobe love of much of its majesty, placing it in the realm of mere emotion and fleshly pleasure.

Finally, there is the freedom and frequency with which we use the very word itself. Some people *love* sports. Some people *love* pizza. Some people *love* the great outdoors. Some people *love* music. Some people *love* old movies. We *love* so many things so much with such an alarming frequency that we have devalued the word to such a degree as to make it very nearly worthless. This has been part of the regression of our language (as discussed in the previous Battlefield) and is an excellent example of how integrated is the ungod's assault upon all of the facets of the Divine Image in us.

THE BELIEVER'S OFFENSIVE

Perhaps the greatest transformation in Scripture was that of the apostle John, who was changed from a *Son of Thunder* who was willing to see an entire Samaritan village destroyed for refusing Jesus hospitality (Luke 9:54) into the John *the Beloved* who penned the inspiring words of First John.

I believe that John loved so fiercely and truly later in life because he personally saw love defined at Golgotha – saw it defined in the commitment of blood and sweat and unspeakable agony. Being alone among the disciples for having followed Jesus to the very foot of the Cross (John 19:26), John saw Jesus hanging where he (John) should be, saw his own sins slaying his Messiah and Savior, and yet through that intense suffering saw that same Jesus forgive John his sins. It was the most selfless event in the history of the universe, and John could not escape it ever after, nor could he ever be the same man.

The Cross is love, and we must know and live this love. The Cross is not a symbol, it is not a bumper sticker and it is not a t-shirt slogan. It is God defining Himself for us, and in so doing defining for us the most noble path for human existence possible. The Cross is the seminal event of all history, and it is therefore an absolute necessity that each of us experience it as John did. We must stand in his sandals and see with his eyes and let our hearts be absolutely crushed with the unbridled and costly commitment of Christ for each of us His enemy and slayer. *Then* we shall know love and be capable of it, and from that foundation we shall be able to love the Lord our God and to love our neighbor as ourselves. And Hell has no answer or countermeasure for such a thing.

BATTLEFIELD: HOLINESS

Holy, holy, holy is the Lord God Almighty;
who was, and is, and is to come
Revelation 4:8c

We now close our study of the Image War for the individual with a brief discussion upon the idea of human holiness. God is a holy Being (Isaiah 6:3), and as beings created in His image we were naturally designed for holy behavior.

THE ORIGINAL IMAGE

When the Scriptures describe God as holy, they are telling us that God is thoroughly good and completely incapable of evil. Since humanity was created in His image, this meant that we were originally designed for holy behavior, or *holiness*. This holiness is best and most simply described as *thought and conduct consistent with the nature of God*.

As discussed in the Battlefield over the human body, in creating humanity as a reflection of Himself, God embedded the idea of holiness in our very genes, for our unique bodies are designed to be *upright* in their carriage – stark and open reminders of Him who is upright in all His ways. This natural carriage is therefore both an advertisement of the nature of God and a call to conduct befitting Him, and is why we still inherently rejoice so greatly at our child's or grandchild's first steps, for it is a grand and noble thing to walk upright. Uprightness has great and deep meaning to the human soul. Holiness is written into us.

THE IMAGE UNDONE

If upright conduct is befitting a race of beings who were designed to advertise the existence of God in the physical universe, then our great

---

Enemy must naturally seek to have us crawling on all fours in issues of thought and conduct, bereft of all behavior noble and chaste in origin, bowed and enslaved to all that is foul and unholy. The Fall itself ensured the genesis of the Dark Image in humanity in this regard, while the sinful nature resulting from the Fall coupled with the influence of Hell will naturally see to its completion and supremacy if left unchecked (Genesis 6:5; Romans 1:18-32).

But as the many Battlefields of the Image War all detail in one regard or another this struggle between holy and unholy conduct, it is not necessary to further detail the struggle here. Instead, I shall break from my established format and take this opportunity to remark upon the disastrous and deadly human consequences of the Fall, and also upon the Divine response to it.

HARD LANDING

God is holy and therefore must by nature always do what is right, and part of doing what is right is the act of punishing wrongdoing – something that we call *administering justice*. From the human perspective there are many degrees of wrongdoing (ranging from the seemingly innocuous *little white lie* to the obviously heinous act of murder), and we administer justice accordingly, with anything from a slap on the wrist to capital punishment. This is rightly so, for some wrongdoing is clearly worse than others and therefore deserves greater punishment.

Yet for all of the many degrees of human wrongdoing, they all still have this one and most important facet in common: they are all *wrongdoing*. If we put aside the *degrees* of wrongdoing, we are still left with the wrongdoing itself, which is an act of unholiness and an affront to God (who must take all wrongdoing personally). The Bible identifies this as sin and, because God is holy, He must administer justice upon the sinner for the sin. He simply *cannot* do otherwise, for to do so would betray His holiness. Whether it is the little white lie or murder (or anything falling between these two extremes), every sinful act must be punished in order for God to remain true to Himself.

There are two forms of punishment administered by God upon sinners – the *temporary* and the *eternal*. The *temporary* punishment is that which is administered during our earthly lives, and may come in the forms of parental chastisement (Proverbs 23:13), governmental chastisement (such as the Law of Moses) or by the direct hand of God upon our lives (Genesis 4:11; 1 Corinthians 11:30). The *eternal* punishment is that which awaits the sinner upon his or her death, and is defined as eternal separation from God (Revelation 20:10; Genesis 3:23,24). The reason for this separation is that those who are unholy cannot dwell in the presence of a holy God (Psalm 5:4) any more than darkness can dwell with light (2 Corinthians 6:14).

It is precisely because of this that God has created a place completely devoid of holiness; in fact, completely devoid of all that He is. The Bible identifies this location as *Hell*, an everlasting dwelling place originally created for the fallen angels (Matthew 25:41). It was not intended for humanity, but humanity doomed itself to the eternal environs of Hell through the sin of Adam, in whose loins we were all then represented (Romans 5:12). And lest we cry foul at being unfairly included in such punishment, let us remember that we daily show our solidarity with Adam's decision by willfully sinning as we have occasion. Through such action we regularly demonstrate that we would have made the same decision as he.

Regarding the notion of Hell, it must be understood that it is a place where God is not, and is therefore a place in which all that God is – in every aspect of His Being – *is not present.*

There will be no kindness in Hell, for kindness is of God. There will be no joy. There will be no beauty. There will be no comfort. There will be no rest. There will be no friendship. There will be no loyalty. There will be no intimacy. There will be no health. There will be no delight. There will be no smiles. There will be no laughter. There will be no open-handedness or honesty. There will be no order. There will be no peace. Simply put, it is the summation of all that is horrible, foul, distasteful and corrupt. *And it is forever.* Above all, it is a place to be feared and shunned, which is precisely why Jesus spoke of Hell far more than of Heaven, that humanity might be sufficiently warned of it.

The Enemy's insidious brilliance here is that in enticing the First Couple into sin and therefore into being clothed by the unholy sinful nature, he pitted humanity (the ultimate object of Divine love and affection) against its holy Creator. By way of this unholiness, in one fell swoop did humanity become the enemy of God and become forever destined to that hopeless place meant to everlastingly house the ungod and his minions. Dire indeed was now the lot of humanity.

Rescue

This changed and degraded human condition that arose from the Fall put at odds with one another God's love and holiness. His love demanded that He should maintain fellowship with humanity, but His holiness demanded that He could not. God's answer to this conundrum was the beautiful and wondrous Plan of Redemption, whereby God could fulfill the demands of both love and holiness and (albeit at a staggering cost to Himself) return humanity to everlasting fellowship with Him. This great Plan is the summation of all of Scripture, and I shall here touch only briefly – though reverently – upon it.

By the sacrifice of animals to provide coverings for the nakedness of Adam and Eve (Genesis 3:21), and later and more fully through the sacrificial system instituted through the Law of Moses, God demonstrated that the guilt of humanity might be temporarily covered by sacrificially shedding the lifeblood of those animals considered *clean*. This was the *model* through which God established that innocent blood shed on behalf of the guilty could restore fellowship between God and humanity.

I use the term *model* because this sacrificial system was only a type and a foreshadowing of that true and real Sacrifice to come (of which more shall soon be written). The idea clearly portrayed through this Mosaic sacrificial system is that those guilty of sin could be forgiven and restored to fellowship with God by the shedding of the blood of one who is innocent. The shortcoming of this model is that the animals involved were not technically pure or innocent, for they had also been subjected to the bondage of decay holding sway over all Creation. They were also merely *animals*, and the sins for which they were being sacrificed were human sins. This is why, though God dwelt among the people of Israel during the sacrificial era of the Tabernacle and Temple, He did so only behind the thick veil guarding the way to the Most Holy Place, behind which no one was allowed to enter (apart from the High Priest on the Day of Atonement). Sin (or unholiness) still separated God from the people, *because it is impossible for the blood of bulls and goats to take away sins* (Hebrews 10:4).

What the model could show (but could not complete) was that it was necessary for innocent *human* blood to be shed on behalf of guilty sinners in order to purchase true forgiveness from Heaven. The problem with such a proposition is the same as it was concerning the sacrificial animals – there is no truly innocent human being, for all are tainted through Adam's seed (Romans 5:12). However, Abraham prophetically showed to us the solution to this problem by his willingness to sacrifice his dearly-loved son upon the mountain to which God had led him. Of course we know that God stopped Abraham from making a sacrificial offering of his son (for it would have accomplished nothing), but God would later offer His only begotten Son as *the Sacrifice* for the sins of humanity upon that exact location (Genesis 22:14).

Since no innocent human blood – without which humanity could never be restored to everlasting fellowship with God – was available, God the Son took upon Himself human form in the Incarnation (John 1:14), becoming fully human and subsequently living a holy and sinless life (Hebrews 4:15). His purpose in doing so was to offer His life and his literally perfect human blood (Hebrews 9:12-14,18b) as the necessary price of human redemption, which explains John the Baptist's reaction upon first seeing Jesus: *Look, the Lamb of God, who takes away the sin of the world!* (John 1:29b). This work Jesus would eventually do upon the Cross, where He reconciled sinful humanity with a holy God.

The great horror of the Cross is that not only did Jesus die upon it, but that He actually became our sin as He hung there (2 Corinthians 5:21). And having become sin, the Son was then separated from the Father and cried out *My God, my God, why have you forsaken me?*

(Matthew 27:46; Mark 15:34). He therefore experienced the separation from God that was ours by right, during which the full might and power of the holy wrath of the Living God was poured out upon Him until the full price for every sin ever committed was exacted from Him. He experienced every bit of Hell (the complete absence of the Father) that could be experienced, for He had to fully complete the Sentence handed down upon guilty humanity by that Heavenly Court.

The act then completed, the Heavenly Judge declared humanity's debt to be paid in full (John 19:30), placing His stamp of approval upon the Sacrifice by raising His Son from death to life and seating Him at His right hand forevermore (Ephesians 1:20,21). And so upon the Cross were the Divine demands of love and holiness reconciled toward man, for the great veil blocking the way to the Most Holy Place was torn from top to bottom (Matthew 27:51), signifying that God and humanity should no longer be separated. Such was the majesty of the Cross, where Divine love and holiness were both satisfied.

And now I must end this discussion of the Cross with a warning for those who may misunderstand its nature. While it is true that the Savior paid the full price for all human sins, that payment is not automatically put to every person's account with Heaven. Here we must look again to the model, which required the individual desiring atonement to choose the animal, bring it to the altar, confess his sins and then offer the animal as a substitute in order to purchase atonement (Leviticus 4). It was available to every Israelite, but not every Israelite asked for atonement on God's terms. Likewise, Christ's forgiveness is available to all, but is good only for those who come to Him on His terms and ask of Him to be forgiven through the work of the Cross (John 14:6; Acts 4:12).

It must be remembered that God is holy, and therefore *all sin* will be judged. If we allow our sin to be judged in Christ, only then are we acceptable to God, for Christ grants us His righteousness in exchange for our sin (Romans 4:24; 1 Corinthians 1:30), and we shall thereby escape judgment. Those who do not come to Christ for forgiveness according to God's terms will themselves pay the everlasting price of their guilt, for the price *must be paid*. Sin is paid for either by the Savior upon the Cross, or (for all eternity) by the sinner if he or she *chooses* to pay the price by rejecting the Savior's free and gracious offer of forgiveness.

THE BELIEVER'S OFFENSIVE

The Believer's heart should pulse with the yearning for holiness in every manner of living, for we are new creatures reborn of that holy and Heavenly seed, and so we should ache to be holy even as our Father in Heaven is holy (Leviticus 19:2). He who died for us and who lives in us is holy still by nature, and thus still hates sin and unholiness. If our lives are therefore not characterized by a revulsion and hatred of sin, we can scarcely say that we know the thrice-holy God (1 John 3:6).

Let us with all honesty acknowledge that sin will always be a struggle for us as long as we inhabit these corrupted mortal bodies so painfully subject to the desires of the fallen nature. And although this effectively means that perfection will never be our lot in this life (despite how greatly we may desire it), let us likewise acknowledge that a life led and filled by the Holy Spirit *will always be one marked by a steady march toward perfection* (2 Corinthians 3:18). The image of Christ, therefore, should always be growing in us, even as the image of the ungod steadily diminishes. Holiness is our birthright in Christ; it is the new native tongue of the child of God. Let us be fluent in it.

THE IMAGE WAR:
THE FAMILY

BATTLEFIELD: MANHOOD

Be strong, Philistines!
Be men, or you will be subject to the Hebrews,
as they have been to you.
Be men, and fight!
1 Samuel 4:9

As we now move on from study of the individual and into study of human affairs, we are met with the idea of the family, for it is with family that all human affairs begin. And such a study naturally has its genesis with the idea of manhood, into which we are now privileged to delve.

THE ORIGINAL IMAGE

Any discussion of family must necessarily entail that we look into the idea of marriage, which in turn demands that we investigate the natures of the man and woman who comprise the idea of it. This requires us to define the issues of man and manhood and of woman and womanhood, something that is usually far too laborious, psychological and/or theological for most of us. But I have found an easier way.

Much may be inferred of an object's function by studying its physical form. During the four years that I spent serving aboard the aircraft carrier USS Eisenhower, the F/A-18 Hornet was introduced into widespread use by naval aviation. By merely walking around and off-handedly studying such an aircraft, I could infer that it was a swift and deadly machine of war, for its form belied its purpose and nature. This is likewise true of the human form in general (as has already been discussed), and so also is true when looking in closer detail at the male and female forms.

Since man was created first, we shall first take the closer look at the male form. When compared to its feminine counterpart, the male form is taller, notably stronger and harder-edged, with a sexuality that is projective and outward. Since form belies purpose and nature, we may rightly infer that the nature of manhood is therefore the projection of power and strength. In short, man is the designed *Hero*, with all that is naturally implied by the idea: steadfast, brave, loyal, selfless, honorable, rugged and dependable. He is a guardian between things Evil and Good; he is a champion of the weak and vulnerable; he is a leader in things righteous. And he is naturally dangerous.

The study of the form of woman (when likewise compared to its masculine counterpart) also yields its own substantial and telling differences. It is smaller, less strong and with a kindness to its softness. Its sexuality is receptive and inward, and is enhanced by the prominence of the breasts, at which her children are most naturally nursed. Whereas the power of the male form demands sufficient space in which to dwell, the softer, kinder and gentler form of woman is an invitation to draw nearer to it. Of the two (as her form would imply) she is far more of the caregiver, and her nature is more gentle, more receiving, more patient, more enduring and more able to develop and rear the children brought forth from her womb. She is designed to be the *Nurturer*.

But before proceeding further upon the study of manhood, I must interject some thoughts on the differences of form just discussed. These differences are notable because they are just that – differences. Yet we must remember that in form (and thereby in purpose and in nature) the male and the female forms have far more in common than in difference, and so by no means should it be thought that the differences are what fully define man and woman. Man is quite capable of nurture – as is woman of the heroic – for God (in whose image both are created) is fully Hero and fully Nurturer. I therefore believe it best, prudent and most reasonable to think of our male and female natures along the lines of collegiate studies, which have a major and a minor thrust. With man, Hero is the major and Nurturer the minor; with woman, Nurturer is the major and Hero the minor.

The Image Undone

When engaged in warfare, a great deal of thought revolves around the leadership of the enemy camp, for the quality of that leadership will often dictate your own fortunes in the conflict. The best situation would therefore be to find yourself arrayed against an enemy whose leadership is ineffective, for such leadership will hamstring your enemy (essentially making the enemy leadership your ally). The worst situation would be to find yourself arrayed against an enemy with experienced and brilliant leadership, for your enemy will then be difficult to overcome. In such a situation, the enemy leadership must be targeted for death or capture.

Although the ungod wages the Image War on a dizzying array of fronts, when he marshals his forces against God's idea of the family, it is therefore the idea of manhood and its leadership within the family that bears the brunt of his assault. Here the Dark One looks to ensure that the male leadership of the family's Hero is either ineffective or nonexistent, and if the ungod finds himself set against a true Hero, he will seek that Hero's death or destruction (Job 1:10,11). By virtue of its nature, manhood therefore exists in the very center of the Enemy's crosshairs, for he knows full well that if he is able to poison or weaken the root of rightful male leadership, the tree and fruit of marriage and family will likewise be poisoned and weakened most effectively.

How the Mighty Have Fallen

The most powerful figure in the marriage and the family should belong to that of the husband and father, for he is the Hero of the household. Such power must not stem from the fact that the male is physically stronger (for this may not always be the case), but rather stem from respect given to the clear teaching of Scripture and his given role as Hero. This is not to say that he must have the most noticeable personality in the household (or even an overbearing personality), for women are usually by far the more personally interesting and complex of the pair. But whether flamboyant or subdued, the presence of the man should be the *weightiest* of the household, and be held in respect (and even a certain degree of awe), for heroes are naturally respected as individuals somewhat larger-than-life, and embody for us the best of what humanity can and should be.

The Hero is someone branded by a notable degree of selflessness, and who puts life, prestige or fortune on the line for the sake of God, country, family, friend or cause. And nowhere is this better demonstrated than in the Cross of Christ, upon which was accomplished the most heroic and selfless deed that the universe shall ever know. This is the Divine mold of Hero from which man is pressed – he is meant to stand undeterred as the selfless bulwark of protection around his wife and children and all things good. He is forged to be strong, constant, faithful and honorable as he faces with unflagging determination and selflessness the storms that would beset the hallowed ground of family.

Needless to say, the ungod has nothing but disgust and hatred for this Divine facet of Hero in man, and must necessarily turn his dark energies toward destroying or polluting it beyond recognition. And since the Hero is defined by selflessness, the Evil One does not have a difficult task before him, for the sinful human nature has at its core the basest degree of selfishness. A selfish Hero is by definition no true Hero, and so all that needs to occur for the ungod's image to reign supreme in the man is for the man to turn selfish. Once this is done, the Hero is fallen – and we inherently find few things more pathetic and pitiable than a fallen hero.

Simply put, a hero is a servant. To act as the designed Hero of the family, then, the man must put aside all self-interest for the sake of his wife, children and home. They (and their welfare) must be what drive the very pounding of his heart and the breath of his lungs. There is simply no room for *self* in the Hero, and when the ungod manages to deter the man by thoughts of self-interest, the Hero rapidly falls. When monetary gain, position, prestige or power is placed before family, the Hero is fallen. When friendship, companionship or sexual desire is placed before family, the Hero is fallen. When hobbies, interests, goals, apathy or entertainment are placed before family, the Hero is fallen. All things for the Hero must submit to the idea of family, for he is its champion, and his hand must never tire of bearing its standard.

For the ungod, then, the remaking of the heroic facet of men into his image chiefly involves turning men toward selfishness, which is the *undoing* of heroism. Once a man is so turned (or to the degree that he is turned) the Hero is fallen and becomes Hell's servant. He has become the Coward.

OLD YELLER

So instinctively reproachful is the term *coward* that no man wants to be thought of in such light, for it is perhaps the greatest slander possible to his innate manhood. In reality, however, the Coward inhabits us all, for he dwells in the sinful nature. Since the Hero is selfless, the Coward is self-consumed. Where the Hero takes a stand, the Coward flees. Where the Hero embraces Truth, the Coward embraces Lie. Where the Hero is loyal, the Coward betrays. Where the Hero protects, the Coward leaves vulnerable. Where the Hero is strong, the Coward is weak. Where the Hero perseveres, the Coward gives up. Where the Hero is engaged in the struggle, the Coward is apathetic.

The sad truth of the matter is that modern manhood far more resembles the Coward than the Hero, for men are growing more and more concerned with (and are loyal only to) themselves. In this we bear that hideous image of the ungod, in whom the Coward originated, for after being created by a selfless God, it was he who became consumed with himself (Isaiah 14:12-14). It is in him that weakness, disloyalty and failing therefore have their genesis, and it is he who would stain all of manhood with the stench of his cowardly nature.

Additionally, as we discuss the heroic, it must be noted that the Hero is quite firmly embedded in men by God's creative hand; so deeply, in fact, that the ungod is unable to convince all men to completely abandon the idea of the heroic. Here it must be remembered that Hero is an attribute of God, and so anything *truly heroic* must be in accordance with the nature of the Divine Personality. For instance, when the Apostle Paul risked his life to spread the Gospel (2 Corinthians 11:23-27), it was something in keeping with the nature of God and His revealed Truth

(Matthew 28:19), and was therefore *truly* heroic. However, when he had previously risked his life to persecute Believers (Acts 9:1,2), it was not in keeping with the nature of God and His revealed Truth, and was therefore *not* heroic. One cannot be a hero *against* Jehovah.

Such misguided heroism as Paul's original heroism is therefore a departure from true heroism, making it a form of cowardice and making each of its practitioners a Coward. Please understand that bravery is not in question here; purpose is. As a persecutor of Christians Paul was quite brave, even as many of the radical Islamists engaging the forces of the West in battle today are technically quite brave. Although bravery alone may make one a hero in the eyes of the world, it does not make one a Hero in the eyes of God (whose is the only view that matters). Only bravery for the sake of Truth makes one a Hero.

Even so, one cannot discount the ungod's monumental success in luring men toward the image of the impressive Coward and who fight so very bravely on behalf of the Lie in its many forms, for their bodies have over the millennia strewn many a battlefield while bearing the standard of an unholy cause, just as they do even today.

GELDINGS

Another mode of attack employed by the ungod upon manhood follows his hatred of the *masculine*, for we must remember that the masculine and the feminine are the ideas of God, and so have both earned the undying enmity of the Serpent. Whereas the feminine has its beauty, the masculine has its strength, and it is against this strength that the ungod so venomously unleashes his fury, seeking to replace it with that which arises in the vacuum of its absence – the idea of weakness. Since strength is the domain of men and inherent to manhood, it should stand to reason that a man without strength no longer fits the mold from which he was pressed; he has, in essence, become an *un-man*, or what once was called an *effeminate*.

I must here interject a reminder that I am speaking of function at least as much as form. Comparatively speaking, let us remember that man is physically stronger than woman (form), from which we derive that the male character is to be the character of greater strength (function). Where possible, men should maintain their physical strength, but should likewise be individuals of moral, emotional and intellectual strength who exhibit strength of character, leadership, judgment and decision-making in all areas of life. Such strength is (and must always be) inherent to true masculinity in light of God's ordering of the roles of the sexes. Where strength is absent, weakness dwells, and where weakness dwells there is no manhood. And since God has given us but to be male or female, where a man ceases to be masculine he has become feminine; he has been emasculated, and an emasculated man is the ungod's model of the perfect man.

Here we find the origin of the male homosexual, who is either completely effeminate or who uses the symbol of his manhood to sodomize other males. Such activity is a deep affront to the Divine Image in him (Leviticus 20;13), effectively making him a Coward in whom the Hero is nearly completely eliminated or polluted (but which is certainly Hell's ultimate template for the remaking of manhood).

BRUTE FORCE

In all honesty, though, it must be admitted that men have brought upon manhood some much-deserved reproach and rebuke, and this by way of the abuse of strength. God gave to men strength; He gave to them also the character of Hero. Men's greater strength is therefore to be used only as the Hero would use it, which is to serve and not to be served. As his family's Hero, the man is to be a protector and a defender – a warrior who challenges the encroaching evil of the ungod upon the sacred ground of family and home. He is the one charged with making that sacred ground a place both safe and secure.

The ungod has a very different idea of how a man should use his greater strength, and it has nothing to do with his playing the role of Hero, but rather of turning that strength against his family. In this way the Hero is replaced by the Tyrant, the Subjugator and the Abuser – a man who rules by fear where he should lead through respect; hate where there should be love; and brute force where there should be willing submission. He turns his home into a place of dread and loathing, and his wife and children into slaves and victims of abuse.

This is the Bully, and he is one of the most heinous remakings of the Hero to come from Hell's dark mind. When unleashed upon culture and society, he has been the cause of the horror of cruel male domination that has so plagued human history, and even still plagues it today in so many hideous forms.

DANGER RANGER

Finally, we must briefly discuss the majesty of manhood. When one sees a woman in the fullness of her glory, one is drawn to her, for she owns the idea of beauty (which is designed to be appreciated). When one sees a man in the fullness of his manhood, however, one is naturally inclined to step back and marvel, for man owns the idea of majesty. And it is the projection of strength within that majesty that naturally causes us to give an impressive man more distance, for he is a dangerous being and is to be considered with caution.

Men receive this dangerous characteristic from the image of God, for He is a dangerous Being. What I mean by this is that God is dangerous to Evil, and Evil therefore fears Him (Mark 5:7). As an extension of the Divine Image, *true manhood is therefore meant to represent a danger to Evil*, which in turn means that the Hero is an inherently dangerous being, and Evil should know the Hero's name and fear him (Acts 19:15).

Since the true Hero represents such a real danger to the ungod and his plans, the ungod must see to the eradication of the Divine characteristic of danger from manhood. This he does by encouraging men to be *harmless*, something usually accomplished through apathy or through the ascendency of radical feminist thought. Through either or both, Evil has nothing to fear from such examples of manhood, for the harmless man does not know how to pose a threat to Evil in the realms of either ideology or of physical battle – he is mentally apathetic and docile, will not engage the realm of Darkness in prayer or study, and is physically incapable of defending himself or his home when Evil deeds come calling. The Enemy does not fear such sheep.

In those remaining males for whom harmlessness does not sit well, the Enemy will channel their characteristic of danger toward embracing Evil (usually a form of the Bully) or toward danger for danger's sake. Being truly dangerous from the Divine perspective means that a man poses a real threat (whether physical, intellectual or spiritual) to Evil, evil deeds and evildoers. For example, an accomplished martial artist is a dangerous being who can use his skills to either defend himself and others or to bully others. In the first case he represents a danger to those who would do him or others ill; in the second case he uses his skill toward evil ends. The Enemy fears the first martial artist, but not the second, for the second martial artist is his servant.

For those males in whom effeminacy, harmlessness or the overt servitude of Evil have little or no appeal, the ungod must turn the characteristic of danger toward the idea of danger for danger's sake. Here we find the bad boy, the tough guy, the thrill seeker and the daredevil – males who look for danger at every turn but who (despite their bravado) inspire not the slightest tremble from Hell or its Darkness.

THE BELIEVER'S OFFENSIVE

Good and honorable manhood is the ingredient most necessary to a successful and enduring society, and though all of true manhood is not yet lost, we must admit that, even amidst true Christendom (where its flame should naturally burn brightest) good and honest manhood burns ever more dimly with the passing of each season. This should be greatly lamented, for true manhood is a handsome thing, a good thing, a noble thing and a necessary thing. Jesus Christ was, and still is, a man. He was, and still is, a Hero of the highest magnitude. He gave not an inch to Evil and the Lie, but always stood His ground and then some, for He literally cleared the Galilee of His day of the ungod's darkness (Matthew 4:16). He used His manly strength righteously (as the money-changers and charlatans in the Temple courts could attest), and never abused it.

He stood the sentry's lonely watch to keep Evil from His loved ones (Luke 22:31,32), and flinched not at the ultimate and selfless sacrifice on their behalf. To Evil, He was a dangerous, dangerous man.

We, likewise, must become dangerous and heroic men – men at the mention of whose names the Enemy does not laugh in derision. Our lives, our character, our minds and our ambitions must be immersed in Truth, and sold out to it. We must stand the sentry's tireless and faithful watch over our wives, our children, our homes and our land, setting the boundaries over which Evil may not pass, *for Evil must be taught to fear us.*

The world is in deep and desperate need of true Heroes, and we are those Heroes. If Evil must prevail, then let it prevail. But let us meet it like true men, and gird ourselves, and stand, and set our jaws, and give it a fight that it shall never forget. Let Evil know that true men still walk this Earth, and that we know how to do battle like Heroes, and that it shall not have our manhood cheaply or easily. Not now. Not ever.

BATTLEFIELD: WOMANHOOD

Adam named his wife Eve,
because she would become the mother of all the living
Genesis 3:20

The line of thought leading us toward marriage now takes us to the study of womanhood, for marriage cannot be understood apart from an understanding of both it and manhood. Since we have just explored the idea of manhood, we now have the privilege of studying glorious womanhood – that last and crowning achievement of Creation.

THE ORIGINAL IMAGE

As discussed previously, the woman is the designed Nurturer of the family, which makes an understanding of the idea of nurturing paramount to understanding femininity, marriage, family and (by extension) appropriate human society. To *nurture* is to cause healthy growth, which means that after being nurtured, something is better, stronger and healthier than before it was nurtured. It is therefore intrinsic to the Nurturer to make something better, stronger and healthier, and implicit within such a nature must be the complex ability to see what nurturing is necessary (or what something can become), to have the patience and ability to supply and apply the nurturing, and to have the desire to see the nurturing take place.

This is precisely what was displayed by the act of the Cross. Jesus saw not just what I was, but what I could become. As the perfect and sinless man, only He had the ability to make me what I could become by the purchasing power of His blood (Hebrews 9:12-14), and He had the desire to see the change in me take place (as demonstrated by His willingly hanging upon Calvary's tree). If the Cross was fully heroic, it was no less fully nurturing for the heroism, nor was it less heroic for the nurturing.

Here we see (as we did with the heroic) the utter selflessness of nurture as displayed upon the Cross. This complete selflessness of nurture demonstrates perfectly for us this facet of the Divine Image – it is always centered upon *others*, every bit as much as is true heroism. Woman, therefore, is designed to selflessly pour of herself into her husband and children, thus making them better, stronger and healthier in every respect. In so doing she bears wonderfully and most beautifully the image Divine.

THE IMAGE UNDONE

Since true nurture is selfless, then, the ungod has as easy a task in reshaping the Nurturer into his sinister reflection as he has with the Hero, for women are as subject to the insatiably selfish sinful nature as are men. He must simply turn her toward one of his many forms of selfishness suited to the fallen nature of womanhood. Once so turned (or to the degree that she is turned), nurture is lost and she has become the Poisoner – the antithesis of that for which she was designed by Heaven.

For those who count such things, it will be noted that the words describing the counter-image in womanhood exceed those written for manhood. This is not because woman is more fallen than man, but rather because man is simpler than woman, which makes his corruption a simpler thing than hers. Because woman is more complex than man, the Enemy has more shades of turning with which to work.

POISONED SAP

As with the Hero, the Nurturer is likewise a servant, and she must put aside all self-interest for the sake of her husband and children in order to be true to her calling. They (and their welfare) must be what drive the very pounding of her heart and the breath of her lungs. When monetary gain, position or power is placed before family, she poisons. When friendship, companionship or sexual desire is placed before family, she poisons. When hobbies, interests, goals, apathy or entertainment are placed before family, she poisons. For the Nurturer, all things must submit to her family, for she is its health.

The Nurturer's gifting (and therefore tasking) is to *believe* in others – to see the potential of what they can be and can achieve, and then to develop them toward those ends. She is the great Encourager: selflessly visionary, deeply kind, wonderfully patient and remarkably giving. The Enemy must naturally respond to such glorious traits as these by corrupting womanhood with his Hellish counter-image, after which we are then left with one who is myopic, mean-spirited, impatient and selfish. Such a person is a Discourager – more commonly known in the vernacular as a *nag* – and is the feminine counterpart to the male Bully.

Nagging is the Discourager's bread and butter, for it bears all of the hallmarks of the ungod's personality. There is in nagging no beauty, no love, no insight or vision, and nothing constructive, for it sees nothing good or worthwhile in another. It knows nothing but condemnation, seeing only that what a person is, is now doing or has done is lacking, and it never misses an opportunity to highlight such lack. It bruises and breaks the spirit of another, and since it is sown in negativity and lovelessness it must likewise reap fruit of identical kind (Galatians 6:7).

The Discourager therefore does not see what her husband or child might become if she actually believed and invested in them. Instead, she sees them only against the backdrop of some perceived and illusory perfection, and hounds them mercilessly into that image, reminding them always of how far short of the goal they are. She cares not a whit for what tremendous damage she does to their lives, or for how miserable a companion or mother she is (Proverbs 21:19), for she is as selfish as she is unenjoyable.

In contrast, the amazing Nurturer is designed as though a consummate artist or sculptor, for the artist sees not only what a blank canvas is, and the sculptor sees not only what a quarried piece of marble is, but rather what each might become when skill, effort, love and patience are applied. She is designed to see the capacity for what might be if nurture is applied, and therefore is meant to believe in others and what they might become. Whereas manhood necessarily represents the sterner aspects of the Cross, womanhood has the privilege of representing the softer aspects of it, bringing to us in caring, human form the love, grace and encouragement needed for us to reach our designed potential. Manhood reflects God's holiness; womanhood is meant to reflect a loving God who binds our wounds, forgives our failings, sees our potential and applies enduring, patient effort to see us succeed.

In short, God does not nag, for discouragement is foreign to Him (John 3:17). Nagging is the realm of human religion, whose author we have already seen to be the ungod. Nagging beats and pounds upon the human soul of its unworthiness, leaving in its wake lives broken and shattered, devoid of all beauty and consumed with guilt. Not so the grace of God, which instead lifts both the heart and soul, bringing life to the dead and purpose and dignity to the lost and disenfranchised. This is the Nurturer's blessed calling, and that for which she is most gifted and capable. But we must know that the Enemy most deeply despises that which the feminine represents of the Divine, and will not let it exist unchallenged.

A Tangled Web

We men often shake our heads in befuddlement at women, because they just seem to us so phenomenally *complex*. And the truth of the matter is that women *are* more complex than men by far. This doesn't mean that men are less intelligent than women – it simply means that we are differently wired by Heaven's design. The Hero sees things in terms of right and wrong and of Good and Evil. He then takes a stand to uphold the right and the Good, or to vanquish the wrong and the Evil. There are not a lot of shades of grey with him, for the Hero is necessarily simple – it doesn't take great complexity to protect your home and family, or to break the teeth of Evil upon the shores of Normandy or Iwo Jima or in the sands of Iraq or the mountains of Afghanistan. It takes guts; it takes strength; it takes a firmly-set jaw. But it does not take great complexity.

To nurture, however, takes monumental complexity, for there is great subtlety involved in the process of making another human being better, stronger and healthier. Here, much depends upon the artful turn of phrase, the nature of a rebuke or a gentle nudge, knowing when to persevere and when to change course, and how to touch someone deeply and personally. Such work is intricate and complex; so also must be the nature of those called to do such a task. It is also deeply personal work, which makes it a deeply emotional endeavor, requiring that the female have a substantially greater emotional capacity than the male.

But yet again we must return to the basic premise of the Nurturer – she is to be the servant of those she nurtures, and not their taskmaster. She is to be selfless. It is therefore most dangerous and destructive when she turns her natural complexity and phenomenal emotional capacity self-ward, for little can stand in the way of the havoc she wreaks when she does so. It also bears a striking resemblance to the ungod, who long ago turned all of his angelic complexity and emotional capacity self-ward (Isaiah 14:12-14), rejecting wholly the opportunity to serve humanity (Hebrews 1:14).

The sinful nature is voracious and insatiable in its selfishness, and when the Nurturer turns selfish there is no end to how far she might fall prey to its abysmal devices, of which two are remarkably common: the Manipulator and the Feeler. The Manipulator is a most fearsome and destructive facet of the Enemy's image, and although men may do their share of manipulating, when a woman orients the glorious inner workings of her nature to selfish purpose, she can manipulate those around her with such head-spinning dexterity as to make Machiavelli look like a schoolboy. When she does so, her family members become her little marionettes, whom she controls with the unseen threads of her selfishness, and she cares not that those threads soon become a trap for them, nor that those whom she most should be serving have become caught in her weavings. Rather than nurture them, she feeds off of them as a spider would do, bleeding them dry as she sits in the center of her web. It takes not much imagination to divine whose image she bears.

FEEL-TY

The Feeler is an emotional wreck mired at the emotional development of an adolescent, for with her everything is processed through the prism of how it makes her *feel*. The Nurturer is by design a far more emotional being than is the Hero (since hers is a deeply caring and personal calling), and so she possesses a tremendous emotional capacity. When she turns this caring inward instead of outward (its rightful direction), she is then in essence attempting to nurture herself, and her emotions then become the only arbiter of right and wrong.

When guided by Truth, emotions make life wonderful. As arbiters of Truth, emotions are an abject failure, for they bear sin's inevitable stain (Jeremiah 17:9). To be controlled, then, by the whim of emotion is to be controlled by the sinful nature itself, and so to bear the ungod's image to near full capacity. In allowing emotions to reign supreme in her life, the Feeler falls prey to an ever-accelerating spiral of emotional pain and need, for there is no end to people or situations to hurt her feelings or cause her to feel lack. She then in her own mind becomes victim to a cruel and heartless world, at which she constantly lashes out for its brutality against her. Her vocabulary gives her away, for it tends to be as limited as is her emotional development, and she is always remarking upon how people and events make her *feel*, for her feelings are the lens through which she views all of life, caring not that those around her wither and die.

TALKING HEADS

Another effective remaking of womanhood undertaken by the ungod involves the polluting of its God-given ability to communicate, for women must necessarily be the more active communicators. The reason for this difference is (yet again) not difficult to understand, for it has its definition in the differing natures of the masculine and the feminine.

Women speak more because they *must do so* – it is what the design of the Nurturer demands. The Hero is a being of fewer words, for he is of simpler makeup and is called to action more than to speech. Contrarily, the Nurturer is tasked with the molding of human lives into those that are better, stronger and healthier. This requires a marked degree of communication, necessitating a high degree of the use of language, which is accomplished primarily through human speech. This is normal and right and in accordance with God's design, for He gifts according to His call (Exodus 4:11,12).

As we proceed with this train of thought, though, let us remember that speech is a form of intimacy, and intimacy is not a bottomless well (for we are finite beings). Whether we are by nature tasked with communicating less (as are men), or more (as are women), we should all be those who are careful and measured with our use of words, for words should not be used carelessly or in excess (Ecclesiastes 5:2).

Women are the designed Nurturers, and nurturing requires a far greater use of words than does heroism. Since the use of words requires communication, and communication intimacy, it is perfectly right and logical to maintain that women have the greater capacity for intimacy. Such a capacity for intimacy, however, must be put to use carefully and thoughtfully, for it is a most powerful – and thereby dangerous – thing.

Bearing in mind once again that intimacy is a thing foreign and detestable to the ungod, it must be expected that he will do all within his power to undo, deplete or so alter it that it bears no resemblance to what its Author intended. Since this deep capacity for intimacy is the natural spring from which a woman's enhanced ability and need to communicate flow, the ungod's most natural means of depleting a woman of her ability to be intimate is to cause her to become *overly communicative*, by which she runs the well of intimacy dry. Here we find both the Chatterbox and the Busybody, and the trail of destruction both leave in their wake.

Of the two, we are most naturally inclined to think less poorly of the Chatterbox (whose sin is that of arrogance) than of the Busybody (whose sin is that of malice). The arrogance of the Chatterbox lies in the assumption inherent to incessant talkers – that others *want* or *need* to hear what she has to say. By her nonstop speech she insists that hers is the greatest insight available, and where possible she overwhelms every other voice, pausing in speech only long enough to catch her breath or to listen for the scarce amount of time it takes her to form another opinion with which to grace her unfortunate listeners. The sheer volume of words she speaks is staggering, and she numbs the hearing of nearly all of those with whom she comes in contact.

If she has a marriage, it will soon be an empty one – hollowed of beauty by her lack of intimacy, for she has no longer any stores of it from which to draw. Her many words have likewise emptied her of true beauty and allure, leaving her as little more than an annoying, buzzing insect that her one-time Hero cannot seem to discourage from his ear. Her children are malnourished of spirit and soul, for in her arrogance she has withheld from them that greatest tool of the Nurturer – the caring and *listening* ear – leaving them to fend for themselves.

PASS IT ON

If less wordy than the Chatterbox, the Busybody is far more overtly dangerous, for she traffics in hearsay, lies, misfortune and misery. Although still many, her words are fewer than those of the Chatterbox only because her trade requires that she listen more. Yet she listens – not out of caring as the Nurturer should – but with Hellish motive as does her dark Master, for her trade is gossip and her aim is destruction. She positively *lives* for the lie, for the tasty morsel of misfortune, for the whispered confidence, for the hint of betrayal. She is always about the business of others – even *addicted* to the business of others – as it is the drug that brings meaning and purpose to her life.

For every tidbit she hears from one, she passes it on to ten; it matters not the damage inflicted or the truth or falsehood involved. She simply *must* be the conduit of personal information, which with forked tongue she must whisper into someone's ear, hissing seductively as did that beguiling Serpent so long ago (Genesis 3:1). Because she knows nothing of nurture, she is the worst of companions and mothers, knowing only how to poison and to use the secrets of her household as currency on the gossip exchange, making her untrustworthy in every respect and despised by those closest to her.

ENCHANTRESS

Just as manhood owns the idea of majesty, so does womanhood own the idea of beauty, for the Nurturer must have her beauty in order to complete her task. Beauty naturally draws people to itself (for it is meant to be appreciated), and so it is natural for us to want to surround ourselves with it. By definition, therefore, beauty has allure and attraction, and the Nurturer must have this beauty, for there must be about her that which makes others desire to be near her or with her in order for nurturing to take place. For this reason, God has given to her the more beautiful (or alluring) physical form, and since form dictates function, He has also given to her the more beautiful nature and character. Simply put, women are more naturally attractive than are men.

It is therefore only natural that a Nurturer should desire to be both outwardly and inwardly attractive. Again, though, as we are reminded that such beauty is God's way of attracting others in order that that they might be nurtured, so we must not fail to see that even beauty is meant to be used selflessly. There was never a truly more beautiful person than Jesus of Nazareth, whose beauty of character and nature most naturally drew others to Him. But never did he use such beauty for selfish gain; it was, rather, used as the vehicle of blessing. Beauty, then, has a purpose – it delights others and draws others to itself. Once drawn to the Nurturer, the Nurturer is then duty-bound to nurture those drawn to her.

When the Hero abuses his greatest asset (his strength) to bend others to his will, he becomes the Bully. When a Nurturer abuses her greatest asset (her beauty) to bend others to her will, she naturally becomes the *Enchantress*.

The Enchantress takes her natural attraction and uses it to draw others into her orbit, and once there they cannot escape any more than the moon can escape the earth, for she has become their master. Her beauty becomes a prison for her admirers, who too late (if ever) learn that her beauty is entirely physical (as there is none of it inwardly), for the Nurturer in her has long since died. She is of her spiritual father, who masquerades as one beautiful (2 Corinthians 11:14), but who is inwardly as corrupt as the grave (Matthew 23:27). Instead of nurturing, her beauty has rotted her husband and her family, for she worships herself and the image she sees (or thinks she sees) in the mirror. It is beauty falsely used.

MAN OVERBOARD

If the ungod desires the feminization of the masculine, he is no less desirous of seeing the feminine made masculine, and his purposes are here again most notably seen through the activities of the modern radical feminist movement. Here, the male is sidelined at best, while at worst is openly disdained or hated, being seen as evil incarnate. While (as has already been admitted) men are not historically faultless in generating such venom from the feminine side of the aisle, it must be remembered that the ungod is the persuasive force behind the Bully in men. Since the Bully bears his image, it testifies to the ungod's genius that he is then able to channel the anger and resentment thus engendered into persuading the Nurturer to clothe herself with the masculine, which is something that also bears his image. It is for him a win-win situation.

Nature abhors the vacuum, and where the Hero is banished there must be that which rises to take its place. For the case at hand, this means that the female must rise to the role of Hero, or become masculine. From the *anything you can do, I can do better* mindset arises the manly female who acts like a man, talks like a man, attires herself like a man and is attracted to other women as though a man. As with the effeminate man, such a thing is unnatural (Romans 1:26,27), and bears the image of him who authors all things unnatural. It is also (as is male homosexuality) destructive of the very idea of family, for family exists only as the natural extension of appropriate sexuality.

THE BELIEVER'S OFFENSIVE

The nature of womanhood is the most beautiful thing given to humanity, and few things are more needed upon this pearl of a planet than the full flowering of womanhood's design into the feminine Nurturer.

It is to be expected that this flower succumb to a slow and withering death at the hands of the ungod in an unbelieving world, but among truly believing women it should – it *must* – flower anew and reclaim the fullness of its natural beauty through lives led by the power of the Holy Spirit (Galatians 5:16).

For the Nurturer (as with the Hero), the answer to what should be lies at the foot of the Cross, from which one might lift her gaze and behold the greatest act of nurture that shall ever be known. Such an act, and the heart that saw it through, must overwhelm and fill the heart, mind, character and nature of the woman who is a child of God. Though you slew Him, even so He did not see only what you were, but rather what you could become. Though you were guilty and undeserving, even so He hung in your place. Though He needed you not, even so He knew that you needed Him, and so saw it through to the end. He saw what you could become, *believed* in what you could become and committed Himself wholly to what you could become.

The Cross therefore signifies nurture in its purest and noblest form. No more beautiful a thing than this nurture is there in all of Creation, and the fullness of such beauty is bestowed upon the nature of womanhood. Live this aspect of the Cross toward your husband and children. Yours is the gift and call to bring and to spread life and health. Let the fragrance of such feminine beauty linger long wherever you have been.

BATTLEFIELD: MARRIAGE

For this reason a man will leave his father and mother
and be united to his wife, and they will become one flesh
Genesis 2:24

Having now discussed some of the designed differences between manhood and womanhood, we move our thoughts toward that which is most natural for the Hero and the Nurturer – their joining one with the other. This brings us to the institution of *marriage*, where we will have the privilege of viewing the greatest honor possible for Image Bearers.

The Original Image

It could not be more painfully obvious that the physical forms of man and woman were meant for one another had God spelled it out for us in large glowing letters among the heavens, for we need look no further than our sexual organs to see the truth of it. And what is true of form will hold true of function, meaning that our masculine and feminine natures were likewise designed to be coupled. By God's design, then, man and woman are simply *best* when partnered together (Genesis 2:18), and His plan for this partnering is the lifelong covenant of marriage between one Hero and one Nurturer, who become to one another husband and wife (Genesis 2:24; Malachi 2:14).

As we explore this joining of the human masculine and feminine by God, we must remember the premise that God has divided aspects of His nature into what has given rise to the very idea of the masculine and the feminine. To the male is given the predominance of Hero, and to the female is given the predominance of Nurturer, both of which are fully represented within the nature of God. The combination of their natures is therefore a formidable and impressive thing, for when so joined, the pair *together* bear the fullness of the image of God: the man brings with him the strength, majesty, heroism and simplicity of manhood; the woman brings with her the beauty, nurture, depth and complexity of womanhood. They thus become a marvelous *one* that is a whole, and in so doing most marvelously reflect the image of the *One* responsible for their existence. Such a wondrous accomplishment infinitely hallows the very idea of marriage.

Yet as wonderful as it is, this miracle of portraying the fullness of the Divine Image is not marriage's only great gift to planet Earth, for marriage also introduces the idea of order into the realm of human affairs. God is orderly and therefore orderly in all that He does and creates, and marriage is no exception. As God's institution, marriage therefore has a Divinely-ordained order imposed through the hierarchy of relationship. Simply stated, each marriage is to have a leader, and that leadership role is given to the husband (1 Corinthians 11:3). In the case of Adam and Eve, this meant that Eve was *positionally inferior* to Adam, making it necessary for us to understand the ideas of positional inferiority and superiority, for without them no institution can for long survive.

Years ago, when I served in the U.S. Navy, Ronald Reagan was President of the United States. As President, he was also my Commander-In-Chief, and due to his superior position he could order the aircraft carrier on which I served to any location on the globe, and we would sail for that location upon receipt of the command. It was a simple expression of positional order, without which the military could not survive. Yet although President Reagan was my superior in the military chain of command, as Americans we were both men of equal worth under the U.S. Constitution. This same concept is seen within the confines of marriage for the husband and wife: to maintain order there is a chain of command, but there is also the equality of worth (Galatians 3:28).

It's important to understand that this order designed into marriage (and by extension all human affairs) is simply an order mirroring the order found in the Godhead. For instance, we know that the Father is fully God (1 Corinthians 8:6); the Son is fully God (John 1:1); and the Holy Spirit is fully God (Acts 5:3,4). Yet the Son submits to the Father (John 14:31), while the Holy Spirit serves the Son (John 15:26). This means that the Divine Relationship itself is a relationship of order, and therefore marriage (which is the genesis of all human relationships) must likewise bear the order of that Relationship in whose image it was made.

Yet because there is so much misunderstanding and chafing by fallen humanity regarding the Biblical idea of the leadership of marriage, it is appropriate to now take some time to discuss why the natures of man and woman so naturally lend themselves to this idea. The headship of a husband over his wife is described in the eleventh chapter of First Corinthians as being a *covering* for her, and a covering is most naturally thought of as something that protects, or shelters. This gives us a fantastic point from which to begin our discussion.

When we put blankets over ourselves on a cold night, the blankets protect us from the cold by covering us. Likewise, a well-built house protects us from the elements by covering us, and a mother hen protects her chicks from danger by covering them with her wings. A covering is therefore a barrier of protection; it represents a strength greater than the danger, and strength is the natural domain of manhood. As a husband, a man is the Hero to his Nurturer, and his natural form and function of strength is the barrier of protection for the (relative) weakness of her form and function.

Leadership may be understood in much the same fashion. When an outside force (such as a strong wind) would assail a family, it first encounters a leading barrier or shelter (such as the walls to a home), which is placed forward of the object sheltered for just such a purpose. The barrier, then, is meant to *lead*, or be at the head of that which encounters what comes from beyond, something that in times past was known as the *vanguard*. The husband is designed to be this barrier, and so he is the marriage's natural and God-ordained leader.

Submission is merely the acknowledgement by the one sheltered of the barrier's strength and ability to protect. When in bygone centuries people would flee from an approaching army to the confines of a walled city for refuge, they were *submitting* to the walls' designed ability to protect them from what was beyond. In marriage, the husband is designed to be the protector (the barrier), while the wife is designed to be the protected (the one who *submits* to the barrier). This actually defines the wife as the more important of the two, for she is the one protected.

This design likewise dictates that the husband has the responsibility to meet the potential danger of all that comes from beyond. This is a particularly sobering point when we consider that God is also among all that is beyond, dictating that the husband is the one held most responsible by God for the health and direction of the marriage. With leadership necessarily comes accountability, and the husband is accountable to God, for we must not forget that the chain of command does not end with the husband; it continues upward to Him who is marriage's Author, and to whom the husband is charged to submit (1 Corinthians 11:3). It is of great importance to note that God did not call to Eve after the Fall, for the man who was her covering and vanguard had to answer to Him first (Genesis 3:9).

THE IMAGE UNDONE

The Biblical idea of marriage is perhaps best described as the *unification* of one Hero with one Nurturer (Genesis 2:24), each of whom is individually lacking the fullness of the Divine Image, but when unified bear that image to the full. Since this unification brings to light the greatest degree possible by which humanity might reflect the Divine Image of Heaven, the ungod must by all means bring about the absence of this unification, which is the idea of *separation*.

Furthermore, the idea of order within human relationships begun through the institution of marriage is a terrible affront to the ungod, for he is the author of chaos and cannot rest until he sees all human relationships awash in it. The destruction or complete pollution of marriage is therefore for Hell a deeply pivotal battlefield in the Image War, for it is the gateway to victory on most all other fronts.

TOP DOG

The struggle for dominance in marriage is nearly as old as the institution itself, having arisen in Genesis 3:16 as a result of the Fall. At the heart of the matter is the idea of *submission*, for submission runs counter to every impulse of the sinful nature, making it a burr under the saddle blanket in any relationship.

Biblical submission does not mean that a wife is her husband's doormat, for nowhere in Scripture is the husband commanded to *dominate* his wife. His charge, rather, is to love her as Christ loved the Church (Ephesians 5:25), which was something modeled for us upon the Cross. Christ does not dominate Believers, for His style of leadership is to serve those under His authority, as He strikingly demonstrated by the washing of the disciples' feet (a task relegated to that era's lowest household servant).

While Jesus does direct the affairs of the living Church as a whole (Ephesians 1:22), and by extension the lives of the individuals who constitute its members, He does not do so with the iron fist of dominance, but rather with the firm and gentle hand of love. For those of us who have the privilege of knowing and following Him, for instance, it is an easy thing to testify that His love and kindness lead us to repentance (Romans 2:4). Likewise, when a husband in this manner loves his wife, his strength is (as is Christ's for us) naturally and humbly given to leading the affairs of marriage and home to her and its benefit. We men would be hard-pressed to find a woman who would not willingly submit to such a handsome example of leadership, for she is loved, served, protected and covered. And herein lies the secret to great unity.

When the ungod convinces the husband and the wife to struggle for dominance, the very idea of marriage is in grave jeopardy, for not only is mutual servitude lost, but so also is the appropriate understanding of order and position in marriage. In Christ's servant-like economy, the struggle for leadership in marriage is the vacuum of it, and where it occurs the image of God is mocked and stained, leading eventually to chaos of every form.

TWO SELFISH

Given what occurs in marriage, it should be understood that the ungod would most like to keep marriage from occurring at all, but due both to the power of the Divine Image in humanity and to the power of attraction that males and females have toward one another, he is unable to keep the great unification from happening. He must therefore resort to despoiling the idea of unification *within marriage*, which will result in separation inside of it – something bearing his Dark Image only all too well.

That marriage involves the idea of love scarce needs mentioning, yet no true treatment of marriage can go without the discussion of it. As we have already sadly seen, few ideas are as misunderstood as is love, and so I will here humbly remind the reader of my definition of the term (from Battlefield: Love), which was gleaned from the pages of John's first epistle: *It is an unshakeable, unconditional and willing commitment to serve another. True, Biblical, God-centered love is an absolutely unselfish giving to the one loved, thinking nothing of oneself.*

Nowhere in Scripture are we asked to be *in love* with God, but are rather *commanded* to love Him (Deuteronomy 6:5). We are likewise *commanded* to love our neighbor (Leviticus 19:18), and husbands are *commanded* to love their wives (Ephesians 5:25). If love is something that can be commanded, it is by definition not an emotional feeling. Love is therefore not a fleeting rush of chemicals and emotions *into which we fall,* and so the Biblical idea of marriage must be completely divorced from this idea. From the Hellish perspective, however, marriage *must be wed to it* for Evil's vile image to prevail upon Earth.

The Enemy knows full well that Heaven's idea of love is defined as a selfless commitment to another; that it is *not* an emotion, but rather is a conscious act of human will. He knows that love is a *decision*. He therefore must redefine love away from its Heavenly origin, and so he has gone to great lengths to bring us to our current state of affairs, where being *in love* is considered love. As has already been mentioned, emotions are a wonderful part of the human experience when guided by Truth, but as Truth's arbiters they are a complete failure.

When an individual marries another person because they are *in love* with that other person, they marry that person because of how he or she makes them *feel*. This is selfish to the core, and literally dooms a marriage to failure because these emotions will one day cease, and the spouse is then left with nothing. Instead, marriage must be something into which we enter selflessly, sacrificing ourselves to serve our spouses. This might be better understood by rephrasing the statement in this manner: *We don't enter into marriage for what we might receive from our spouse, but rather by what we can give to our spouse.* The husband selflessly enters into marriage to supply to (and for) his wife what she is lacking of the Divine Image. She does for him the same.

When a marriage is thus a unification of a servant-Hero with a servant-Nurturer, the Divine Image is gloriously magnified and portrayed upon Earth, which is precisely why the ungod would have a man and a woman marry under what is really the false pretense of love. Once begun under such a pretense (which is selfishness wearing a clever mask) he would then have them continue further down this same path, which naturally leads to many of those dark facets described in the previous Battlefields on manhood and womanhood. That always-cunning Serpent knows well that the very idea of the fullness of unification in marriage is wed to servanthood and selflessness. Selfishness in marriage, then, dictates that unification is in many ways absent, and this absence is a form (or degree) of separation, and bears the Dark Image.

Christ's love dictated that He die for me. Likewise it is for us: on the day that we marry, we too must die. It is a death that we die to ourselves, committing to live only thereafter for our spouse. God owns nothing of selfishness, and neither is His institution of marriage meant to own any of it.

AHOY, SOUL MATEY!

One of the more destructive lies unleashed by the ungod upon the institution of marriage is the dangerous idea of the *soul mate*, and so we must take some time to explore the idea and its consequences. Setting aside until a later time its effects upon the search for a spouse, we will here focus our thoughts toward the havoc wrought upon a current marriage by the concept.

The thought behind the idea of a soul mate is that there is that one special and kindred soul with whom we are meant to be linked, and in whom friendship's greatest potential for blossom rests. It is a hauntingly romantic idea that makes for wonderful storytelling, but is nevertheless an idea never mentioned nor hinted upon in Scripture.

The danger inherent to such an idea lies in the fact that there is no way to *prove* that someone is your soul mate, for it is a completely subjective idea, entirely dependent upon emotional interpretation. Hence, when troubles beset a marriage (and they always will), one enamored of such an idea is given easily to conclude that one's spouse must not be one's soul mate, and thus that the opportunity for truly penetrating happiness is lost or must be found in someone else. The eye and heart then turn elsewhere or grow dark and aggrieved toward one's spouse, leading to the bitterness of disappointment. The unity of the marriage is in this way undone, and separation while still married is produced, allowing the ungod's image to triumph.

THE GREAT DIVIDE

Sadly, no discussion of marriage would be complete without touching upon the issue of divorce, for it is both the Enemy's crown jewel of separation and his idea of marital perfection. Since God hates divorce (Malachi 2:16), divorce will be that which causes the very beating of the ungod's dark heart.

Before proceeding further, it must be noted that in a world populated by a humanity utterly stained by the fallen nature, such heinously selfish acts will occasionally be committed that will require the dissolution of a marriage. Both God and the written Word bearing the representation of His nature make allowance for such a necessity (Deuteronomy 24:1; Matthew 5:32), for so dreadfully and completely fallen is humankind that there are times when a spouse must depart a marriage, both for his or her own protection and for that of the child or children. But I must be as clear here as the Scriptures themselves make it: God hates divorce. He does not hate the divorced person, but He does hate divorce.

There are, perhaps, an unfathomable number of reasons why God hates divorce, so I shall here list but a small number of them as seem most appropriate to me. First, for whatever the reason the divorce, it is to some magnitude a triumph of selfishness, which is a thing foreign to Him. Second, the idea of separation is unknown to the Trinity, which knows only the perfection of unity. Third, what God has knit together cannot be *un-knit* by man – it must be *torn apart*, leaving the Hero and the Nurturer forever (in this life) scarred from the rending (Matthew 19:6). God can and does heal from the pain and suffering of divorce, but its consequences will remain.

The fourth reason is that this tearing apart shatters that ultimate reflection of the Divine Image marriage is intended to proclaim, and therefore falsely represents Him. And finally (although it will be explored more fully in the Battlefield to come), divorce is utterly devastating to the children of the marriage.

For these reasons (and many others) is the ungod positively enthralled with the idea of divorce, as it is a thing owned by him from start to finish – he conceived it, birthed it and is perfecting the art of it.

ONE FOR ONE

It is clear both by example (one Adam and one Eve) and by the simplest reading of Scripture that God intended His institution of marriage to be that which was between *one man and one woman* who are committed to one another for as long as they both live. It is true that the Scriptures do record many instances of polygamy (even among the lives of Biblical heroes), but the practice is never condoned. On the contrary, in every instance of such occurrences recorded in the Bible, we see the inherent dangers and pitfalls involved as events unfolded over the course of family and time. The Bible simply records what actually happened (as opposed to what we wished would have happened), and the Israelites were certainly warned most clearly against the practice by God (Deuteronomy 17:17).

It is logical to assume that since God created one man for one woman, each has but the inherent capacity to bring to fullness the Divine Image with but one other. Against such a designed capacity the ungod must naturally throw himself with full force, and so the idea of polygamy would have been given birth in the Hellish mind, for if the capacity of an Image Bearer is exceeded, then the Divine Image in such a relationship would necessarily become diluted. In essence, when a man takes more than one wife (or vice versa), he simply does not own the capacity to bring into its fullness the reflection of the Divine Image with either (or all) of them. When this occurs, the Dark Image waxes while the Divine Image wanes, advancing Hell's standard in the battle.

Here we now find ourselves in an appropriate place to remark upon the Levirate marriage of Scripture (Deuteronomy 25), for the astute student or critic may point to this as an example of God decreeing (and thereby condoning) the practice of multiple marriage partners. Of first importance is to note that the Levirate marriage was instituted only in the case of a childless widow, and that the new husband was to be the closest male relative available. Secondly, such a marriage was instituted to ensure that the land owned by the deceased stayed in his family, and that the name of the deceased not perish from among Israel (something most wonderfully played out for us in Scripture in the Book of Ruth by Naomi, Ruth and Boaz). The Levirate marriage insured against either of these things happening, and also provided a safe covering for the widow (who had no means of worldly support or protection).

Finally, it must be noted that God's institution of the Levirate marriage should be regarded as an *allowance*, for He deals with reality. There would be no death had there been no Original Sin; but there was Original Sin, bringing with it death that is often most untimely and tragic. The Levirate marriage was God's gracious manner of dealing with the widow thus affected by the consequences of the ungod's heartless handiwork.

DO OVERS

This probably is the most appropriate place in which to insert a discussion upon the subject of *remarriage*, for while it does not strictly fall into the category of polygamy, much of what was just discussed is appropriate to this topic as well. It should first be stated that God's Word does allow for remarriage in the case of a widowing (Romans 7:3) or a Biblically-justified divorce (Deuteronomy 24:3), as God is gracious, forgiving and the loving Master of the second chance. However, the Word does not make allowance for *serial remarriage*, which is a thing greatly common today, and which bears the stench of the fires of its birthplace as surely as does polygamy.

It must be remembered that divorce (whether justified or not) is a breaking of a sacred covenant, after the making of which a Hero and a Nurturer were in every sense knit together by marriage's Author, in order that in their unity they might proclaim that wondrous Heavenly image. The failure of that covenant (and its subsequent tearing asunder of the two natures that were one) carries with it loss and pain both personal and deep. When two pieces of fabric are sewn intimately together and then subsequently ripped apart along the seam, it is not a clean thing, and both of the original pieces end up less than what they were prior to the joining.

In the same manner, any divorced person has been *lessened* as a Hero or a Nurturer, and the capacity for bringing to its fullness the Divine Image with a subsequent Nurturer or Hero no longer exists. A second marriage simply *cannot attain the potential of a first*, nor a third of a second, and so forth. Serial remarriage, then, is one of the ungod's methods for diluting the Divine Image that marriage was designed to proclaim, and is one of his best methods of cheapening the institution itself.

It should be noted that in the case of a widow or widower, the betrayal of the sacred bond has not occurred, and while the pain and loss are most severely experienced, it is not due to a tearing asunder, but rather to a natural expiration (if death may be considered a natural thing) in accordance with the vows taken. In such cases the fabric of Hero or Nurturer is left largely intact, and a second marriage may yet fulfill the potential of a first, especially if that first marriage was a blessed one.

ANYTHING GOES

The foundational idea behind the Biblical institution of marriage is that it is between a man and a woman. It is *not* an institution between two men or between two women. God did not create Adam and Steve, or Madam and Eve. Yet we more and more often see a movement afoot to redefine marriage in just such ways, for when God has been removed from consideration regarding this His institution, the ungod is free to redefine marriage into his loathsome likeness. It is in this vein that he puts forth such Herculean effort into persuading modern humanity of the rightness of his Hellish idea of *homosexual marriage*, which is (Biblically speaking) a ridiculous oxymoron. It is simply something than cannot exist in the realm of Truth, but which flourishes well in the realm of Lie.

Another of the ungod's acts of the redefining of marriage is the idea of the common-law marriage, which is a nice way of describing the act of a Hero and a Nurturer living together outside of a covenant. This used to be known as *shacking up* or *living in sin*, but we have now whitewashed this tomb by describing it as simply *living together* or *cohabitation*, and in the age of the prospering Lie this ungodly act is seen as more desirable than marriage itself.

Yet we must remember that (according to the example of the Cross) love does not and cannot exist apart from commitment. In marriage, the commitment is the lifelong covenant *made at the altar* between a husband and wife. By definition, their love (as Biblically defined) cannot therefore truly begin *until* they are married; so to think that living together is marriage's equal or superior is senseless on the face of it, for there is absolutely no true love involved. Couples that live together are doing nothing more than using one another while hoping to reap the beauties of marriage without its commitment, and are thereby doing something both cowardly and selfish. If and when such couples decide to marry, they are far less likely to succeed than others, for they have already laid a foundation of tremendous selfishness that will be difficult to overcome in their relationship.

Marriage is not failing because of any flaw intrinsic to it, but rather because it is an institution misunderstood in its many facets, is entered into by those who know little or nothing of love, and is viciously and without pause being assaulted by that vile Lord of Darkness, for he would snuff out the last of the glorious Light that it portrays.

THE BELIEVER'S OFFENSIVE

Marriage is the grand and wondrous institution of our Creator and Savior, and must among us be a most hallowed and revered thing. We must each and every day approach it with wonder, respect and awe, for what greater privilege is there upon this earth than to combine the differing natures of the Hero and the Nurturer into a marvelous reflection of the Divine Image?

We must therefore be those who enter this lifelong covenant not for what we might receive from our spouse, but for what we can give to them in the complementing of what the other lacks of the fullness of that Image. We must daily put aside that old and wretched selfish nature, submit ourselves to the Holy Spirit, and with humble servitude live the utterly selfless life of the Cross toward our spouse, and do so without end until one of us draws their final breath.

We must *believe in marriage*. We must be its champions by the examples of our lives and by our defense of its sanctity and beauty. We must be those who fight to once again foster an atmosphere of Truth in our culture, that marriage may once again rise to its rightful place of prominence, for all of human society hinges upon the strength or weakness of this Divine institution.

BATTLEFIELD: FATHERHOOD

Like arrows in the hands of a warrior are sons born in one's youth.
Blessed is the man whose quiver is full of them
Psalm 127:4,5a

Marriage is something that would naturally lead humanity into parenthood, thereby expanding the roles of the husband and wife into those of fatherhood and motherhood. For the man and husband, this meant the added duties and glory of being a father, and it is into this idea that we now explore.

THE ORIGINAL IMAGE

Under the Divine ordering of Creation, the idea of family began with the partnering of one man with one woman (one Hero with one Nurturer), who were forever committed to one another through the bonds of Cross-like love in marriage. This love would lead naturally to sexual intimacy, from which life would be conceived and children brought forth, ushering in the now-expanded family roles of father, mother and child. Each child would enter the world fully stamped with the image of God, yet knowing nothing of that Image. The privilege of forming fully in each child the conscious and knowing Divine Image would fall naturally to the father and mother (Deuteronomy 11:19), whose lives, natures and relationship would provide the haven and instruction necessary to accomplish this formation.

Once that image was sufficiently formed in the younger Hero or Nurturer, each would then have the joy of marrying (Genesis 2:24) and continuing the process through their lives and their children. It is in this way that the Biblical idea of family (beginning with marriage) is the foundation upon which was to be built all human relationship, for from this foundation would extend all of society and culture (which are simply

---

the idea of human relationships on a grander scale).

Most central to this molding of the young Image Bearer would be the role of the father, for although both motherhood and fatherhood are indispensable in the raising of a child, it is fatherhood that carries the greater burden of the Divine reflection, for God is Father (Matthew 6:9).

THE IMAGE UNDONE

When you poison the root, you will poison the tree and thereby its fruit. If the ungod is able to poison that which is the root of society and culture, he will then be able to reap the greatest harvest of the Dark Image possible among humanity. And since it is through the Biblical idea of family that the hated Divine Image is bred, nurtured and spread, he must at all costs and by all means remake such an idea with his own, and so must concertedly attack the family on all fronts. Because the man is at the head of the family (and bears that hated title of *father*), we should expect that the ungod will attack the idea of fatherhood most viciously of all.

Once a child is old enough to think and to reason, no figure is as important to him or to her than is the father, who is the child's Hero. In Scripture, God is always referred to in the masculine and as Father; He is never referred to in the feminine or as Mother. This means that the earthly father has the solemn responsibility of modeling to a greater degree the attributes of God to his children than does the mother, and is *in this sense* the more important of the parents to the children.

Simply stated, men have the privilege of reflecting the sterner aspect of the nature of God – that of His holiness – just as women have the privilege of reflecting the softer aspect of His nature, which is that of His love. And whereas God is described as thrice holy (Isaiah 6:3; Revelation 4:8), He is never described as thrice loving, which wonderfully illustrates that while God is fully holy and fully loving, holiness *dominates* His nature and character.

It is therefore in the ungod's deepest interest to deprive children of that great masculine reflection of the Divine, and so he must necessarily influence fathers to be absent from their children. Please bear in mind that I am not speaking of those things that will call the Hero away or abroad in the effort to stay or vanquish Evil (such as military service), for such things are necessary in a fallen world. But I am speaking of that willing physical absence from the home so prevalent and preferred by fathers today, and also of the absence of availability, wherein the father is physically present but cold and removed from his children.

ABSENT FROM DUTY

The giving of our time to our children is the primary way that we influence them and prove to them that we love them. Childhood's Enemy must therefore convince fathers to spend as much time apart from their children as possible, and this is fairly easy to do with us. We men are by nature protectors, and so it is natural for us to put our masculine efforts into supplying and maintaining a home that is safe and secure, which is a right and good thing. As protectors, we also desire to protect our family from what the future might hold – also a right and good thing – and so we store away for the future (2 Corinthians 12:14). But while our children are still in our homes, we must guard against putting our efforts into anything more than these basic things if it costs our children time with us. Fame, money, power, prestige or the excess of material goods are not worth our child's character, and should not be pursued at the expense of a child still in the home.

As one who worked with teens for the better part of two decades, I can testify readily enough that they have a tremendous surplus of *things*; what they too often do not have is anything even approaching an adequate amount of their father's time, for he is off either building his selfish kingdom or using his time in supplying his family with more than is needed for their safety and security. A humble and adequate home with a present husband and father is far better for a family (and especially a child) than an ostentatious or materially wealthy home from which he is largely absent.

Apart from this idea of excessively providing for his family, the Enemy is also able to influence men toward physical absence from their homes through the pursuit of selfish pleasure or gain. Here we should all be reminded that when we marry we are to technically die to ourselves, and are to ever after live to serve our spouse, for there is no room for selfishness in God's institution of marriage. What is true of marriage is doubly true of parenting, and so the father ever and always should live to serve his children, thinking nothing of himself (as is appropriate for a true Hero). There is nothing on the planet – not a single pleasure, not a single hobby or pursuit, not a single relationship – worth one more minute of a father's time away from his children than is absolutely necessary. We cannot mold when we are not present, and when we are not present the Dark Image tends to flourish in our absence.

PRESENT, BUT NOT ACCOUNTED FOR

Another method used by the ungod in achieving the absence of the father in the lives of his children is through ineptitude, where despite the fact that he may be physically present, he is a horrible representative of the Hero to them. The many fallen forms of the Hero that we have previously studied all have in common the thread of selfishness, and to the degree that a father is selfish, he is technically unavailable to his children, making him an absentee father despite the fact of his physical presence. His unavailability (which is a form of absence) is in this case one of emotional, mental and/or spiritual unavailability, which is a terrible representation of God, who to His children is *never* unavailable (Matthew 19:14; 28:20).

Since God is available to His children, it means that He is likewise warm and inviting to them. In Romans 8:15 and Galatians 4:6 it is taught that God's children are able to call Him both *Abba* and *Father*, with the term *Abba* being very similar to our terms of *daddy* or *papa*, which signify warmth and emotional closeness. Put simply, God wants His children with Him personally and emotionally, and so must the earthly father. To this the ungod's counter-image is the idea of the cold, impersonal, detached and unemotional father who seems to have not the slightest joy with the presence of his children, nor even care for them at all.

DERELICTION OF DUTY

At the other end of the spectrum is the father who is so highly engaged with his child that he is considered nothing more than a friend by him or her. Here there is great warmth and joy of relationship, but the father fails in one of his duties as the child's Hero, for in his desire to befriend his child he neglects to set and maintain firm boundaries of appropriate conduct. This setting of firm boundaries is something that will naturally put a parent at odds with a child's sinful nature, making it an uncomfortable and painful thing, but it is something that must be done. And as the reflector of Divine holiness, it is the Hero's charge to do so.

It is true that God is our Friend (John 15:15), but friendship with God cannot exist apart from right conduct (John 15:14). Our friendship with our children must exist in like manner if we men are to faithfully discharge our fatherly duties before God. This should not be done to the point of exasperation (Ephesians 6:4), of course, but it should be done. The joys of deeper friendship await father and child later in life, but in the child's younger years the father must not work to be seen as a peer to his child, for Hell's tentacles will find many a way into his child's life if the father does so.

Closely akin to the friendship father (and often the same person) is the father who fails in his sacred duty as that of the home's sentry, for he is its designed watchman against the ungod's incursions upon it through the influence of Evil. We men are charged with setting and maintaining the boundaries past which Evil and the Lie may not pass, and none are in greater need of having those boundaries firmly and lovingly set and maintained than are the impressionable young Image Bearers entrusted to us.

In this light, mention must also be made of the father who is living with his child's mother without marrying her. As a form of fornication, such a thing is inherently wrong and contrary to the nature of God, and the wrongness of it is compounded by the utter selfishness of the idea itself. Such a confluence of dark behavior leaves the father without any moral authority whatsoever, and dooms any attempt at setting godly boundaries around his home to abject failure, something for which his children will eventually pay the price.

This work of the dutiful sentry is now perhaps more important and needed than ever, for the Lie and the image of Evil wax in magnitude and greatness and assault our homes and children in every conceivable manner, especially with the growth of technology. Here the Enemy would influence the watchman to be absent from his post so that the Darkness of Hell may find entry into the home, where it will steal, kill and destroy (John 10:10).

MOTHER KNOWS BEST

Before moving on to different subject matter, discussion must be had regarding the growing popularity of the Hellish idea of the purposeful single mother household. I am not speaking of the home where the father has been tragically lost to death or where the mother is forced to raise her children apart from the influence of their father, but rather to the idea of *purposeful* single motherhood. Here it is decreed that a father is unnecessary, and that a woman alone can do a far better job of child rearing if the (unwholesome) masculine influence is completely absent. Such an idea can be viewed as a paragon of familial excellence only through the tinted lens of Hellish thought and through minds already subjugated by Darkness (Romans 1:21; Ephesians 4:18).

That such thinking is man-hating is fairly obvious; that it is child-hating may not be so, and so must be briefly explored. Any child who is willingly and knowingly brought into this world with the *design* of being raised in a vacuum of masculinity is doomed to miss – in nearly every conceivable manner – anything even approaching a realistic representation of God to the child. This is a wholesale failure of childbearing's greatest responsibility, and it is therefore child-hating in every respect to celebrate and promote something so naturally devastating and debilitating to a young Image Bearer. But such is the influence of Hell.

MALE BONDING

We move now from a discussion of the ungod's influence toward absentee fatherhood into a discussion of its ramifications upon a father's children, and we begin by looking at how it affects a son. When we discuss the young Hero, we must remember that manhood is an inherently dangerous thing, for a man fully grown is meant to pose a danger to Evil and the Lie. This characteristic makes boys more naturally dangerous than girls, and is why boys tend to do more dangerous things, for they must develop the idea of danger within their character. For this to be done most appropriately and naturally requires the presence of a full-grown Hero, who should most naturally be the boy's father, for he is half of the boy.

Fire is an excellent example to use when speaking of the male propensity for danger, for just as fire is an inherently dangerous thing, so also is manhood. When the danger of a fire is respected and confined to the hearth, it is a most wonderful thing. When this dangerous thing is loosed, it destroys. In like manner, a boy needs his father to model the Hero for him in order to develop his dangerous and masculine nature appropriately, and to show him that being dangerous is a good and fine thing when bounded by Truth (as is a fire when bounded by a hearth). He must grow to understand that his masculinity is irretrievably and wonderfully dangerous, making the most important thing for the young Hero to learn that of becoming *appropriately dangerous*. This designed role falls squarely upon the shoulders of his father.

A boy with a physically absent or inept father will typically be at a loss as to how to develop properly into a man, for it is the father's duty to bring his son into the fullness of Biblically-defined manhood. This means that the boy most deeply of all needs the thoughtful structure, guidance and *approval* of his father, for the father is meant to be his model. Without such a model to provide a compass bearing for his dangerous nature, a young man will often move in the direction of extremely destructive and violent behavior in order to prove this masculinity that he does not understand. Such boys are likely to one day find themselves as gang members, violent felons and abusers of women and children, for their dangerous nature has been unleashed wildly.

The other sad direction of the fatherless boy is toward the forsaking of the dangerous, which is often done at the hands of an overbearing and protective mother. As Nurturers, most women are naturally poor at developing a dangerous masculinity in their sons, for it is the Nurturer's marvelous tendency to desire the lack of harm to those she nurtures. The development of a dangerous nature, however, requires a boy or young man to become acquainted with stepping into harm's way, and so when a young Hero is thus always shielded from harm he never has his chance to grow dangerous, which causes his masculine nature to wither and his character to become emasculated. He will at best end up as what is deemed a *mama's boy*, with no strength of nature or character. At worst he will be confused regarding his manhood, or else a despiser of it, and such young men often add to the ranks of male homosexuality.

DADDY'S LITTLE GIRL

As we move the discussion in the direction of the absentee or inept father's effect upon his daughter, we must remember that womanhood (when compared to manhood), is a thing of great beauty, but also of comparative weakness. Regarding the young Nurturer's feminine weakness, it is imperative that she be covered and protected with (and by) the strength of manhood, which is designed to be provided most naturally by her father, for he is half of her.

Her father's handsomely bold and masculine presence must always overshadow and protect her, and he must represent to her the glory of God by maintaining boundaries of holy conduct around her. He must not smother her, but he *must* keep her safe, and she must know that she is made safe by the strength of his hand and his character.

The young Nurturer is also beautiful (for the feminine is the true owner of beauty), and it is her outward beauty of form and her inward beauty of function that provides the draw for others to one day come to her for nurture. This naturally makes her a being who desires to be appreciated, for that is beauty's purpose. And the ultimate purpose for the Nurturer's beauty is that she might draw her children to herself in order to nurture them, which requires first that her beauty attract a Hero whom she can nurture and with whom she can complete the fullness of the Divine Reflection to her children. This gives her a decided need for *masculine* appreciation of her beauty, something meant to be filled by her father while she is under his shelter. He must therefore be the first to encourage and praise beauty in her, for she must have such encouragement and praise to blossom.

I recognize that it is a difficult subject, but we must now speak plainly of the physical contact necessary for a girl to receive from her father. Being affectionate with one's children is a handsome, manly and necessary ingredient to fatherhood. Furthermore, there is simply no substitute for human touch, and this should come every bit as much from the father as from the mother. Sons and daughters alike need the affirmation that is given from physical closeness with their home's Hero, and while they may shy away from public displays of such affection during their latter adolescence and teen years, the healthy home is one where such affection will continue during these years and always.

The young and developing Nurturer is deeply dependent upon such masculine affection, for she is an inward being and her *need* is to be appreciated by the masculine. Tender and physical fatherly affection is therefore required for her to blossom into the wonderful fullness of her womanhood. This is something most easily and naturally accomplished during a daughter's early years, but something from which many fathers shrink when the curves of physical womanhood come upon their daughters (for reasons that any good man will understand). Yet it is at this time that the wholesome and masculine affection of her father must most sincerely continue for her to achieve the fullness of her womanhood's promise.

Given the tremendous importance of the father's role in the life of his daughter, we must now look upon what handiwork is wrought in the Enemy's counter-image of the young Nurturer when he manages fatherly absence or ineptitude. As we do so, it must first be noted that with a father's absence the young Nurturer is not covered by the masculine, which is a thing unnatural for the feminine (1 Corinthians 11:3).

Such an uncovered young Nurturer will naturally seek to be covered by the masculine, and she may very well go outside of the home to find such a covering – something that leads her into danger at every turn. Her seeking after a masculine haven of protection is ready-made for the ungod's hideous plan of childhood and teen romance, as these are things for which the young Nurturer is not in any way prepared.

In the same manner, a young Nurturer who doesn't have her father's appreciation of her beauty will go elsewhere to be appreciated for it. For this she will most naturally go to the ranks of the masculine, and she will find many there who will appreciate her beauty to the point of abuse. Additionally, the lack of physical, fatherly affection will naturally have the same effect upon her, driving her into the preying arms of any man or boy who willingly offers such needed affirmation to her, and she will often turn promiscuous. In such cases where the young Nurturer's experience with her father (or the masculine) is horrible or devastating, she might turn even to the feminine to find shelter, appreciation and affirmation, for her very nature demands them.

When a daughter's father and Hero fails her, all roads for her will tend to lead away from home, and the wolves do not wait far down that path.

BROKEN MODEL

I must now insert the promised discussion on divorce, despite the fact that it no more truly belongs to fatherhood than to motherhood. But since in our culture it does more often lead (via the legal system) to a greater degree of the absence of the father than of the mother, we shall discuss it here under the banner of fatherhood.

The marriage of a child's father and mother (who are his or her Hero and Nurturer) is meant to be the institution through which the bonds of love and intimacy bring about the child's conception, birth and growth into maturity. This parental union is meant to both reflect *and model* the image of God to the child, thus providing the shelter and nurture needed for life's journey. From the marriage of his or her parents, then, the child is meant to derive a sense of stability, safety and purpose. When that marriage fails, the child's world and existence are shattered, for life's very foundation is stolen away.

Misguided people may speak of *clean* divorces, of *amicable* divorces, or of *good* divorces. But for the child there is no such thing as these. Divorce tears the very heart from a child's chest, and not a surgeon in this world has the ability to mend such a wound (which will in some ways be borne by the child until the grave is met). Although we may sugarcoat the issue or fool ourselves, we do not fool our children, for divorce devastates a marriage's children, sending them spiraling toward the Dark Image (Malachi 2:15).

As mentioned previously, divorce is to some degree always a triumph of selfishness. Since marriage is meant to fully portray God in the child's eyes (and God owns nothing of selfishness), divorce effectively hobbles a child's ability to comprehend God as He is, for God has now been most poorly represented to the child. I do not say this because I doubt the ability of God to reach the child of divorce (for I am one), or of His gracious desire to do so. I say it simply because it must be said: divorce makes it difficult for a child to believe in God, and Jesus warned us most sternly about such a thing (Matthew 18:6; Mark 9:42; Luke 17:2).

We must also bear in mind that the marriage's young Hero or Nurturer is meant to one day be married, and the marriage of the parents is the primary model forming the mold from which their own marriage will be cast. The strengths and weaknesses of the manhood of their father and the womanhood of their mother will be taken with them into their adult lives and marriages, and will be mimicked and mirrored by them. The ungod therefore has a deeply vested interest in sowing his counter-image in the characters of the father and mother, that their children might more fully reflect him at a younger age, and also have more of his Dark Image to pass on to their own children.

His crown jewel in this effort is, of course, the divorce of the child's parents, for the child will grow to adulthood without the benefit of seeing a marriage work – something essential to future success. For this reason it is to be expected that such children will have even less a chance at marital success than did their parents, and their coming children even less so than they. It is the snowball effect of Hell.

As to the many facets of the Hellish counter-image discussed in the Battlefields detailing manhood and womanhood, I believe it appropriate to here insert a solemn reminder concerning what these model to our children. Just as our children grow to physically resemble us, so too will they grow to resemble us in our character and actions. How they see their father treat their mother, their mother treat their father, and how both treat their children they will most naturally carry with them into their own marriages, for it is a profound and lasting model. This is to be expected, as it is the natural course of events. But a solemn and sobering thing is this, for we realize how it calls us to account in our own lives and through the legacy of our children's character.

Our children should be – must be – the most important thing in our lives, and we need to put action behind such words. The children with the greatest natural chance for success in every noble avenue of life are those who come from a stable, loving home where the father is an admirable and godly Hero who remains married to their caring and godly mother. There is no way around such an idea – it is simply Heaven's designed way of the family. Parents should therefore do all that is within their power both to stay married to one another and to stay married *well*, not allowing the selfishness of the ungod to mar or destroy the very foundation of their children's lives.

> *Author's Note: As I have thus far spoken solely upon the subject of the natural, biological parents of children, I will now make mention of those of us (for I am a stepparent) who do not fit into the mold of the original design of parenthood. I have not maintained such focus because I am lost in the unreal world of the Biblical ideal, but simply because I believe we must pay homage to God's original intent and design, for it is best and must be acknowledged as such.*
>
> *In this sinful and ungod-stained world we experience death, widowing, divorce and remarriage. Some children are therefore orphaned and abandoned, others are removed from their homes over*

concern for their safety, and others have parents or near relatives abuse them in one or many of the myriad fashions inspired by that vile hater of childhood. And so reality brings to us the adoptive parent, the foster parent and the stepparent. That these are not the ideal has already been discussed, but I would not for that reason shame those who bear what to me are titles of great honor and distinction.

Mordechai could be considered the adoptive or foster parent to the beautiful Esther, and he is a remarkable and brave hero of Scripture. In like manner, Joseph of Nazareth was technically our Lord's stepfather, for Jesus had none of Joseph's blood. What we parents of the second choice do is admittedly not ideal, but it must be allowed that what we do is real and lasting and difference-making in a child's life. It is in many ways the harder road, for we do not have the legitimacy of the natural parent girding us. Let us therefore bloom where we are planted by lovingly serving these children of another as a true Hero or Nurturer should. There is no doubt that many of God's greatest heroes are those who have walked (or are now walking) in the shoes of the parent of second choice.

To the divorced and single parent of either gender I would also like to add my encouragement, for I am well aware that such a frank discussion about the effects of divorce upon your child or children may have felt like nothing so much as a cleanly-landed blow to your very soul. If by such a frank discussion I have seemed to excoriate you, I would not have it be so, for in so doing I would be excoriating my own dear but divorced parents (both of whom have always been to me pillars of love, encouragement and support).

Damage is done by divorce. Always. But please take heart, for all is not lost. The ideal is lost, but all is not lost. God is greater – by the magnitude of infinity – than is the ungod, so do not give up or lose heart. The divorced parent must return to the original intent of marriage, which was to bring children to knowledge of the Living God. Therefore do your best to lead your children to God by devoting yourself to bringing them up in the beauty of His Word, remembering that He is the great Healer and can make beautiful any mess of ours (as David and Bathsheba can certainly testify). Always bear in mind that the ungod cannot muster enough power to even qualify as a speck against the omnipotence and magnificence of God, whose living Word can in an instant undo the filth and despair sown by the Enemy.

You must do your best and soldier steadily on, for there is much yet of the good and wonderful that you may impart to your children. Though there is no way that one parent can fully manage the part of two, it must be remembered that God has given to the Hero the minor of Nurturer, and to the Nurturer has given the minor of Hero. Because of this, God can still be represented to the marriage's children in the absence of the other parent. Although this representation is somewhat dimmed, let us remember that the dimmed glory of God is still vastly superior to anything this world has to offer (Exodus 33:18-23). But your focus must now be upon your children, and you must more fully die to yourself than ever before.

As a general rule I think it wise to refrain from remarriage until your children are grown, so as not to further dilute your time, affection and availability, for your children are now in greater need of these than ever. If already remarried, I have no need to speak to you of the weighty challenges involved (especially where stepsiblings and half-siblings are involved) for this can be difficult. If not remarried, enter into such situations only when God's leading to do so is clear and unequivocal – and we must be reminded that our loneliness does not qualify as God's leading. The children must come first, and it is never too late for us to begin making this so.

The Believer's Offensive

Such a wondrous and grave calling is the institution of fatherhood, that to a man should be given the opportunity to represent to his child the holiness of our thrice-holy God! Of all that may be done by us upon this earth, all else pales in comparison, and the life of the believing father must in all ways prove this true.

As reborn sons of the Most High, we know well that though we may often fail our Heavenly Father, He never fails us, for He is ever present with us. His Fatherhood is always that of availability and presence, and our fatherhood must be the same. We must, therefore, make every possible sacrifice to be present in our children's lives while they are in our homes. Jesus cried out in despair at being forsaken by His Father upon the Cross; let us do all within our power to ensure that our children never do.

We must also understand that God's fatherly presence is an *available* presence, and so we must be physically, emotionally, mentally and spiritually available to our children – available to touch and be touched, available to laugh and play, available to teach and mentor, available to correct and rebuke, available to urge and encourage, available to listen and understand, available to commiserate and cry, available to watch and learn, and available to pray and teach of God.

We must also be their Hero in every respect, which means that we must protect them from Evil's ruthless assault upon childhood and the home, and from the vices of their sinful nature as well, understanding that this often means sacrificing being seen as a friend for the sake of being a parent. We must mold godly danger into our sons so that they might one day stand as Evil's stalwart foes, and we must mold godly beauty into our daughters so that they might one day be the fountains of grace, nurture and healing so desperately needed upon Earth.

We must be men faithful and true to our wedding vows – true and devoted lovers of our children's mother until death parts us – for nothing better models God to a child than the healthy marriage of his or her parents. God is a wonderfully stable Being; let us therefore be stable men of stable marriages. If we have succumbed to divorce, let us then redouble our spiritual shepherding of our children, for the Divine Image meant to be modeled by marriage has failed them.

Fatherhood is designed to be the most powerful force in a child's life, and God has given to us shoulders strong enough to bear the weight of this calling. Let us therefore bear it as the Hero should, ever reflecting through service to our children that most glorious image of our Heavenly Father.

BATTLEFIELD: MOTHERHOOD

Her children arise and call her blessed;
her husband also, and he praises her
Proverbs 31:28

From the pages of fatherhood we now turn to that more blessed and wonderful idea of motherhood, where all that a human being is capable of becoming lies waiting to be discovered and encouraged. It is a look at the very fount of human greatness.

The Original Image

If fatherhood's glory is its greater importance and power in a child's life, motherhood's glory is its greater *blessedness* in a child's life (Proverbs 31:28). Our mothers are simply dearer to our hearts than are our fathers, for they have typically had with us more time, more personal involvement and more physical contact.

Motherhood derives its blessedness from the remarkable form and function of the female body and nature, which make the woman a Nurturer. It is in her womb that the child is conceived and grows; it is from her body that the child is brought forth; and it is at her breasts that the child is nursed. She has, therefore, a greater *connection* to the child than does the father, and this connection is Divine in inspiration and design, for it is needed over the course of the long and arduous process of nurturing.

What is true of form is also true of function, and so just as it is natural for a mother to physically nurture her child, it is likewise natural for her to nurture her child's character and personality, for by design her business is the health and growth of her child. Since this nurturing is a lengthy process, she has great patience; as this is a personal process, she has great insight; as this is an involved process, she has great complexity; as this is a varied process, she has great ability and flexibility; and as this is a process of nearness, she has great beauty.

Each human being is a unique blend of gifts, talents, abilities and dispositions, but each human being is born only with the *potential* to see such things to the greatness that is the Divine fingerprint in them. To the mother has been given the unique ability to discover that potential and to nurture the child toward his or her inherent greatness, which means that sons and daughters are meant to become who they were designed to be at the patient and caring hands of their mothers.

In the nine months that a child spends in its mother's womb, he or she grows from a relatively simple single-celled life into a complex multi-trillion-celled child. What it was at birth it had the potential to be at the moment of conception, but it needed the nurturing womb of its mother to realize that potential. The character, nature, personality and giftings of the child likewise exist at birth, but they await the long process of nurturing at the hand and heart of their possessor's mother in order to be discovered, nourished and then finally blossom into the greatness for which they were meant. Such sustained, patient and loving effort make our mothers very dear and blessed to us, and explains why Mother's Day is much more widely celebrated than is Father's Day.

THE IMAGE UNDONE

Given this tremendous and important role of the Nurturer in the life of her child, it should come as no surprise to us that the ungod makes every effort to ensure that Biblical mothering does not occur, for he both fears and loathes true greatness in humanity. His tactics here are largely the same as they were with fatherhood, which dictate that he place great emphasis upon the absence of the mother in a child's life.

It should by now be obvious that the Nurturer is one who *nourishes*, and so the mother is designed to nourish her children in both body and person. When she is absent as their Nurturer (either through true absence or the absence of selfishness), nourishing does not occur and she then bears the ungod's counter-image of the *malnourisher*, either fully or by degree. As we have already learned, the ungod despises human health in the physical sense (Job 2:4; Luke 13:16), and we must know that he likewise despises health of the human character, for it is ground all too fertile for the Divine Image. Our Enemy would therefore have all of the human experience suffer the throes of malnourishment, and the absence of the Nurturer is the surest way to see this occur.

Since we have already discussed the general idea of absence in the previous Battlefield on fatherhood, we now find the heavy lifting that would normally be required in this Battlefield has already been done, allowing us to treat the issues plaguing motherhood more generally and with far fewer words. This will allow us to limit our discussion on motherhood to a brief look at the causes of modern motherly absence from the home, followed by a short discussion of its consequences in the lives of her children.

Career Day

One of the two primary methods used by the ungod to keep the mother absent from her role as her child's Nurturer is the pursuit of an overly-high standard of living that forces even loving and caring parents into a needed two-income situation, dictating that the mother must work in order to keep up with the financial requirements of the household. However, in nurturing there is no substitute for time and sustained focus, neither of which is truly possible for a mother who must work away from her child. Such a standard of living should therefore be shunned for the sake of the child, and both parents should look for ways to either lower their standard of living or to establish a home where the standard is more reasonable and achievable. Again (as with fatherhood) a modest and stable home with a very present mother is far better for any child than an ostentatious or materially wealthy home from which she is largely absent.

The other primary method used by the Enemy to absent the mother from the home of her children comes to us as part of the Lie, and finds its deceptive packaging at the hands of the modern radical feminist movement. Here it is purported that a woman's career is more important than her children, or that a career can be pursued without detriment to them. But time away is time spent away from nurturing, and I have yet to see any career (including my own) more important than one's child, and so I must most strongly submit (for I cannot demand it) that there is no more *important* a career than that of nurturing one's own children into noble and dignified adulthood.

It doesn't matter how much the mother pays a nanny or a daycare center – no one else can nurture her child as she does; no one else is as connected to her child as she is; no one else can love her child as she does; and no one else can understand her child as she does. Since she is half of the child and is married to the man who is the other half of the child, who else could be better qualified to see and understand the potential within her child? That mothers can be so easily convinced to leave the nurturing of their children to another (or leave them to fend for themselves) is an idea that reeks of the sulfur of its birthplace, as did the child-sacrificing altars of Molech so long ago (Leviticus 20:3).

Women are quite capable – even immensely capable – of successful careers outside of the home, for the very makeup of the Nurturer is a most formidable thing. It is a fine and good thing for a woman to be well educated, and it is a fine and good thing for a woman to be successful at her career. But it is *never* a fine and good thing to be either or both at the expense of nurturing one's child. It seems to me a strange thing that women should need reminding to nurture their children, but so it is with us today. In any event, it needs to be understood that while children are in the home they need their Nurturer to hang up the briefcase, for the world will still be there when the children move on, at which time professional pursuits will again be appropriate.

STUNTED

Through the marvels of modern technology, we have all most likely seen the horrors of malnutrition and malnourishment experienced in some places in the world, and most heartbreaking of all is to see the stunted and malformed bodies of the children so affected. While there is typically some human culpability for such tragedy, it must be understood that such a state of affairs has the ungod as its ultimate author, and what he has accomplished with the physical bodies of these poor children he is likewise bent upon accomplishing in the characters and personalities of all children, for he would see all of human existence caught in the throes of malnourishment.

To do so he has enlisted mothers to neglect the inward nurturing of their children, who (while they seem hale and whole physically) are inwardly stunted beyond imagination. It is vitally important that we understand that a child is a magnificent person *waiting to be discovered* – a world of possibility and potential yearning and straining to be unlocked. There is a *greatness* in that child, and it awaits its Nurturer to be set free and soar. There are gifts, talents and abilities crying out to be developed, and it is the mother's keen insight, patience and beauty that are by Heaven's design meant to do so. But the Enemy will have none of such greatness from our young (for it is too dangerous a thing for him), and so he must persuade mothers to abandon their children for the sake of selfish pursuit. When they do so – and to the degree that they do so – their children's lives are relegated to the ash heap of mediocrity.

I at times with sadness wonder how much human greatness there is among us that will never be achieved – what literature is left unwritten, what music never to be heard, what innovations never discovered, what cures never found, what beauty never seen and what records never set because true motherly nurture exists more and more rarely in our midst.

An Apple a Day

Finally, touching upon the idea of the inward malnourishment of our children offers us an excellent place to reflect upon their need for physical nourishment. Both the womb and the breasts indicate to us that it is the natural responsibility (and design) of the mother to be the one who generally sees to the physical health and nourishing of her child. And since the three great components to robust physical health are a healthful diet, regular exercise and sufficient sleep, the ungod must seek to influence the Nurturer away from seeing these supplied in the life of her child. While I will spare the reader a repetition of those health issues that have already been covered in the Battlefield on the human body, I must note that this form of malnourishment is usually accomplished with expedience in mind, for it is a consuming thing to prepare fresh and wholesome food on a regular basis (especially when there is more than one child involved). Even so, every inch given to expedience in the issue of a child's health is a form of absence for the Nurturer, whose child depends upon her for his or her physical well-being.

The Believer's Offensive

To the mother God has given the great privilege and responsibility of being the parent most naturally connected to her child, and from her are meant to spring forth the waters of beauty, love and nurture into and upon that young life. As their Nurturer, she holds the keys meant to unlock the possibility and purpose of their existence, for she is the natural possessor of the insight, complexity, patience and beauty needed to see this done.

The believing mother must, therefore, make every effort to be physically and qualitatively present in her child's life, setting aside all that would hinder her from truly nurturing her child into the strong, healthy, stable and godly young adult that he or she was meant to be. She must diligently apply herself to the joy of discovering the intricacies of her child's unique blend of gifts, talents, abilities, disposition and calling, and then forge courageously on toward nurturing her child into what he or she should rightfully and naturally become.

As is true of her husband, she must be faithful to her wedding vows, exhibiting a stable and loving marriage for her child to see and later imitate. She must remain devoted to her Hero (for she is his Nurturer first), and together they must model to their child that full and rich representation of God for which marriage was designed. If this model has already failed the child due to divorce, she too must redouble her efforts at spiritually shepherding her child, knowing well that all is never lost at the feet of our gracious and loving God.

Mothers, to your child you are the blessed one - the *beautiful one* -

of their existence. Model these characteristics with the deepest sense of calling, for you are irreplaceable in your child's life, and you have but one go at it with them. Therefore do all that you can to see them through to the excellence and greatness that lies at the heart of who they are.

BATTLEFIELD: CHILDHOOD

Train a child in the way he should go,
and when he is old he will not turn from it
Proverbs 22:6

At long last we now arrive at the destination of childhood, where we find all of the Enemy's efforts against the individual and family most powerfully converge, for given the relatively short lifespan of humanity, it is by sowing his destructive seed in childhood that he can most bountifully reap the harvest of his Dark Image upon our planet. He therefore targets our young with the focused concentration of every weapon in his unearthly arsenal, but as we have already studied the lion's share of this arsenal in the previous Battlefields, we are now able to narrow our focus on but a few of the more outstanding engagements of the battlefield at hand.

The Original Image

Childhood and youth were meant to be that wonderful and blessed time of life when a young Image Bearer was to be shaped toward the fullness of the human being's ability to reflect the image of God as a Hero or a Nurturer, finally to arrive at the threshold of manhood or womanhood as a person dignified, noble, capable, and wise – worthy reflections of God's image in them. From that threshold they would naturally move toward marriage (the completion of what was lacking of the Divine Image in them), and from that marriage's natural intimacy would be brought forth another blessed Image Bearer, beginning the wondrous process anew.

THE IMAGE UNDONE

The primary idea behind childhood, then, is that of *training and development*, things most wonderfully and naturally supplied by a child's father and mother, who were to train and develop their children under the light of Truth (Deuteronomy 4:9,10; 11:19). As this would naturally tend to result in the advancement of the Divine Image among humanity, the ungod must therefore do all that he can to see that children are trained and developed under the darkness of the Lie, and his success at this is truly breathtaking.

OUT OF OUR HANDS

Let us for a moment suppose that in the early days surrounding the foundations of the idea of public schooling in this nation, the founders of such a system had proposed that they be able to train all of our children according to the following guidelines:

- The Bible may not be taught in school
- Prayer will not be allowed in the classroom
- It will be taught that there is no God, and that all things exist by chance
- It will be taught that there is no such thing as absolute truth
- It will be taught that no culture is superior to any other culture
- It will be taught that homosexuality is healthful, wholesome and good
- It will be taught that there is no such thing as sin
- Reading and writing will be taught in ways proven to fail
- Most high school graduates will be fortunate to read at the sixth grade level
- Grading will not be based upon merit, but upon a child's perceived need of self-esteem
- National sovereignty and love of country will openly be despised in the curriculum
- The schools will teach children how to express their sexuality

- Birth control devices will be given to children at their school without parental consent
- Abortions will be granted without parental consent or knowledge
- Children will engage in sexual activity on school property
- Illegal drugs will be readily available to all children on school property
- The social development of children will be greatly slowed
- Teachers will be able to maintain little control over their classrooms

I daresay that not a decent person of that (or any) era would have inaugurated such a system, yet today most of our children spend nine months of each year for twelve or thirteen of their first eighteen years of life being trained in such a Lie-belching system of public education, where graduates are little more than the well-trained lapdogs of Hellish thought, and who then move on to collegiate studies of even worse influence.

While public education was once a noble endeavor, it is barely so any longer, and the only explanation capable of making sense of such a detrimental transformation is this: Evil is real, the ungod exists and he is about the business of training and developing our children into his dark and hideous image.

Responsibility is a thing that cannot be delegated, and the responsibility for the training and development of a child is in Scripture given to the parents of the child (Deuteronomy 4:9,10), and *never* to anyone else. And since that responsibility is given *by God*, it is expected that parents will train and develop their children under the light of Truth and only under the light of Truth. Everything else borders on an abdication of parental responsibility, and when that abdication involves allowing one's child to be trained and developed under the darkness of Lie, it is tantamount to child sacrifice, whose author is the ungod (Jeremiah 7:31).

We must understand that the Enemy is after the very souls of our children, and his success in the world today is truly astounding. In the impoverished world the children are being trained in nothing, which is almost as bad as the Lie; in the large swath of the Islamic Crescent all children are being trained in the Lie; in the Buddhist and Hindu nations, most children being schooled are being trained in the Lie; in the Communist nations all children are being trained in the Lie; in the socialist West, all children being taught in government-run schools are being trained in the Lie; and here in once Judeo-Christian America our schools have become little more than their European and Canadian counterparts, leaving most of our children under the tutelage of the Lie.

We must stop and consider this for a moment. Do we realize how small a percentage of the world's children are trained in Truth, and thus how close we are to the absolute oblivion of the Dark Image's full ascendency upon Earth? We must stay this advance of Darkness, and staying that advance begins with us fulfilling our responsibility to train and develop our children according to Truth and Light.

HOUSE OF WORSHIP

We are inclined to believe (due mostly to the overwhelming influence of public education in society) that the ideas of education and of worship are separate things, when in truth they are inseparable. Fealty to Truth is the very foundation of the Heavenly idea of education (Proverbs 9:10), and Truth is inseparable from the existence and person of God (John 14:6). When we consider that the responsibility for the education of their children was given to the parents – and that it has always been most natural and right for such education to occur in the home – this makes the home the primary place of worship.

Our Enemy knows this only too well, and although he places great emphasis on seeing the school systems indoctrinate our children into intellectual worship of Hellish ideology, he has by no means neglected influencing our homes into becoming places where the stench of his Darkness is only too welcome. Would we not as parents be appalled to find our adolescent being taught to play a savage and violent video game at our church, or to hear of our teen watching R-rated (or worse) sex scenes with the youth pastor in the youth center?

If such things are out-of-place in our churches, they must likewise be out-of-place in our homes, for to have it otherwise is hypocrisy. And if we don't want such Darkness plaguing our corporate place of worship, we must likewise keep it from our homes, for not only is our home the primary place of worship for our families, it is also the place of the training and development of our children into godly Image Bearers, and therefore should be a place as devoid of Darkness as possible.

YOU-THE MINISTRY

Another idea we unthinkingly borrow from our experience with the public schooling system (where we are programmed to drop off our children so that they may be trained and developed by others) is the idea that a church or its youth pastor are responsible for the spiritual training and condition of our child. But as has just been discussed, spiritual training is inseparable from education, and the responsibility for educating and training one's children has never been removed from the parents. This means that the parents bear the responsibility for their child's spiritual development and condition, and to give that responsibility to another is a serious abdication of parenting.

After nearly twenty years of involvement in youth ministry, I can sadly say that most parents will drop their children off at a church's youth center without ever bothering to investigate what occurs within or to inquire of the character and nature of the person leading the ministry. This unfortunately tells their child that his or her spiritual condition is of little consequence to the parent – something most damaging to the young Image Bearer.

Youth ministry is a thing of modern making, and while it may exist to deal with the breakdown in the structure of the family specifically and of society in general, blessed will be the day if and when it is lost in the rearview mirror of time. It would be far better to see all children shepherded by the ministry that proceeds from home (Ephesians 6:1-4), and all churches would be wise to at least encourage such a model.

THE IMAGE UNDONE PART 2:
TOWARD THE RINGS AND THE ALTAR

Apart from seeing our children enter into a relationship with the Living God and of bearing richly His glorious image, our other great hope and responsibility is that of seeing them prepared for (and entering into) the covenant relationship of marriage (Genesis 2:24). That we best do this by modeling for our children a healthy and stable marriage has already been in many ways discussed; what we will do now is table some Biblical thoughts upon the modern ideas of romance and of choosing a spouse.

CHASTITY BELT

Males and females have a tremendous natural attraction for one another, since without it God's design of marriage wouldn't work. The problem with this issue of attraction is that the human beings possessing this attraction also possess the sinful nature. This is a most dangerous combination, and is used to great effect by the ungod, who has a large stake in seeing to it that our children engage in sexual activity outside the boundaries of marriage. At this he has been highly successful primarily because our children are not appropriately supervised.

It is insanity to think that sinful, sexual beings will not get into sexual mischief if left unsupervised, which is why all sane peoples have historically made efforts to keep their unmarried children (especially while young) separated from those of the opposite sex. Today, however, most children (including a high percentage of teens) spend tremendous amounts of unsupervised time with members of the opposite sex at school, at church, at home, on the phone, on the computer or even through texting and other written correspondence. All of this leads to inappropriate intimacy, which in turn leads to inappropriate sexual involvement. And since it is the parents' responsibility to deliver chaste young men and women to the threshold of marriage (Deuteronomy 22:14), such lack of supervision is nearly criminal in Heaven's eyes.

The best method to ensure that our children understand the idea of chaste behavior is to model it for them. A child should never be given any reason to even *suspect* that his or her father is ever alone with any woman who is not his wife or a close relative, or that his or her mother is ever alone with any man who is not her husband or close relative. It should simply be the manner in which we structure and live our lives, despite what this world may expect or allow.

During His ministry, Jesús was *never* alone with a woman, for He was not married. Even the very public meeting with the Samaritan woman at a well in Sychar took place in the presence of John, who recorded the event (John 4:4-38). Jesus was accused by His enemies of being one illegitimately born (John 8:41) and of being a friend of tax collectors and sinners (Matthew 11:19), but He was never open to the charges of fornication and adultery – something for which His enemies would have accused Him were there even a hint of evidence for it available.

Finally, we must understand that the idea of chastity is not merely an idea that encompasses the physical, but is also an internal issue (Matthew 5:27,28). Outward chastity is so difficult for our children to manage today because the idea of internal chastity is given such little thought, even as the Enemy positively bombards them with his non-stop sexual imagery, sexual innuendo and sexual ideology. As parents, we are not just the guardians of our children's physical chastity, but also of their internal chastity, and our homes must therefore be places where this virtue is extolled. We should have chaste television sets, chaste computers, chaste music, chaste reading materials, chaste conversation and chaste conduct.

GO ASK YOUR DAD

Our journey into preparing our child for marriage now takes a turn in the direction of the need for the choice of an appropriate spouse for him or her, and given the dismal statistics on divorce today (especially among Christians), we are in need of a major overhaul of thought and practice in this realm. We will begin that overhaul with a look at the Biblical method of choosing a spouse.

Jacob taught us that if you really like a woman, you can work seven years for her father only to be given the wrong sister on your wedding night, and then have to work seven more years for the correct one (Genesis 29:15-30). Samson taught us that if an attractive foreign gal catches your eye, you can act like a spoiled brat and demand that your parents go get her for you (Judges 14:2,3). Abigail taught us that you can give your husband a heart attack and hope that the handsome, young, future king will give you a better proposal (1Samuel 25). Or (as the two hundred remaining men of Benjamin taught us) you can hide in the vineyard while the maidens come out to dance, then pick one that you like and carry her off when her father and brothers aren't looking (Judges 21:20-23).

Yet if we set aside these humorous anecdotes, we find that a closer and more serious look at Scripture shows to us a Biblical model of marriage that is a combination of the arranged marriage and personal choice. Now I understand that we are a people prone to thumb our noses at the idea of the arranged marriage, but this is primarily because we're enthralled with the idiotic idea of marrying because we're *in love*. I don't want to imply that the idea of the arranged marriage cannot be (or is not) tainted by the ungod or fallen humanity, but I must teach the truth of the Biblical model, despite the fact that it may take us to places we find uncomfortable. And despite our attachment to the idea of absolutely choosing our own spouse, it must be admitted that a loving, caring, prayerful and discerning parent of noble intent who knows well his or her child is as capable (or more so) of choosing a suitable spouse for their child than is the child himself or herself. Isaac certainly had no issues with his father's choice for him (Genesis 24:67), as Rebekah was beautiful (24:16), hardworking (24:19, 20), adventurous (24:57) and trusted in God (24:50).

I think it safe to say that the only perfect union between a man and a woman that has ever existed was an *arranged* one, for God wrought Eve from Adam's side and brought the two of them together (Genesis 2:21,22). Abraham *arranged* for his son's wife to be found from among his own people (Genesis 24). Pharaoh *arranged* a marriage for Joseph in Egypt (Genesis 41:45). Caleb *arranged* a marriage for his daughter to a valiant man (Joshua 15:16,17). Jehoiada the priest *arranged* two marriages for the orphaned King Joash in order to rebuild the decimated Messianic line of David (2 Chronicles 24:3). And our Heavenly Father is currently *arranging* a marriage for His only begotten Son (Revelation 19:9).

Having now established the Biblical legitimacy of the idea of the arranged marriage, we must now look at the flip side of the same coin, which is the consent of the individual being married. In the case of Isaac, Abraham *did* commission his servant to find a suitable wife for his son, but Rebekah was free to deny the proposal (Genesis 24:57). We are never told that Moses was forced to marry Zipporah (Exodus 2:21), and though there was some kind-hearted matchmaking being pursued by Naomi, the marriage of Ruth and Boaz was strictly a consensual matter (Ruth 3-4). And, of course, the beautiful and intelligent Abigail was free to deny David's proposal of marriage after the death of her previous husband (1 Samuel 25:39). We therefore see that the Scriptural model for marriage is one of both parental arrangement (usually at the hand of the father) and the choice of the individual, bringing us now to the heart of the matter.

God is Father to Believers (Matthew 6:9; John 20:17). As our concerned and discerning Heavenly Parent, He is both capable and desirous of arranging the marriage best for us, just as He did with Adam and Eve, for He does not show favoritism (Romans 2:11). When God does this for us, Believers will most naturally give their consent to the union (as did Isaac), for the Hero or Nurturer chosen will be a wonderful match, and a most wonderful example of this is played out for us through the story of Ruth and Boaz.

THE DATING GAME

Ruth and Boaz didn't meet in the ancient version of a chat room; they never played the singles' scene or went to the singles' Bible studies; nor did they mow through all of the eligible bachelors and bachelorettes of Bethlehem to find one another. They each simply served God: she by taking care of her aging mother-in-law (Ruth 2:11), and he by being a faithful steward of his portion of the Promised Land (Ruth 2:4). That they were two people lonely and in need of their complementary Hero and Nurturer I have no doubt, for they were human adults designed for marriage (Genesis 2:18). Yet Ruth and Boaz simply served God, and God showed Himself as concerned for their loneliness as He had been for Adam's, for in the appropriate course of time He brought them together through both Providence (Ruth 2:3) and His idea of the Levirate marriage, to which each gave their willing consent.

Yet how different is the ungod's plan for finding and choosing a spouse, which is a process that leaves a person so scarred by the time the choice to marry is made that it scarcely gives the eventual marriage a chance at even mediocre success! I submit that it is intrinsically wrong (and shows utter lack of faith in both the Biblical model and the fatherhood of God) to become romantically involved with person after person in our search for the perfect spouse, only to hang them back on the rack when once we are dissatisfied with their fit, as if they were nothing more than department store clothing that was meant to be tried on in the fitting room of romance and replaced if undesired. That the world thinks this an admirable thing I am not at all surprised; that Believers should treat their sisters and brothers in this manner is appalling.

Apart from leading to sexual promiscuity due to its unsupervised nature, this modern system of spouse selection is personally damaging and dangerous, for it hurts deeply to be rejected in this manner. Such a system simply involves too high a degree of trust and intimacy to be shared by two people not married to one another, and when one is rejected after such a relationship, it leaves a person hurt (and possibly even devastated). With many such relationships under one's belt, very little of trust and confidence survives into marriage.

Such broken trust and confidence going into marriage is a dream-come-true for that institution's Enemy, as is the damage done by the out-of-bounds sexual activity typically accompanying such non-Biblical ideas of romance. It is a far better thing to embrace the Biblical model, which is simply to serve your Heavenly Father with all your heart, soul, mind and strength wherever He has you (Mark 12:30), and to trust in His fatherhood of you. Something as important as your partner for life is of tremendous importance to Him, and so He will prepare the two of you for one another and in His time will bring you together. When He does so you will recognize one another through the goodly and godly character that you each possess (just as it was with Ruth and Boaz), at which time you will delight in giving your consent to marriage, for the arrangement is a fantastic one.

It is now appropriate to insert a thought or two again upon the idea of the soul mate, for what I have just described may sound dangerously akin to that hideous idea, and it is most important that I not be misunderstood. If I seem to be saying that God has the intent of arranging a special someone for another, it is something I believe readily enough, for it is the testimony of the First Couple. But this is true *only* of the unmarried person, and must not be used to justify breaking up a marriage because one believes that his or her special match has been missed. Once married, spouses are knit intimately together by the design and hand of God – something that is infinitely greater in scope than any pre-marriage preparation. The great truth of the Biblical model of marriage is that it can work beautifully between *any* Hero and *any* Nurturer if properly applied. Your spouse is to remain your spouse. Bloom where you are planted.

Parents, I submit that God is a better matchmaker than we. Our task is to prepare our young Image Bearers to be ready for marriage and to be ready to recognize their eventual spouse (for whom we should already be praying). Let us bid a hearty farewell to the Hellish dating game for them, as God has much better in store for our children.

THE BELIEVER'S OFFENSIVE

No greater and more wonderful human responsibility is there than to be given a clean-slated, malleable and ultimately ignorant newborn Image Bearer who is literally bursting at the seams with potential and greatness, and who is meant to be delivered at adulthood's threshold as a strong, intelligent, wise, dignified and noble Hero or Nurturer beautifully and deeply reflecting the Divine Image. I can imagine no more blessed or solemn a thing.

For the believing parent, then, all that enriches the training and education of our children toward these noble ends must be embraced most fully by us, even as that which hinders it must be most fully rejected. It is our responsibility to see that our children are educated in the light of Truth, and not in the shadow of Darkness. This charge we cannot (and must not) give to those who do not dwell in (and love) the light of Truth, which in turn demands that we (as parents) be people of Truth and of the Biblical worldview, and that our lives, characters and homes reflect Truth and the Biblical worldview.

Every facet of our children's lives must be fashioned by training according to Truth, and the Lie must not be allowed the space for even a foothold in the midst of this training. To reap Truth in their lives we must sow Truth, we must water Truth and we must nurture Truth. To do anything but these – to willingly and knowingly in any manner give our children to the Lie – is child sacrifice, which is an idea anathema to our Heavenly Father (Jeremiah 7:31).

Better it is by far that we sacrifice all in order to one day see our adult children standing strong and fair and noble as sons and daughters of Truth. Let us see to it then, heart and soul, for the mature dignity, nobility and beauty of our adult children is life's greatest crown of glory – it can be matched by no other.

BATTLEFIELD: AUTHORITY

Honor your father and mother,
so that you may live long in the land
the LORD your God is giving you
Exodus 20:12

In our study of the family we have thus far focused the heaviest share of attention and responsibility upon the parents, for so it must be. This has not been done in order to exasperate those of us who are parents, but rather to highlight the deep, wonderful and solemn charge of parenting given to us by God. If both parent and child have therefore been wondering as to when I would arrive at the responsibilities and Divine expectations of the child, wonder no longer, for we are there.

THE ORIGINAL IMAGE

Apart from the First Couple, all human beings were designed to be born and then raised by their parents into mature adulthood. If we suppose (for the sake of argument) that Adam and Eve had never sinned, and that humanity had then been free to flourish upon Earth without influence from Evil, each child would have been raised by his or her father and mother, whom they would willingly and naturally honor, and to whom they would willingly and naturally submit. This is true because honoring one's parents (Exodus 20:12) and submitting to one's parents (Ephesians 6:1) were later commanded by God, and all commands of God are extensions of His perfect nature, and therefore good (Romans 7:16). Since those without the sinful nature are only capable of good, our hypothetically sinless humanity would have resulted in a state of affairs in which parents were honored and respected less than only God Himself, giving rise to a perfect and orderly society.

The Image Undone

The ungod despises everything of Heaven, and since a perfect and orderly society upon Earth would resemble and reflect Heaven, he would naturally have to see to the flourishing of an imperfect and disorderly society upon Earth. He accomplished the foundation of this idea most admirably through engineering the Fall, and has ever since been working by degrees to see to its completion among humanity – something most naturally accomplished through an attack on the understanding of the idea of authority in childhood.

As the human population naturally expanded, human society was designed to grow from the root of the idea of family, which means that *as goes the family, so goes society*. If the ungod is therefore able to bring into adulthood sufficient numbers of people who despise authority, the entirety of the planet will be his in short order, for all structure and order will be lost.

Rebel-utionaries

Since obedience to one's parents is a good thing, the Enemy will naturally work to influence children into disobedience of their parents at every turn. To disobey against the established order (structure) is to *rebel*, and the ungod is the author of rebellion against the established order of God (Isaiah 14:13,14). Since the family is God's established structure for humanity, to disobey one's parents is therefore a form of rebellion against God Himself, and is a thing near and dear to the heart of Hell. Furthermore, since Satan is a direct creation of God, it may be properly said that he is a *son of God* (Job 1:6 KJV), making him the first to rebel against parental authority. And though Satan lost that first Rebellion against Heaven (Isaiah 14:12), he will never surrender the fight, but instead enlists the sinful nature of humanity's children to continue the battle with him, and that sinful nature has every selfish and sociopathic tendency necessary through which to work his dark scheming.

It is the duty of children to recognize that they are possessors of this sinful nature, and that it is the God-given right and responsibility of their parents to govern (limit) that sinful nature until adulthood is reached, by which time the child has hopefully learned how to govern it appropriately himself or herself. To the child, to the adolescent and to the teen I must submit the following painful truths: Your parents did not have to teach you to lie; they had to teach you to tell the truth. They did not have to teach you to be selfish; they had to teach you to share. They did not have to teach you how to be a slob; they had to teach you to be orderly. They did not have to teach you to be lazy; they had to teach you to be disciplined and industrious. They did not have to teach you to be cruel; they had to teach you to be kind. These are but a few of the many evidences of your sinful nature and its hideousness, and your parents have been given the tasks of governing its expression and of training you in right living, with the ultimate goal being that of seeing you one day appropriately govern it yourselves.

Such training and governing is a difficult and uncomfortable thing, but your success as an eventual adult hinges upon it. Despite the difficulty and discomfort involved, you must obey your parents in the Lord (Ephesians 6:1) and learn to *appreciate* them for their position of authority in your lives, for if you do not learn to do so you will never be able to appreciate God's loving authority over you, over your eventual marriage or over your children. You will also be unable to function meaningfully in an orderly society, since an orderly society has necessary authority at every level.

And so the ungod would have all children disobedient and rebellious, for they will then become his disobedient and rebellious adults who will infect all of human society with anarchy until his Hellish image of planetary chaos and disorder are complete. The anarchy now seen among our youth (as evidenced most deeply in our inner cities and in the growing chaos of our public school systems) is but a small foretaste of what awaits us in the not-too-distant future if this trend is not reversed.

Regarding the issue of complete obedience, it must be noted that the Scriptures do allow for an exception to obedience of one's parents, for Ephesians 6:1 tells us that children are to obey their parents *in the Lord.*

What this means is that children may only choose to rightly disobey their parents (the established authority) when the commands or wishes of their parents go against the obvious will and nature of God. In such a circumstance we must always obey God rather than human authority (Acts 4:19), and a good example of this would be if a parent told a child not to pray to God. Since we are expected to pray (Matthew 6:6) and commanded to pray (1 Thessalonians 5:17), a child would be justified in disobeying such a parental demand.

HONORABLE MENTION

Apart from obedience, there is for the child that higher calling toward his or her parents contained in the Fifth Commandment (Exodus 20:12), which tells us to *honor* our father and mother. Since it is quite possible (and all too common) to obey one's parents without honoring them, it is more than a little appropriate for us to explore the term *honor* as it is used and meant in this verse. To honor our parents means that we recognize their right to our respect and give it to them; that we render to them love, devotion and even a degree of awe; that we willingly submit to their wisdom and judgment; and that we see to it that their good name and dignity are upheld by us and by those around us. It is the highest degree of reverence reserved for fellow human beings, and is surpassed only by the idea of worship – something that is reserved for God alone (Revelation 19:10). If we honor our parents, we will not only obey them, but we will inwardly delight in doing so.

Admittedly, this is a particularly tall order, for all of our parents are of the imperfect variety, and some much more so than others. However, this Commandment was given even in light of the imperfections of earthly parents, and so honor must be given despite what failings earthly parents may or may not have. A commandment is not a suggestion, and this Commandment dictates that our hearts be humble and appreciative of our parents.

Since this honoring of our parents is an expression of the Divine nature, the ungod is necessarily its avowed enemy and will see to its absence, which is the idea of *dishonoring* one's parents. Those who dishonor their parents will therefore not recognize their parents' right to their respect and will give to them none; will render to them no love, devotion or awe; will despise their wisdom and judgment; and will take delight in seeing their good name and dignity disparaged. Obedience (if given at all) will be reluctantly and hatefully done, for there is no inner disposition of beauty toward one's parents.

It is here that we must take stock of ourselves as a people, for we have become one that places more value upon youth than upon age and wisdom, and this throws the idea of honoring one's parents to the wolves. Most of advertising is now geared toward youth (despite the fact that most of the dollars desired by advertisers are held by those well beyond the years of youth), and huge sums of money are spent each year in the pursuit of turning back the hands of time, as if age were something to be despised. Hollywood, too, is guilty of the dishonoring of parenthood on a magnificent scale, for rarely can a sitcom, television show or movie be seen in which the parents exhibit any kind of character deserving respect, while the children portrayed are those in whom reside the founts of clear thinking, sense and wisdom.

This is deliberate parental character assassination of the highest order, and bears the under-worldly stench of the ungod to its very core. I have nothing against those who possess youth, for it is a wonderful thing; but youth are *young*. And since they are young, they lack experience and thereby wisdom, a fact that should drive them toward living in deference toward their seniors. The Israelite tribes and towns of the Old Testament were governed by the Elders of its people (Joshua 20:4; Proverbs 31:23), and never by its *Youngers* for this very reason. The young were, in fact, required to rise in the presence of the aged as a sign of deference and respect (Leviticus 19:32); not respecting the elderly dearly cost the young men who taunted Elisha (2 Kings 2:24), and cost Rehoboam most of his kingdom (1 Kings 12).

Rotten to the Core

Children are born into a universe awash in structure, for its Author is an orderly Being. The Godhead has structure (John 6:38;15:26), the angelic realm has structure (Daniel 10:12,13), physical Creation has structure (Genesis 1:14-18), human government has structure (Exodus18:21,22), humanity has structure (1 Corinthians 11:3), the Church has structure (Ephesians 4:11) and the family has structure (Exodus 20:12). Since a child's first experience with the idea of structure is through the family, his experience with – and attitude toward – family will shape how he later views all institutions of structure (up to and including God). If the parents are able to shape a favorable view of the blessing of Divine structure in his mind, he will then have a natural appreciation for order at every level, and the Divine Image will flourish with (and in) him. If this is accomplished on a large-enough scale within a people or nation, the disorder of Darkness can be pushed back significantly.

It is therefore imperative for the ungod to poison or destroy the idea of structure, and he must necessarily focus such destruction upon the child of the family, for this will cause the Dark Image to flourish with (and in) him, and if done on a large- enough scale, Darkness will eventually prevail upon Earth. His work here is focused mainly upon the attitude of the heart of the child, for if the child despises his parents even while he obeys them outwardly, he is still despising the ideas of structure and authority.

This is why the Fifth Commandment carried with it a promise, which was that the Israelites might live long in the land that God was giving them (Exodus 20:12). And although this is described as a promise (Ephesians 6:2), it is a promise because it is a simple fact of reality. If the Israelites were to honor their parents, they would be delighting in the idea that there is a Divine structure to the family. If they were delighting in the Divine structure of the family, they would be delighting in the nature of God. If they were delighting in the nature of God, they would be a good and moral people. If they were a good and moral people, they would know Heaven's blessing (Deuteronomy 28:2). If they knew Heaven's blessing, they would be a strong people (Deuteronomy 28:7).

If they were a strong people, they would hold possession of their land (Deuteronomy 28:10).

That this would result in the Divine Image flourishing needs no explanation, and a fantastic example of how such national goodness caused the light of Heaven to shine upon Earth may be found in ancient Israel during the middle part of Solomon's reign (1 Kings 4:34). From the ungod's perspective, then, such light must never be allowed to shine, and his answer was, of course, to attack the very idea of family through that nation's king, who would eventually take three hundred wives and seven hundred concubines. The light of Heaven's reflection was then largely extinguished by the time Solomon's son took the throne (1 Kings 11), and never thereafter shone from that land with its former brilliance.

Simply put, the despising of one's parents is the root of all decay in human society, which is why it is pursued with such dedication by that ancient Rebel in whom the idea originated, for he was the first to despise his Father (Isaiah 14:13,14).

THE BELIEVER'S OFFENSIVE

The Fifth Commandment has a promise; it also has no end (Mark 7:9-13). While we as believing children are required to obey our parents during the time that we live under their covering, honoring them is that higher and inward and far better thing to which we are called, and it must never stop, for we would then be failing to honor God.

Honoring our parents has the natural and wonderful effect of rendering obedience nearly irrelevant, for if we honor them, obedience will never be in question. And when we honor them, we honor God and the order He has authored, thereby causing the Divine Image to flourish in our lives, our families and (by ultimate extension) our society and our planet. We therefore must see to our hearts and humble ourselves before God and our parents so that Heaven's blessings may flow and its light shine upon our fair world.

THE IMAGE WAR: HUMAN SOCIETY

BATTLEFIELD: LIFE

This day I call heaven and earth as witnesses against you
that I have set before you life and death, blessings and curses.
Now choose life...
Deuteronomy 30:19

We move now into study detailing the ungod's assault upon the idea of human society, where we find ourselves discussing issues of immense weight and planetary consequence. The first of these issues is the very idea of life itself, and as we shall see in the coming pages, how a people view this issue will shape both their society and their culture.

THE ORIGINAL IMAGE

The Scriptures begin not with an explanation of God, but with the acknowledgement of His eternal existence, for when it states that *in the beginning God created* (Genesis 1:1), it is a recognition that He existed prior to matter, energy and time. And if He existed before these things, then He simply always has been – an idea consistent with how He introduced Himself to Moses, which was as *I AM THAT I AM* (Exodus 3:14), from which we derive the hallowed Name of Jehovah or Yahweh.

Things can only reproduce after their own kind (Genesis 1:12,21,24), and life is no exception to this rule, dictating that all things living must have had a source of life in order to exist. Since God is eternally alive, He *is* Life, and so defines the very idea of it. As Life, only God can be the Author of all things living, and of all things living, humanity was the crown jewel and recipient of a greater degree of Life than any other (Genesis 1:26,27; 2:7). This meant that in the realm of physical Creation, humanity was more alive than anything else in existence.

THE IMAGE UNDONE

As the absolute absence of God (who is Life), the ungod is Death itself, for he knows complete and utter separation from God (the finest definition of *death* available). He must therefore see to it that all evidence of Life is eradicated from existence, and as the greatest recipients and reflectors of Life, humanity would most necessarily find itself lodged in the crosshairs of Death. It was therefore not long before the fatal wound of the Fall was inflicted, severing the silver cord between humanity and God.

Yet even with his tremendous success of engineering the Fall, there were three issues most certainly not resolved to the ungod's satisfaction through it. The first is that the spiritual death experienced by humanity was not permanent, for humanity was redeemable (Genesis 3:15) where the ungod was not (Matthew 25:41). The second issue was that physical death was not immediate for humanity (Genesis 5:5), while the third issue was that the Divine Image had not been entirely vanquished in them, a state of affairs which called humanity ever Heavenward and made it possible to think and live in a manner befitting Heaven. Such things must be remedied by the Evil One.

ORIGIN OF SPECIES

A people's belief in the origin of Life will fundamentally affect who and what they are, and therefore how they will choose to live. If a people hold to the Biblical view of God and Life, they will have great love and respect for the concept of life, since they will recognize that they are answerable to its Author for their deeds (Revelation 21:7,8). This will result in conduct befitting Heaven. If a people hold to a non-Biblical view of God and Life, they will lose love and respect for the concept of life, thereby embracing Death and its destructive ideologies to the great detriment of humanity.

For the ungod, such a Death-embracing and non-Biblical view of God and Life is paramount, and so we see the importance and fury behind his battle to supplant Truth with Lie, for where his Lie holds sway, Death will naturally reign supreme. Hence the brutal ages-long war against the Scriptures and its adherents (Matthew 23:35), and by extension against the marvelous truth of Redemption contained within Holy Writ (Romans 10:14). The Enemy is many things, but dense he is not, and he understands that our chance at redemption ends at physical death (Hebrews 9:27), and if not redeemed by that point, we belong to him and will experience the fullness of Death forevermore (Mark 9:48), as will he (Revelation 20:10).

Murder, He Wrote

Since physical death forever seals a Hellish eternity for those not redeemed, in the mind of the ungod it is naturally most desirous to see physical death occur as early in life as possible, for it logically limits a person's chance at salvation. Even more important, however, is the fact that any living, breathing human being is a constant reminder of Life and its Author, which dictates that the ungod must work toward seeking the death of every human being whenever, wherever and however possible, with an ultimate view of human extinction in mind.

The first two chapters of Job teach us that Satan wields tremendous destructive power in this world, and would use it to utterly destroy humanity but for the restraining hand of an omnipotent God. This restraining hand therefore leaves the ungod with the necessity of influencing human thought and behavior toward the idea of the wanton and wholesale taking of human life. Since human life begins at conception (Psalm 139:13; Jeremiah 1:5; Luke 1:39-44), those in the womb are his first and most hideous target for the idea of murder, and his target practice does not stop through any stage of life, but continues through the full spectrum of the human lifespan.

Since there is much confusion about what constitutes the idea of murder, this is an excellent place to define the term. Simply put, murder is the act of willingly and knowingly taking human life without proper sanction, and as the Author of human life, only God has the authority to issue such sanction (something we shall study later under the banner of human government). The ungod, however, has always been a murderer (John 8:44), and is therefore the author and inspiration for every type of murder upon Earth (regardless of who may physically commit the act itself), since it is ultimately his doing and therefore is a reflection of the Dark Image.

To this discussion we must also add the idea of human death due to tragedy and the cataclysms of nature. Death was not part of human existence until the Fall (Romans 5:12), nor was accident or injury, for it seems it was either not possible or prevented by the angels (Psalm 91:12; Hebrews 1:14). Since the ungod was the engineer of the Fall, all of the blame for the injury and death associated with it and its continued consequences must therefore fall upon his dark shoulders, for he is their originator.

Regarding the cataclysms of nature, although they are deemed *acts of God*, they are merely the continuation of the process by which nature itself is slowly moving toward the chaos that is the Decay Laws' natural and ultimate end (Romans 8:22), and so the blame for any tragedy and death associated with them belongs also to the dark author of chaos. True *acts of God* are actually quite rare, as demonstrated by the Flood (Genesis 6) and by the destruction of Sodom and Gomorrah (Genesis 19), which were done because the level of human wickedness required Divine judgment.

Make It Stop

As to the ongoing tragedy that we call human existence, some words must now be put forth in defense of God regarding it. In a nutshell, the question regarding tragedy naturally becomes: *Why would a loving and holy God allow suffering and tragedy?* The Enemy's answers to this question would lead (and have led) many away from faith and fealty to God, and so must first be briefly stated. His first answer is that a loving God would not allow suffering, therefore God must not be loving. His second answer is that an omnipotent (all-powerful) God would stop suffering, therefore God must not be omnipotent. His third answer is simply that God is an absentee landlord unconcerned with humanity and planet Earth.

But, of course, the ungod does not traffic in Truth, and so we must take some time to discover it regarding this issue. The appropriate answer to this conundrum lies with the exploration of two trains of thought: the issue of human free moral agency (free will), and the issue of the responsibility for planetary affairs. Simply stated, planet Earth was created for humanity. When completed, it was a place of perfection and perfect delight, and existed without pain, tragedy or death. It was then given to those for whom it was created (humanity), and they were made lords of it (Genesis 1:28-30), which meant that planetary affairs were henceforth human affairs. That is simply the way God created things, and it would not be uncreated even if it changed detrimentally (any more than God uncreated Lucifer after his changing), for even the affairs of the new Earth will be human affairs (Revelation 21-22).

As lords of the planet and planetary affairs, Adam and Eve then willingly and knowingly brought the stain and scourge of sin, death and decay upon the planet and its affairs through their participation in the Fall – something their freedom gave them the perfect right to do (however we may wish it otherwise). This could not change the fact that the affairs of Earth were permanently designed to be the affairs of humanity. That being understood, let us now continue the argument from the standpoint of human free will.

Having free will means that one has the ability to legitimately choose between differing courses of action (an idea which brings to us the wonderful thought of *freedom*). But as we shall more fully discuss in later Battlefields, freedom must be balanced by responsibility, which means that any holder of freedom must squarely face the consequences of the choice he or she makes. This was true of Lucifer, and is just as true of humanity. For Lucifer it ultimately means an eternity in the Hell created for him (Matthew 25:41). For humanity and the case at hand it meant having to deal with the consequences of every horrible thing that would come with the Fall: tragedy, sickness, disease, decay, corruption, death and every other vile facet of the Dark Image (Genesis 3:16-19).

At the heart of our cry to see human tragedy stopped is therefore the cry to be absolved of the consequences of human action, and lest we complain that it is unfair that we face the punishment for Adam's sin, let us be reminded once again that we daily show our solidarity with him in our choices to willingly sin (even though we know far more than he the consequences of this). But even were God to end suffering, we would not like the result, as He would have to remove our freedom from us in order to do so, for if God were to put an end to everything evil (which He must do to end suffering), He would have to remove our ability to choose. This would leave us as little more than robots programmed to do His bidding, and that which we most cherish about our humanity would effectively be lost.

Finally, we come to the idea of the absentee landlordship of God, which is a fantastically hideous idea of Hell, for as the great *God With Us* of Matthew 1:23, God is intimately and passionately involved in human affairs. Indeed, all of Scripture is a record of His loving involvement with humanity, culminating in the deep, personal, painful and costly involvement of the Cross.

As both a holy and a loving God, He will eventually make all things right and end all suffering when the sinful nature is destroyed and all things have been made new (Revelation 21:4). But this will not be done at the expense of our humanity.

QUALITY CONTROL

Any discussion of Life would be incomplete if the idea of the *quality* of Life was not included, for Jesus said that He came that we might *have life and have it to the full*, whereas Satan came only *to steal and kill and destroy* (John 10:10). Life therefore means far more than the mere beating of a heart and the breathing of lungs and the firing of neurons in the brain. For to be *truly alive* means to be connected to Him who is Life itself, and to reflect His image and attributes as our own.

True Life, then, is about ideals such as greatness, magnificence, beauty, nobility, honor, loyalty, heroism, wisdom, eloquence, love, grace, nurture, compassion, fairness, humility, intimacy, freedom, responsibility, order, delight and joy, all of which are humanly represented in the person of Christ, who is the exact representation of God in human form (Hebrews 1:3; Colossians 2:9). To the degree that human thought and life are connected to (and inspired by) these highest of ideals, human existence will trend upward toward the Divine Image, and life on Earth will mirror that of Heaven, a wondrous state of affairs I define as *High Humanity*.

Since the Holy Spirit is transforming Believers into the image of Christ (2 Corinthians 3:18), Believers are those most likely to achieve High Humanity upon Earth, and where their influence reaches critical mass, High Humanity may be achieved on a grand and magnificent scale. The ungod therefore not only wars against Truth in a general fashion, but he wars against Redemption and the Redeemed most fiercely of all, for they must not be allowed the spreading of their Heaven-like existence and ideology. Hence the ruthless and unrelenting attack upon Biblical Christianity from its inception (Acts 4) until today, for the High Humanity it brings in its wake is anathema to Hell.

Jesus called His followers *the salt of the earth* (Matthew 5:13), and since salt was the preservative of the day, this meant that Believers were to keep humanity from absolute corruption and spoil. Without the influence of Believers, then, the sinful nature would inevitably lead humanity into the dark abyss where every noble thing is lost (Genesis 6:5; Romans 1:28-32). In such a state, conditions upon Earth mirror those of Hell, which is something I define as *Low Humanity*. Although they physically live and breathe, those poor souls living in the shadow of Low Humanity are technically the walking dead, for they are nearly devoid of Life.

THE BELIEVER'S OFFENSIVE

Our loving Redeemer is the idea of Life fully defined. Apart from Him there is no Life, and in Him there is only Life. Over the date and time of our physical death we have little control, except to live wisely and to treat our bodies well. But over the depth and quality of the image of God that is reflected in us we do have tremendous control. Our once-dead lives are meant to be made more and more alive by Him who is Life, something that is accomplished by exerting our energies in the direction of Christ-likeness, wherein we submit all thought, attitude and action to the principles of Scripture. When we do so, the Holy Spirit will mold the likeness of Jesus in us (2 Corinthians 3:18), which is High Humanity perfectly defined. We should be cups positively running over with Life (John 7:38).

But let us remember that Life naturally begets Life, and we neither cannot nor should not stand or sit idly by while the vast majority of our fellow human beings are the walking dead and are slowly moving toward their rendezvous with eternal Death. We must equip ourselves, we must pray and we must go out to seek and see saved those who are lost and held as slaves to sin and Darkness (Luke 19:10). We have the light of Life (John 8:12) and are the light of the world (Matthew 5:14), and light is meant to shine (Matthew 5:15,16), leaving no room for the Darkness that is its absence. So let us shine with all heart and soul, for *how beautiful...are the feet of those who bring good news!* (Isaiah 52:7).

Furthermore, as those who have by grace inherited the Father's gift of eternal life, we should be those upon Earth who more than all others safeguard the idea and sanctity of human life whenever and wherever possible. We must champion this idea by protecting human life from womb to grave, for each human being is an Image Bearer, and must be allowed the dignity of existence unless otherwise sanctioned by Scripture.

And finally, let us see to the arranging of human affairs according to the principles of Scripture in order to lessen the dominance of evil and tragedy in our midst (Deuteronomy 28). Let us also humble ourselves and invite God to be gracious to our land (2 Chronicles 7:14), and let us offer the hope and love of Christ to all who suffer loss, for He is able to turn what is meant for evil into good (Genesis 50:20; Romans 8:28).

BATTLEFIELD: FREEDOM

It is for freedom that Christ has set us free
Galatians 5:1a

Few ideas can brighten human existence as can that of freedom, for the sound of the word has an almost magical quality to it. Toward this concept we must now turn our gaze, for it is a fierce Battlefield in the Image War, and it has a great impact upon human existence and society.

THE ORIGINAL IMAGE

When we study the issue of freedom as it relates to the nature and image of God, we're in for quite a surprise, as we find that freedom is not quite what we assumed it was. While the fallen human nature would love nothing more than to define freedom as the ability to do whatever one wants whenever and however one chooses, this is not so with how freedom works within the nature of God.

God is an absolutely free Being (Psalm 135:6), but His freedom doesn't mean that there are no limits to what He can do. This is because God is also a holy Being, which in turn means that He is incapable of doing anything sinful (James 1:13). God's freedom is therefore *limited* by the reality of His holiness. When something is limited by something else, the thing that does the limiting is considered the greater (or stronger) thing, and technically owns the weaker thing. Regarding God's freedom and holiness, this means that His freedom is owned (or limited) by His holiness. Since humanity was created in God's image, this meant that the true and original freedom known by humanity prior to the Fall was defined as *the ability to do anything in keeping with the nature of God*. Adam and Eve's actions were *owned* solely by the idea of holiness, and holiness was as natural to them as breathing.

THE IMAGE UNDONE

The absence of freedom is the idea of *slavery*, and since freedom is defined as having one's actions owned by the idea of holiness, slavery is naturally defined as having one's actions owned by anything other than the holiness of God. With this definition in mind, we are much better equipped to understand the inherent slavery of the sinful nature, for it places our actions under the natural ownership of unholiness.

The Fall therefore made slaves of Adam and Eve (and by extension all of humanity), for they became owned by the sinful nature, which made unholy (sinful) conduct natural for them from then on. The principle of slavery had thus been introduced into the human condition; the ungod would now war by degrees against human freedom until the last remnants of it were removed from Heaven's hated Image Bearers.

CHAIN GANG

If humanity must exist at all, the ungod's perfect idea for our existence is the concept of *absolute slavery*, in which human lives are completely devoid of choice and owned fully by another who cares nothing for their welfare. The great Biblical example of this is the plight of the Hebrews in Egypt, who cried out to God for relief from their utterly miserable existence at the hands of Pharaoh (Exodus 1-12). Since living under such a condition crushes the human soul and empties a person of hope, delight, purpose and dignity, it is the dark idea toward which Hell influences all of human existence.

Here we see the plight of the true human slave – someone who lives in a choiceless dungeon, unable to pursue the higher ideals of human existence and who is forever mired in the mundane. His eyes are not allowed to wander upward, and he knows nothing of the beauties of choice, growth, excellence or achievement. The despairing soul, the numbed mind, the lifeless eyes, the bent back, the broken body and the broken spirit of the human slave testify to the meager existence of the hopelessness it engenders, and is the goal toward which the ungod drives all of human thought and society. It is the absolute bondage of the spirit, mind and body.

It may be argued by critics that the Bible institutionalizes slavery, but great care must be taken when accusing Him who is the Author of both freedom and Scripture of such a thing. God's Word has too much to say concerning slavery for such a topic to be reduced to simple sound bites, and we must remember that Egypt was punished most severely for their harsh enslavement of the Hebrews (Exodus 7-12). Above all, God deals with reality, and in a fallen world then devoid of our dangerous ideas of modern welfare, slavery was often the only manner in which a person or family might survive destitution (Leviticus 25:39).

When such was the case, the Israelites were allowed to take foreigners as their slaves (Leviticus 25:44), but were admonished to treat them with dignity and respect, for they themselves had known the yoke of brutal slavery in Egypt. It must be remembered that the decrees of the Law were being given during the great Exodus, when the memory of brutal Egyptian slavery was still fresh in their minds and a deeply odious thing to the Israelites. When employed, Israelite slavery was therefore designed to be a far kinder and more humane thing than was practiced elsewhere (Exodus 23:12; Leviticus 25:43).

Regarding their countrymen, the Israelites were forbidden to make slaves of their destitute fellows, but were only allowed to make indentured servants of them for seven years (Exodus 21:2) or until the Year of Jubilee, and were commanded to treat them honorably (Leviticus 25:39-43). Such a system worked so well that many servants willingly entered into a lifelong covenant of servitude to their masters by becoming bondservants (Exodus 21:6).

SLAVE-OLOGIES

Pursuit of the ideals of High Humanity will always result in greater freedom, for High Humanity always directs toward Heaven, where freedom is complete. The pursuit of the ideals of Low Humanity will therefore always result in slavery, for Low Humanity always directs toward

Hell, where slavery is complete. But since absolute slavery is so odious even to fallen humanity, the Enemy must work to achieve the slavery of Low Humanity in a roundabout fashion, which he does by using the Lie.

By virtue of the nature of its author, the Lie will always lead to absolute slavery as its ultimate destination, and since slavery is defined as being owned by anything other than the holiness of God, we see that a wondrous universe of sly temptations is opened up to the ungod. Here he will take advantage of every possible facet of the Lie in order to enslave humanity, and the greatest example of this is in the realm of religion, where any departure from Scriptural worship will suffice, and where the examples are many.

Islam openly seeks to subjugate the entire world under the severity of Sharia Law, while the caste system of Hinduism is notorious for its virtual enslavement of the major portion of its population. The karma of Buddhism has largely robbed its adherents of the thought or desire of betterment, and the pseudo-Christian cults (such as the Latter Day Saints and the Jehovah's Witnesses) enslave their practitioners to a soul-numbing list of regulatory do's and don'ts in order to inherit salvation.

To these dark facets of the Lie we must also add the idea of secular humanism in its many shades, for although it purports to be religion-free, it actually qualifies as a religious belief system. While this may sound like a strange thing to say, secular humanism actually answers all of the great questions that religions answer: *How did the universe originate? Where did we come from? Why are we here? What happens when we die?* Simply because it answers these questions without God (in any form) in the answers does not take away from the fact that it answers all of the questions. And answering these questions soundly qualifies it as a system of religious thought. The dark brilliance of this false religious thought lies in the fact that because it originates with the premise that *God is not,* belief in secular humanism is actually an indirect manner of rendering worship to the ungod by those who purport to worship nothing.

As proof of who its ultimate Master is, one has but to look at the short and bloody history of communism (which is the governmental system secular humanism has inspired), for it is something that has resulted in the near-total suppression of freedom in the lives of countless millions of people, despite its brief existence. It is not the only form of government that enslaves, of course, but it is an excellent example of how the amazingly deceptive Lie will always lead to slavery.

DEBTOR'S PRISON

No Biblical discussion of slavery would be complete without discussing the idea of financial indebtedness, especially because it has reached such epidemic proportions among us. In Romans 13:8, Paul charges us to *let no debt remain outstanding, except the continuing debt to love one another*, a charge certainly inclusive of monetary debt. Since Scripture therefore teaches that it is best to have no debt, the ungod finds debt a fantastic idea and encourages as high a degree of indebtedness as possible on people, thereby enslaving them to the lender. Apart from instances of difficulty and tragedy, this is most often done due to the impatience of the sinful nature (which wants everything *now*), or to its laziness. In all cases, however, freedom is lost.

When we owe, we are *owned*. As beings created in God's image, we are meant to be free, and we are not free when we are owned by anything other than God's sense of holiness. When we have need or want of something, the Bible (and good sense) teaches that we should save beforehand and then buy it outright, whereas the ungod encourages us instead to purchase it with *someone else's money*. He does this because he is slavery's biggest fan.

I CAN'T STOP

Finally, having dealt with the issues that tend to cause widespread slavery among humanity, we must touch on those things of individual choice that enslave us as well. The Scriptures state that we are slaves to whatever has mastered us (2 Peter 2:19), which is why the freedom-loving Paul would write that despite everything being permissible for him, he would be mastered by nothing (1 Corinthians 6:12). Here we face the idea of that thing that we simply *must do* (or what is called an *addiction*), and it can range from being something seemingly innocuous (such as the need for constant texting on one's cell phone) to something obviously dangerous and wicked (such as drug abuse). But in all cases, our ability to choose has effectively been lost, which means that we are slaves to the thing.

THE BELIEVER'S OFFENSIVE

The Biblical idea of freedom that burns in the human breast is made full in Christ (Galatians 5:1). As those already made free by Him, then, Believers should always seek to be mastered by nothing but holy behavior, for it is our birthright and new native language.

As reborn Image Bearers of the Living God, we also have a duty to see human affairs move toward the ideals of High Humanity (Matthew 5:13,14), and must therefore seek the destruction of every enslaving heresy of Hell. As Heaven's ambassadors of true freedom, we should be those who most strenuously and openly oppose the idea of absolute slavery wherever it is found upon Earth, for it is in many ways the most hideous expression of the Dark Image possible, and we are the sworn and mortal enemies of that Image.

We must lift freedom's fair banner high and proud, that the eyes of the enslaved and hopeless might gaze upon their salvation, and receive hope, and be set free in Christ, for He is the only answer to slavery of every form (including the eternal slavery of the human soul).

BATTLEFIELD: RESPONSIBILITY

Am I my brother's keeper?
Genesis 4:9b

With our discussion of freedom now in the rearview mirror, we move on to discussion of its fair cousin *responsibility*, for they are the two sides of the same coin within the Divine Image. Although our words will be few due to the simplicity of the concept, it is nonetheless a concept of tremendous importance, for it lends itself greatly to the idea of social cohesion.

The Original Image

Strength of character is one of the most admirable traits in humanity, and comes to us by way of the idea of responsibility, for God is a responsible Being. As a responsible Being, God owns up to the consequences of His choices and actions, which together represent the exercise of His freedom. This may seem a strange thing to say about God, but Scripture brings three excellent examples readily to mind. The first is that the universe was put into bondage to decay (Romans 8:21) through no fault of His own, yet because He was responsible for its creation as an act of His freedom, God has taken responsibility to see that it is eventually renewed (Revelation 21:1-4). The second is that national Israel has forsaken Him many times over (Judges 10:13; Jeremiah 5:19) through no fault of His own, yet because He was responsible for calling them and making of them a nation as an act of His freedom, God has taken the responsibility to see that they will always remain a nation (Jeremiah 31:35,6). The third is that humanity was lost to sin through no fault of His own (Genesis 3:1-7), yet because He was responsible for our existence by an act of His freedom, God has taken the responsibility to provide (at tremendous cost to Himself) the Plan of Redemption.

THE IMAGE UNDONE

Such strength of character is foreign to the ungod, for he is necessarily the absence of it. And if strength of character is contained within the idea of responsibility, then the absence of strength of character will effectively be the idea of *irresponsibility*. Sadly, the Fall brought ample evidence that humanity had been deeply corrupted by this facet of the Dark Image.

HE SAID, SHE SAID

This weakness of character did not take long to rear its ugly head, for when the newly-fallen First Couple were confronted by their Creator as to their deed, neither was willing to accept responsibility for their actions (Genesis 3:11-13). Consequently, Adam blamed Eve, and Eve blamed the Serpent. Since God had created both humanity and the Serpent, Adam and Eve were essentially blaming God for what they had done. Such a reaction gives us great insight into the workings of the sinful nature, and should serve as a warning for all people through all ages.

Adam and Eve had just authored their own deaths (Genesis 2:17), had just doomed Creation to decay (Genesis 3:17,18), and had just doomed human posterity to enslavement to sin and death (Romans 5:12). But in their first *post mortem* conversation with God they blamed *Him* for what they had done. Such a Hellish and irresponsible attitude raises deep issues for humanity, and the first of these is that it puts a person at odds with God (for He deals with reality and not illusion), and since fellowship is not possible when there is no agreement (Amos 3:3), it destroys any chance of cohesion between God and humanity. The appropriate response to our choice to engage in sinful behavior is the response of David, who recognized that he had sinned, and that the sin was ultimately against God Himself (Psalm 51:4).

Part of taking responsibility for one's actions is acknowledging that one must face the consequences of those actions – something that is a great natural deterrent for bad behavior (which is why we have the Law and its associated penalties). Sin has dire and tragic consequences not just for the one committing the act (Genesis 2:17), but also for those around us (Joshua 7), our posterity (2 Samuel 12:10) and the world itself (Genesis 3:17,18). This means that either not believing or not knowing that one will have to face the consequences of one's irresponsible behavior (behavior guided by Evil) will only encourage such behavior. And such behavior will naturally cause a tremendous increase of suffering and tragedy upon Earth, for the sinful nature will be free to sink as often and as quickly as possible to its baser instincts.

We have already discussed the issue of tragedy and natural cataclysm associated with the decay to which this fallen world is subject, but it is worth reminding ourselves that such tragedy and cataclysm is the result of unholy *human* action, and that all tragedy therefore has a direct correlation to the irresponsible use of human freedom. When an attitude of irresponsibility prevails, tragedy and suffering upon Earth are therefore greatly multiplied, which suits Hell just fine.

VICTIMOLOGY

The whining of Cain provides us with the next sterling example of the majesty of the sinful nature and its irresponsible conduct. Cain was the first child born upon Earth, and he eventually murdered his younger brother for the crime of having had the audacity to serve God appropriately (Genesis 4:2-8). When confronted by God for his actions, Cain proved himself a true son of his parents, for he refused to take responsibility for what he had done (Genesis 4:9).

But even worse than his parents (who to their credit never complained of that which resulted from their actions), Cain complained about the just consequences that were imposed by God upon him. In this he not only blamed God, but claimed that the consequences of his actions made him the true victim of what had transpired (Genesis 4:13,14), *even before his brother's blood had dried from the ground!* It is worth noting that by their acceptance of the consequences of what they had done, Adam and Eve proved humble enough for repentance. Abel had apparently learned this lesson, but not his older brother.

Here we see that absolute weakness of character so intrinsic to the Dark Image, for Cain appears to us as no more than a spoiled brat of a child who sees all things through the lens of unfettered selfishness, and who whimpers and cries when things don't go his way. And true to the sinful nature's natural arrogance, he saw all things contrary to his whims through the prism of selfish victimhood: *He* was the victim of Abel because Abel offered an acceptable sacrifice to God. *He* was the victim of God because God did not view his sacrifice with favor. It was this perceived victimhood that gave Cain license to slay his own brother, and then gave him license to believe that he was himself the true victim of the slaying.

It is fitting that such whining and weakness of character should surround the scene of the first murder, for it shows us that self-absorbed victimhood is the natural enemy of social cohesion, pitting each person against his neighbor. It is a most dangerous idea that (if left unchecked) will lead to absolute social breakdown and thereby the absolute ascendency of the Dark Image.

The Divine answer to this facet of Darkness is the idea of restitution (Exodus 22:3-12), which God personally modeled for us in the examples mentioned earlier. For humanity, restitution is therefore not just the act of admitting guilt, but also of correcting the wrong. Jesus taught that to serve Him one must be willing to make restitution to all (Matthew 5:23,24), and true restitution demands the desire to be forgiven, which in turn is a sign of true repentance (a return to holy conduct). But to a yet greater idea are His followers called, for they are commanded to forgive others (Matthew 5:12), which necessitates putting aside the ugliness of selfish victimhood (Matthew 6:38-41). Such inner strength of character reflects the Divine most wonderfully, and leads naturally to the ascendency of High Humanity upon Earth.

THE BELIEVER'S OFFENSIVE

As followers of Christ we must be those who travel upon the high road of strong and enduring and responsible character, for this most wonderfully mirrors the tremendous depth of our Savior. The idea of responsibility dictates that we use our freedom in holy conduct, and so we should be people of such conduct (both because it is right and because it is our native language in Christ). But when we fail the idea of holy conduct – and we shall do so (1 John 1:8) – we are to admit our wrongdoing, willingly face the consequences and be those who make restitution.

Above this, though, there is a still higher road that we (like God) must travel, and it is the road that refuses acknowledgement of victimhood and forgives all wrongs against it. Such conduct will lead humanity upward in thought and action, for it is the Cross made plain among men.

BATTLEFIELD: PURPOSE

The LORD God took the man and put him
in the Garden of Eden to work it and take care of it
Genesis 2:15

The battle for human society continues now through a look at how humanity views its reason for existence, and so the question of the *why* of human life must be explored. This leads us to the idea of *purpose*.

The Original Image

As we have already seen, everything created by God has structure. Such structure signifies order, which signifies design, which in turn signifies purpose. This teaches us that God has designed all things with a purpose (a reason for existing). For instance, the angels have a purpose (Hebrews 1:14), the sun has a purpose (Genesis 1:16-18), Israel has a purpose (Deuteronomy 4:6) and the Church has a purpose (1 Peter 2:9). Humanity must likewise have its purpose, but since humanity is the crown jewel of Creation, its purpose must be the highest purpose there is.

This highest degree of purpose is found in Genesis 1:26, where the first mention of humanity is done in conjunction with the first mention of the image of God. This makes humanity inseparable from the idea of the image of God, which in turn makes humanity's great and noble purpose that of reflecting the likeness of God upon Earth. As this great idea is the subject of the entirety of this book, we will not delve further into the idea in this Battlefield, but shall rather look at the subordinate purposes for humanity that spring from that blessed Image. And we have but to peer into the Garden of Eden in order to do so.

From this view into the Garden we see that humanity was meant to walk with (or personally know) God (Genesis 3:8). We also see that humanity was meant for stewardship of the Garden (Genesis 2:15) and of all of Earth (Genesis 1:26-29). Finally, we see that humanity was meant to fill the planet (Genesis 1:28) and was meant to delight in existence, for the term *Eden* is equivalent to the terms of *pleasure* and *delight*.

THE IMAGE UNDONE

Since humanity has such fantastic and high purpose, the ungod must bring about the absence of purpose in us in order for the Dark Image to reign supreme in humanity. This absence of purpose is *aimlessness*, and because humanity's purpose is a thing of Divine origin, the perfection of the idea of aimlessness would be for humanity to be led to believe that there is no Supreme Being in whose image they were fashioned. If there is no God, then there could be no purpose stemming from His nature.

IT WAS ALL AN ACCIDENT

Since God eternally is, the idea that *God is not* is the ultimate form of the Lie, and belief in the ultimate form of the Lie will therefore have for humanity the ultimate form of consequence, which is the fullness of the Dark Image upon humanity, upon its society and upon Earth. If humanity was not the object of a special act of creation by a Supreme Being, the only other possible explanation is that humanity came into existence through the idea of chance operating randomly over time. This puts the idea of chance directly in the shoes of the Supreme Being – effectively *making it* the Supreme Being. When this is done, impotent chance is transformed into Chance the Almighty, who was able to bring into existence all of life by random interaction with a dead rock hurtling through space.

This idea of divine Chance effectively means that humanity may do as it pleases, for there is no accountability to the idea of a holy God. And since God does not exist in this invented scenario, there is likewise no set standard for right or wrong conduct. This allows the strong to dictate what is right and wrong to the weak – a standard which is as cruel as it is ever-changing. The result of worshipping Chance (for that is effectively what atheism and Evolution do) is therefore a people or society in which there is ultimately no order and there is no accountability for conduct. In short, atheism gives free reign to the sinful nature, which always results in the stench of Low Humanity.

Getting to Know You

Since purpose dictates that we know God, aimlessness dictates that we should not know Him. The perfect example of this we have just seen, but because humanity has eternity set in its heart (Ecclesiastes 3:11) and is therefore a natural worshipper, the ungod does not have tremendous success with the model of atheism. He therefore employs the tactics of Distraction and the Lie to further his image of aimlessness.

Regarding the Distraction, the concept of knowing God implies a personal relationship with Him, and a personal relationship takes time and effort to be a thing of success and quality. In the case of the non-Believer, it becomes a fairly easy thing to distract him or her away from contemplation of God, for we have already seen how the sinful nature is consumed with thoughts of self, the mundane and the mediocre.

For those who have been redeemed and restored to fellowship with God (Romans 8:15), however, the ungod primarily employs the Distraction in order to lure Believers away from quality with God. This lack of quality is our old friend *mediocrity*, whose dark influence is why so many Christians today have so little of the Divine Image reflecting from them – they barely know the God who has paid such a high and personal price to redeem them.

The sad issue here is that it is God's deep desire to be with us, as signified by one of the names of Jesus being that of *Immanuel*, meaning *God with us* (Matthew 1:23). God did not create and walk away; He created and walked *with* (Genesis 3:8). It is we who walk away (Luke 15:11-13), not He.

Regarding the Lie, its many shades have already been discussed, and so here it is left for us but to remark that every degree or facet of the Lie held close to the human heart and mind promotes aimlessness, for it moves humanity away from understanding its purpose. When this occurs, so does the rotting of human society.

IDOL HANDS

The next facet of human purpose to be discussed is that of labor, for Adam was tasked with working the Garden and taking care of it (Genesis 2:15). He was therefore not designed to sit around eating coconut pies while the chimpanzees did all the work, but was designed (as was humanity by extension) for steady and beneficial labor. The Garden was undoubtedly a place of unsurpassed beauty, artwork and landscaping, but it was (above all) a place filled with living plants, and living plants tend to outgrow the boundaries set for them.

Adam was therefore tasked with the purpose of maintaining the beauty of the Garden and its flora, probably with the idea in mind that he would add to its beauty as his skill and artistry grew, for (like his Heavenly Father) he would learn to make *everything beautiful in its time* (Ecclesiastes 3:11). This verse from Ecclesiastes helps us understand that after God has imparted effort into something, that something is always better for it – whether we speak of the ordering of the elements of Creation (Genesis 1), of the status of the Israelites after their deliverance (Exodus 15) or of humanity's plight after the Cross and the empty Grave.

Such a facet of Divine purpose could not go unchallenged by the Enemy, and into this arena he must introduce his counter-image of aimlessness, which brings to us the sluggard, the mediocre worker and the one who destroys. The sluggard is someone who is the embodiment of laziness (Proverbs 19:24; 22:13), and who will never lift a finger more than needed to survive (if that). He is selfish and unindustrious and is accustomed to living off of the welfare of others, and finds a ready-made home in today's Hell-inspired system of income redistribution, for he is also akin to the leech (Proverbs 30:15), who never gets enough of what other people have. Society groans with the likes of him.

The Dark Image also brings to us the mediocre worker, who has none of the greatness or drive necessary to this facet of purpose, for he is as unremarkable as he is unskilled, and leaves nothing better than he finds it. Worse still is he who spends his efforts upon things that destroy, for he is the one who makes *everything repulsive in its time*. This is best demonstrated by the rise of the urban gang members, who like dogs urinating on trees and hydrants mark their territory by defacing all they see, leaving a trail of rape, destruction, mayhem and murder in their wake. That these bear the Dark Image needs no explanation.

GENDER SPECIFIC

We must now resolve the issue of whether or not the woman is meant to work in the same manner as is the man. To Adam was given the task of working the Garden and taking care of it (Genesis 2:15), for Eve was not yet created when this purpose was given. While I have no doubt that in the absence of children Eve shared this duty with her husband, it is instructive to note the nature of the effects of the Fall on their expected duties as a man and a woman. Adam was told that working the ground would now be painful for him (Genesis 3:17-19), while Eve was told that childbearing would now be painful for her (Genesis 3:16).

Since the Garden may legitimately be thought of as the First Couple's home, the significance underpinning these Divine statements is that Adam was tasked with the idea of maintaining the idea of the home itself, while Eve was tasked with the idea of maintaining the idea of the family within it. This idea is wonderfully displayed in the Biblical example of the wife of noble character (Proverbs 31:10-31), who while certainly as diligent, intelligent, capable, industrious and wise as any man, was always about the business of her family. Her husband, however, was about the business of the workplace, through which he supplied the financial foundation for the existence of his home and family.

Though it may rub many the wrong way, Heaven's design (and therefore purpose) here is as clear in Scripture as can be made: the mother's focus was to be on the family and the nurturing of her children, and (given the Divine command to fill the earth in Genesis 1:28) this was meant to be a full-time endeavor. A people tamper with this model at their own peril, for such tampering pollutes the idea of family, and polluted family begets polluted society.

THE NEW MATH

The previous point brings us to the facet of purpose that dictates that humanity fill the planet with their presence, for Adam and Eve were told to literally multiply (increase rapidly in number) and fill Earth with humanity (Genesis 1:28). This command was later repeated to Noah's family after the Flood (Genesis 9:7), and has never been rescinded. To fulfill such a purpose, each marriage should therefore try to produce a minimum of three children, with the ideal being that of producing many more (as we see from Genesis 5). The ungod's answer of aimlessness for this Divine purpose is his less-dark facet of breaking even or that of the mathematical idea of *subtraction*, where each marriage produces two or less children (and preferably zero). His darker facet would then be that of mathematical *division*, where the human population is rapidly decreased by tragedy, war and disaster.

While we are on the subject of the need for humanity to fill the earth, it may have been noticed that I have failed to mention the *subdue the earth* portion of the command and purpose of God for humanity (Genesis 1:28). This is because it encompasses the idea of earthly stewardship, and so deeply misunderstood an issue is this today that it requires we deal with it through its own Battlefield, which shall immediately follow this one.

DELIGHTED, I'M SURE

Our last look from within the Garden at human purpose is simply that – to look around. When we do so, we will notice that there is present in that Garden everything necessary for the full pleasure of the human senses, of the human body, of the human mind and of the human heart and soul. Put simply, one of the purposes for which God created humanity was to enjoy life and to enjoy it fully (John 10:10). Our

Creator is not a cosmic sourpuss, and there was nothing about Creation and life that was not wonderful and enjoyable and pleasing for humanity. *Eden* was not just a garden; it was a fact of existence.

We may therefore readily understand that our ancient Enemy has a particular distaste for the very idea of the enjoyment of life, and so must see to its absence in humanity if the Dark Image is to fully prevail upon Earth. In this light I believe it may properly be said that God's purpose for humanity is to take great delight in life, whereas the Enemy would have us wallow in its absence. This brings us to the idea of *misery*, and the ungod's most potent and complete example of it is the condition of absolute slavery.

The facets of misery that are less complete than absolute slavery (but which lead ultimately to the debasement of Low Humanity) are shades of ideas discussed thoroughly enough in the Battlefields for the individual, and so must only be lightly touched upon here to be understood in Evil's battle against purpose. The first of these shades is the idea of the need to be God-ward in all things, for when delight is expressed God-ward (which includes experiencing delightful things in a manner in keeping with His holy nature), it is appropriate and fulfills the idea of human purpose. But when any delight is expressed or experienced away from God-ward, it is a turning Hell-ward and leaves empty the idea of human purpose, and the aimlessness of misery fills the void thus created.

Another shade of aimlessness is the idea of the worship of delight or pleasure (Romans 1:18-32), which we studied in the Battlefield for human sexuality. A people engrossed in such a state will not long know any degree of freedom or dignity, and the darkness of their thinking has already blinded them to their misery, for their supposed delight utterly lacks keeping with God's holy nature.

The final shade of the ungod's counter-image to Divine delight that we shall study is the detestable imposition of false and religious piety that disallows experiencing one or more forms of Edenic (and therefore Heavenly) pleasure for the sake of a perceived degree of righteousness. This may include such things as the imposition of lifelong celibacy upon members of clergy (such as in Catholicism or Buddhism), and since it requires abstinence from a delight designed by God for humanity, it represents an imposed misery. This is sheer genius by the Serpent, for he is able to use the idea of *worship* to turn us from enjoying our lives as our Creator meant us to do.

THE BELIEVER'S OFFENSIVE

The true Believer in Jesus Christ is one who has already succeeded in that great and wondrous purpose of knowing God, for if we know Christ then we know God (John 14:9). Yet as truly wonderful a thing as this is, we must understand that it was only the first step of a lifelong process, and we must therefore exert unceasing effort toward the purpose of knowing Him more and more fully each and every day.

As those who love the idea of Divine purpose, we should see to the spread of dignified humanity, dignified family and dignified human society upon Earth. Furthermore, our hands and our lives ought not be those of idleness, but rather those that honor God through noble and dignified efforts, bearing always in mind that our Savior improved everything He touched and every place He went.

Finally, let us remember that we serve Eden's God, who is the Father of all delight and life. Let us therefore be alive with delight, for misery is not our heritage. Yes, there are trials and tribulations, sufferings and hardships, toil and death and struggle, for it is a fallen world yet to be fully redeemed, and we are part of it. But *joy* is ours in all things (James 1:2), and the Dark One has no answer for it, for joy is beyond him, and bears most nobly that image Divine.

BATTLEFIELD: EARTH

The highest heavens belong to the LORD,
but the earth he has given to man
Psalm 115:16

We have yet to finish discussing the idea of human purpose, for much of humanity's purpose is bound physically to Earth. But so horribly mutilated is today's thinking concerning our fair planet that I find I must treat this grave issue independently, giving rise to the necessity of this Battlefield. It is a serious and difficult Battlefield, and will lead us where we may not want to venture, but we must follow Scripture where it leads, despite the offense it might give us.

THE ORIGINAL IMAGE

Our look into this Battlefield begins with discussion of two ideas: the singularity of the Garden of Eden, and the concept of stewardship. Regarding the Garden itself, we must note that it was unique upon Earth, for it was the only garden then in existence (Genesis 2:8). It was into this Garden that God placed Adam – and in which Eve was brought to life – making it their proper home. As with any garden, it was a cultivated, manicured, landscaped and designed place, and since it was a garden designed by God Himself, it was undoubtedly the most beautiful and wondrous place in the physical universe.

It is appropriate and necessary to pause and consider life as it was in that Garden, for it defines human existence as it was meant to be. The term *Eden* itself tells us what we need to know, for it means *delight*, and signifies for us that all things necessary for the delight of human existence were met in that place. The Garden therefore gave Adam and Eve beauty, order, shelter, comfort and sustenance. In essence, it gave them the highest standard of living possible.

The rest of Earth, however, was not a garden, but existed as a wild place in which there was no landscaping or artistic design. The charge given to Adam and Eve to fill the earth and subdue it (Genesis 1:28) is therefore best understood through the lens of landscaping and artistry, for the First Couple (or more probably their descendants) were to bring the artistry and cultivation of Eden to the rest of Earth. This would be in keeping with the heart of their Father, who makes *everything beautiful in its time* (Ecclesiastes 3:11). In effect, they were to *Edenize* the wilds of Earth, bringing to us the idea of *stewardship*.

A steward is someone who is given charge over the care of something while its true owner is away (Luke 12:42-46), but who is answerable to the owner for the care or negligence exerted over the object. It is also expected of a steward that he or she will return control of the object to the owner in a better state than it was received by the steward (Matthew 25:24-27), which means that a steward must *improve* the object under his care. Since God retains ultimate ownership of Earth (Psalm 24:1; 50:10,11), humanity's stewardship of it required that we improve the planet while it was under our care. This would have resulted in a slow and steady transformation of Earth from wild to cultivated by using Eden's marvelous and artful template, making earthly beauty a thing of ever-increasing proportion.

THE IMAGE UNDONE

As we consider humanity's relationship to Earth and Earth's relationship to humanity, we therefore see that all that is necessary to bring about the destruction of Earth is for the ungod to pollute humanity's understanding of the idea of our planetary stewardship. When this is accomplished, the idea of Eden will be lost, and both humanity and Earth will trend toward the Dark Image, resulting in the blighting of our planet and the ascendency of Low Humanity.

No Man Left Behind

Since it was the Divine command for humanity to *fill the earth* (Genesis 1:28), it rightfully follows that every bit of Earth was intended to be inhabited by humanity. And while it is true that the catastrophic upheavals of the Flood have essentially rendered portions of Earth uninhabitable, this Divine command has still never been rescinded, but was in fact repeated to Noah upon completion of the Flood (Genesis 9:1). All of Earth is therefore meant to know the habitation of humanity, the footsteps of humanity, the grooming of humanity and the cultivation of humanity. This is the primary purpose of Earth.

If it is the Divine plan (and therefore part of the Divine Image) for humanity to spread out fully upon the face of Earth, it is easy enough by now to understand that the ungod would naturally desire the absence of the spreading of humanity, and the response of the Dark Image to such a command is therefore that humanity gather together in perpetual assembly. In this way was born the idea of the *city*, in which large numbers of people occupy a relatively small portion of land, leaving vast areas of Earth uninhabited and untended. This trend began with Cain (Genesis 4:17) and continued with such tenacity even after the Flood that God had to confuse the language of humanity at Babel in order to force them to spread upon Earth (Genesis 11). Sadly, it is a natural and deep-seated desire within fallen humanity to remain assembled and leave our planet as a perpetual wilderness.

Man Vs. Wild

Apart from the issue of humanity's natural, sinful predilection to leave Earth largely uninhabited, we must now begin our exploration of the use of environmentalism in pursuit of the Dark Image. Environmentalism is simply the idea of exercising concern for the well-being of Earth, and in its simplest and most natural state should be the friend of any faithful steward of this planet. But (as with most ideas of noble origin) the ungod has hijacked this wonderful idea, and has unfortunately turned the principles of environmentalism into tools that destroy and enslave to Darkness.

Since land was meant for us, land that doesn't know our touch is aimless land; it is a sad and sorrowful thing, devoid of its purpose of granting us harbor, delight and sustenance. Such land (even when plentiful with life) is of great delight to the dark heart of the ungod, and so he is fully behind the modern environmental movement seeking to ensure that large swaths of Earth are deemed *too good* for human habitation. We have many fancy names for such places today, but the idea that humanity is deemed unworthy and a danger to such places comes from non-Biblical thinking, which is something that always originates in Hell (Genesis 3:1). And while we use words like *pristine* and *unspoiled* as license to stop the tread of humanity's footfall, by so doing we leave much of Earth to rot for lack of our touch and stewardship – something that suits the ungod just fine.

Contrary to modern thought, *wild* is not the ideal state of nature (Isaiah 5:6; 7:23-25). If we look closely at the wilds, we see a world of death and struggle where plant vies with plant for soil, space and sunlight, and where the victor strangles or muscles out the vanquished to such a degree that there is scarcely a place for the sole of a foot. Where there is no thinning, no clearing, no loving and intelligent design and stewardship of land there is only the pitiable and unending struggle that our hands and hearts were meant to stay. I am not saying that there is no beauty to be found in such places; what I am saying is that such beauty could be enhanced (and even greatly so) by appropriate human stewardship. The land needs our touch, and the Dark One would keep us from it. Despite modern thinking, wilderness is not ideal. Eden is.

An excellent template of how Earth is meant to be inhabited is given in the apportioning of the Promised Land to the Israelites from God (Numbers 26:1-27:11; Joshua 13-21). Here, the land was divided into twelve parts, which were allotted to twelve of the Tribes. In each tribal portion, land was given to each clan, and each clan allotted its land to its families. In this way, *every square inch* of Israel was designed to be under the care, grooming and ownership of a private Israelite citizen. There were no protected wetlands, no wildlife refuges and no national parks, which consequently meant that no areas were off-limits for habitation and cultivation.

But before the alarm bells begin ringing a bit too loudly over such an idea, we must discuss the appreciation of Nature's beauty. As a great lover of Nature, I readily admit that there are places upon Earth of such astounding beauty that the hearts of good people cry out for them to be preserved for beauty's sake. Beauty brings delight, and both beauty and delight are appropriate uses of Earth according to Eden's template; it is therefore not inappropriate to set aside a place for appreciation of its beauty. But this must be done carefully and judiciously, so as not to set aside the commands to fill and subdue Earth any more than is absolutely necessary. I have had the privilege of spending a great deal of time in Israel, and I can testify to its amazing and varied places of extraordinary beauty, but the Biblical reality is that God exempted none of these from human care, touch and habitation when He apportioned the Promised Land. This should be taken deeply to heart.

ME TARZAN, YOU JANE

Another facet of Hellish environmentalism is the notion that primitive living is best for the environment, and so we are led to embrace the implausible thought of the *noble savage living at one with Nature* as the ideal for humanity. We must at all costs resist the ridiculous notion that Adam and Eve in the Garden were nothing more than cavemen in a jungle or forest. Quite the contrary is true, for they were exalted beings who lived in the most magnificent place ever known to humanity, and were individuals of the highest thought and speech, deeply capable of fellowship with the Living God. As beings of such a tremedous order, they didn't swing from trees or wallow in the mud, but instead knew a dignified standard of living that could not be bettered.

Such a standard of living calls to us still today, but the comfort, ease, health, dignity and delight it represents may only be approached through the overcoming of the disastrous results of the Fall. In many ways the Fall of humanity therefore pit humanity and Nature against one another (Genesis 3:17-19), and these degrading physical results of the Fall may only be overcome on a large scale through applied science and technology, but they *can* be overcome to a great degree. However, this Edenic standard of living is anathema to the ungod's design for humanity, and he must not allow humanity to attain or sustain it. Instead, he must influence us into limiting ourselves to the low and degrading standard of living of a basic existence, where we know nothing of the higher and more enjoyable things for which we were designed.

GROSS POLLUTER

Toward this end the ungod works at convincing humanity that all pollution of the environment is wrong and must therefore be avoided. However, human offal is detrimental to the environment (Deuteronomy 23:13,14), yet God commanded humanity to fill the earth despite this reality (Genesis 9:1). This shows us that in the fallen state of affairs we must actually pollute Earth to a certain degree in order to fulfill the Biblical mandate. The issue then becomes the degree to which pollution is allowable under the standard of good stewardship.

When we consider that part of the call to earthly stewardship was that of Edenizing the expanse of Earth, we understand that this would have included the spreading of the dignified standard of living found within the Garden. This effectively means that in our fallen world we are allowed to pollute to the degree that doing so elevates our existence toward the Edenic standard. Simply stated, the object must be worth the price.

But before proceeding further, we must speak of the idea of the wanton and wholesale pollution of our planet, by which we leave it destroyed, permanently blighted or unlivable. Such a poor example of stewardship (to say nothing of the state of heart and mind which allow it) cannot be further from the Biblical ideal, and will surely bring those who do so into ultimate conflict with the true owner of this planet (Revelation 11:18). Such an attitude of destructive stewardship suits the ungod quite well, however, for his picture of a perfect Earth most likely resembles the surface of the moon.

GIVE A HOOT, DON'T POLLUTE

Although sometimes used inappropriately, advances in technology have always tended to raise human existence from a base and savage level toward that Edenic ideal for which we were originally created, as evidenced by our own amazing standard of living today. But because he chafes at such human dignity and delight in life, the ungod must war against the applied sciences that bring them to us, and nowhere is this more evident than in the environmental war being waged against large-scale electricity production and the internal combustion engine.

Let us first quickly consider the idea of electricity, which brings to us the amazing comforts and delight of modern life. According to the irrational environmentalists, nuclear energy is simply evil; coal and oil power plants pollute too much; natural gas plants cause (fictional) climate change; wind turbines make too much noise and kill too many raptors; and solar plants endanger the desert tortoise. Such people would simply box us into a corner, for those impotent methods of power production that may survive their imperious environmental scrutiny will leave us with a Stone Age level of power production, which is precisely the point desired by Hell's master (and is why I like to refer to the Environmental Protection Agency as the Early Paleolithic Agency).

As embodied in the availability and use of the internal combustion engine, the idea of modern personal transportation is the greatest expression of personal freedom upon planet Earth, and wonderfully elevates human existence. But because human freedom so nobly expresses an aspect of the Divine Image, the internal combustion engine is likewise under withering attack by that Image's enemy. The ungod's environmental disciples are therefore busy proselyting the fossil fuel engine out of existence (using their misguided belief in the phantom of man-caused climate change as ammunition), and this is being done with no viable, large-scale alternative to such transportation available. That if they are successful we will be left once again to a horse-and-buggy existence makes no difference to these true believers, for they simply loathe the idea of modern existence, and seek to destroy it any way they can *for the sake of the planet.*

SCARFACE

The preceding discussion leads us naturally into thoughts of how much physical damage we may do to our planet, for human existence and progress demand that we in some ways alter or scar Earth. Here again we meet our good friends *pristine* and *unspoiled*, for they are used by the ungod and his disciples to keep us mired in primitive living by staunching humanity's spread and progress. And so the idea of physical damage to Earth must be explored.

I cannot imagine that the splendors of ancient and modern landscaping – with their works of stone and metal, their fountains and works of water, and their architecture and terracing – either had or have anything to match that Divine Garden near Eden, in which every type of metal, gem, mineral and stone was in all likelihood artistically used by Heaven to the delight of the human eye and mind. Not only should we put out of our thought that Eden was merely a wild jungle or forest, but we should do the same with the idea that it was made up merely of plant life. Our own gardens are so much more; how then shall we limit that supreme and great Artist to less?

Furthermore, we must seriously consider the idea that Eden was also the proper home of the First Couple, and it only seems appropriate to think of their being housed as befitting the royalty they were. If Solomon in all his splendor was not adorned as beautifully as the lily of the field (Matthew 6:28,29), was his great palace of stone and timber (1 Kings 7:1-12) more splendid than that of the First Couple?

The point toward which I'm driving is that humanity is not (nor was it meant to be) merely caretakers of plant life. With the exception of the Tree of Knowledge of Good and Evil, every resource in or upon Earth was given to humanity in the command to subdue (Edenize) the planet to its farthest reaches. And since that Tree was destroyed in the Flood long ago, we are now free to make use of every single planetary resource, bar none. There is therefore nothing intrinsically wrong with our use of the planet's stores of oil, or of its stores of uranium, or of its stores of wood or any other resource. God has given all of Earth to humanity

(Psalm 115:16), and we may use it as seems best to us in the effort to Edenize our planet and existence.

The idea of delight must also be briefly looked at here, for a proper understanding of it is essential to our discussion. It is more *delightful* to be comfortably and safely housed than not. It is more *delightful* to be well fed than not. It is more *delightful* to be free than not. It is more *delightful* to be healthy than not. Yet the pursuit of such delights (and others) can only be done at the expense of a *pristine* Earth, for Earth must be changed, remade and even scarred to accomplish this. If we are unable to physically change or scar our planet, most of the delight known in Eden is forever out of reach to us, leaving us to the cruel claws of misery (which is in keeping with Hell's design for humanity).

The question then becomes whether or not such a changing, remaking and scarring is Biblically permissible, and Scripture shows that it is. Again we need only look to how God structured certain elements of the ancient Israelite nation to see the truth of this. The Israelites were to maintain permanent homes for themselves, which at a minimum required the felling of trees and the moving of stones (Leviticus 14:45). They were to maintain a militia (Numbers 26:2), requiring weaponry, which in turn required mining and metallurgy. They were to build and maintain roads to the Cities of Refuge (Deuteronomy 19:3), which necessitated scarring the land. Finally, God's own Temple required lumber from Lebanon and vast quantities of rock to be quarried in the vicinity of Jerusalem (1 Kings 5-7), and the plans for that Temple came directly from the Holy Spirit (1 Chronicles 28:11-19).

All of these activities required moving natural resources from one place to another, often leaving the place from which the resource was taken somewhat scarred (either temporarily or permanently), but this is the unfortunate reality of life on this fallen planet. To pursue an Edenic standard of living, we must change, remake and scar our planet, for we must find, mine and use Earth's resources toward these noble aims.

There are two critical points being made here: The first is that the resources of Earth belong to us, and are meant to be used by us. The second is that we cannot use our resources without changing and sometimes scarring Earth. But we must bear in mind that the entire post-Flood Earth (despite some breathtaking beauty in parts) is actually horribly scarred from its original condition due to the cataclysmic upheaval of the Flood. As breathtaking as it is, for instance, the majestic Grand Canyon is simply one gigantic scar testifying to the massive and rapid recession of the waters of that event. Earth lost its pristine status long ago.

Yet to say that it is inevitable that we must mar our planet in order to pursue Heaven's noble purposes and plans for humanity is not to say that we should do so joyfully, wantonly or callously. It was decreed that by painful toil and the sweat of our brow would the blessings of Earth now come to us (Genesis 3:17-19). We should find it sobering (both individually and collectively) that we must in effect war with our planetary home in order to attain that which once was ours by virtue of Creation's birthright, and we should therefore humbly set our vast capacity for intellect and innovation in the direction of maintaining a beautiful planet as we pursue Eden's call.

BOTTOMS UP

Creation is a thing of tremendous order and (like the idea of family) has an established hierarchy. Atop this hierarchy is the Creator, beneath whom is humanity. Beneath humanity is the animal kingdom, and beneath the animal kingdom is the plant kingdom, resulting in a hierarchy that is essentially the Creation Week in reverse. This tells us that humanity supersedes Nature in importance and dignity, and so when Nature is allowed to supersede humanity in importance, this hierarchy is turned upon its head. When this occurs, it is both an affront to the Creator and a boost to the Dark Image and its Low Humanity, and is something under which human dignity suffers tremendously.

It is therefore natural for the ungod to influence thinking in this direction, for when it occurs, humanity becomes enslaved by cosmos, beast or plant. This has historically been accomplished through the idea of false worship (2 Kings 23:5; Romans 1:23), but in the supposed enlightened secularism of today is being accomplished through the guise of non-Biblical environmentalism (which has become little more than modern, secular worship of Nature). Regardless of what it is called, though, the result is the same, for humanity is denied dignity, space and progress for the sake of earth, water, beast or plant, and finds itself under the boot heel of Nature.

Simply put, humanity has a mandate to Edenize the planet. In the fallen state of both humanity and Nature, this mandate will at times bring the two into conflict (Genesis 3:17-19; 9:2). When this occurs, the only reasonable solution is to remember Heaven's ordained hierarchy and to decide according to that scale. When human life or existence come into conflict with an aspect of Nature, human life or existence must prevail. When legitimate human progress toward Eden's standard of living comes into conflict with an aspect of Nature, human progress must prevail.

Humanity – and not Nature – is always the appropriate trump card when legitimate conflict between the two arises. The Enemy, however, would have us bent and begging before each tree, insect or rodent for the right to pass, build or change.

ANIMAL RITES

This human enslavement to nature is in few places more evident than in the modern animal rights movement, which is populated by those unable to see or appreciate the difference between an Image Bearer and a lower form of life, and who then invent fictional rights for animals by which humanity becomes enslaved. Animals are wonderful and special, but they are not Image Bearers. Only humanity was made in the image of God (Genesis 1:26-28).

The first point to be made here is that such thinking represents a mindset in utter rejection of both Scripture and the obvious. Humanity is simply singular in existence and construction, and singular in its capacity for things like greatness, love, language and relationship (to name but a few). Humanity possesses a nature, glory and calling that is degrees higher than that of any animal, for God Himself became human and dwelt among us in the Person of Jesus of Nazareth (John 1:14). That

God could be expressed to us in human form therefore sanctifies the very idea of humanity far above that of any other form.

What this naturally means is that the life of any human being is worth more than the life of any animal, or of any number of animals (Genesis 9:5). When the upward calling of humanity to Eden's high water mark is therefore hindered by the animal kingdom, the decision must be made in favor of humanity. While Scripture does admonish us to treat animals kindly (Proverbs 12:10), animals are considered property in Holy Writ (Exodus 22), and have no more rights than does a farming implement. They could be sacrificed (Leviticus 1-7), they could be hunted (Deuteronomy 12:22), they could be slaughtered and eaten (12:21), they could be ridden (Zechariah 9:9), they could be trained (Psalm 32:9), they could be used for labor (Deuteronomy 25:4), they could be bought or sold (Exodus 22:1) and they could be captured and put on display (1 Kings 10:22).

The idea of *rights* (as we commonly think of them) properly exist only in the human sense, for these rights derive their existence from the image of God in humanity. For instance, God is alive and the Author of Life; as beings created in His image we are uniquely alive and therefore we alone *own* the right to life. God is also free and the Author of freedom; as those bearing His image we therefore *own* the right to freedom. This means that as Image Bearers we naturally own life and freedom, which make life and freedom our inherent property. The right to own property (whether real or ideal) is thus the sole right of humanity. When such an idea is ceded to the animal kingdom, the designed hierarchy of Creation is in danger of being undone.

Humanity is tasked with stewardship of Creation, and that stewardship includes the animal kingdom. This stewardship represents a relationship of trust between God and humanity, and this trust implies an *expectation of conduct*. An expectation of conduct, however, is much different than Biblical ideas of human government, which are a *limitation* of human conduct and therefore include a penalty if the limitation is surpassed. Earthly stewardship, on the other hand, is an expectation of human conduct toward Creation, and the Divine expectation regarding stewardship of the animal kingdom is humane treatment.

The mistreatment of animals is a horrible thing, but it is not in the eyes of God a criminal thing. To the King of all beasts will every earthly steward one day answer (Exodus 20:10), but we must not allow any beast anything even close to an equal footing with humanity. Image Bearers are – and must always remain – singular and unassailable as beings of the highest and noblest order. Animals naturally possess no rights to life, freedom or anything else, and must not be granted any by us.

Human subservience or enslavement to the animal kingdom turns the Divine hierarchy upon its head, and is thereby degrading to the very idea of humanity's glory and position. Such degradation demeans humanity, and a demeaned humanity is an ignoble, bestial humanity – something tailor-made for the Dark Image.

EXTINCT-SHUN

But because we are beings of the highest and noblest order does not in any way give us license to rid the world of the lesser kinds, for such an idea runs counter to the very idea of good stewardship and to the revealed heart (and will) of God.

Good stewardship requires that we leave our planet in better condition than we found it, and it is not a better place when it has lost a unique form of life designed and placed here by our Creator. Furthermore, there is no getting around the fact that when God destroyed the entire Earth through the Flood, He went out of His way to ensure that every kind of creature was allowed to survive the event and to flourish afterward (Genesis 6:19-21; 7:8,9). This makes it abundantly clear that we are meant to share our planetary home with the full spectrum of animal life, and that God cherishes their existence.

Although no creature has the inherent status of the human being, we must understand that all other creatures exist because the mind and heart of God created them – making them wondrous testimonies to His creativity and design. When such creatures are lost to Earth, our planet then becomes a diminished place, and the delight of Eden is dimmed yet further because of it. Humanity must therefore find a way to ensure that every species still left upon Earth remains here (even while we pursue the Edenization of nature and the quality of life represented by the Garden).

It is a horrible thing to forever lose a species, and we will do well to remember that our Enemy hates every single creature ever designed and given life by God. Hell will therefore always influence the affairs of Earth (and especially of humanity) toward the removal of every last reminder of God's amazing creativity.

CLIMATE CHAINS

The ungod is the great enemy and despiser of human freedom, and one of the most effective methods he uses to reduce human freedom today is through environmental regulation, and so some words on this issue are required. The Divine idea of private land ownership and stewardship began in Genesis 1:28, and long predated the establishment of even the barest framework of human government (which began after the Flood in Genesis 9:6). Land ownership was something never thereafter ceded by God as a prerogative of government when government was later instituted, meaning that both the ownership of land and its use (stewardship) was left in the hands of its owner. Simply stated, God has not authorized human government to regulate the environment.

Just as with stewardship of the animal kingdom, God has an expectation of good stewardship of land use, but there is no criminal punishment for poor stewardship of it listed in His Word. For instance, God commanded Israel to observe every seventh year as a year of rest for their land (Leviticus 25:4), but no punishment for non-observance was codified. Israel eventually ignored this expectation of God, and He therefore removed them from their land for seventy years so that the land could know its needed rest (2 Chronicles 36:21). This shows us clearly that humanity was not meant to answer to government for our use of the land. We answer instead to God and to the nobility of the Divine Image in us.

Sadly, though, we have today become near absolute slaves to an army of environmental legislative bodies. Citing great concern for the health of the environment, nearly every facet of modern existence is dominated by the far-reaching tentacles of such governmental agencies, essentially leaving no person free to do with their land as they please. This lack of freedom we now recognize as a form of slavery, and it both degrades and thwarts progress toward High Humanity, which is exactly as its Master would have it.

Nowhere is this presently more evident than in the ridiculous and illogical approach to the fictional idea of man-made global warming (which due to the gracious lack of cooperation by Nature has had to humorously be altered into the equally-fictional man-made climate change). So purportedly worried about the possible destruction of Earth are the proponents of this ideology that they are willing to sacrifice all of the advances of modern living to ensure that Earth's climate doesn't change at the hands of human industrial activity. Such a notion is so utterly absurd that it should hardly need refutation, but so muddled, timid and backward is modern thought that we must address the issue all the same.

Despite what these alarmists say (and ridiculously predict), humanity simply cannot in any way and to any measurable degree compete with the sheer volume of British Thermal Units pumped into our atmosphere by our sun. To think otherwise is akin to a colony of ants contemplating the damage they have done to a hillside by excavating enough earth to build their tiny colony, while a thousand feet away a fleet of bulldozers is really going to work. It's preposterously insane, and needs to be seen for what it is – the ungod's attempt to influence humanity into the misery of primitive living. We simply need to be reminded that our sun is not a Swiss watch, for its output waxes and wanes over time. When it waxes, we're warmer. When it wanes, we're colder.

Of course, the real issue here is not climate change; it is the ideology of enslaving humanity to a degraded standard of living. If people were truly concerned over man-made climate change, they would look to history for its two greatest episodes and learn something from them. The first and more serious example of such a climate change was the Flood. The second was the episode of Sodom and Gomorrah. In both cases the change of climate was induced by rampant sinful living, and not by technology. If climate change is truly a worry, I recommend holy living.

THE BELIEVER'S OFFENSIVE

We serve an amazing God, who is both the ultimate defender of Earth (Revelation 11:18) and One who has always exhibited great concern for the animals upon it (Genesis 6-8; Exodus 20:10; Jonah 4:11; Matthew 6:26). Care, concern and good stewardship of this planet and the life upon it should therefore be something natural and wonderful to those who are reborn of Heaven's seed, in turn giving rise to the enlightened and truly beneficial idea of Biblical environmentalism.

This Biblical environmentalism leads us to Edenize our fair planet, through which we will bring order, beauty and cultivation to the wilds, and through which we will be compelled to carefully use its vast resources in order to bring Eden's wonderful standard of living to Earth's most important inhabitants – humanity. We have in this regard the excellent example of Solomon, who was both the finest naturalist the world has ever known (1 Kings 4:33), and one who physically remade much of Israel through the pursuit of the ideals of High Humanity (1 Kings 5-10).

Finally, we must always bear in mind that God makes all things beautiful in their time (Ecclesiastes 3:11), and that His idea of stewardship therefore requires that we always leave something better than when we received it. Jesus left Earth a far better place than He found it. It should be the same with us.

BATTLEFIELD: VIOLENCE

---

*So he made a whip out of cords
and drove all from the Temple area
John 2:15a*

It may surprise many, but a discussion regarding the use of violence is neither out-of-place nor inappropriate when related to the image of God and to His nature. Accustomed as we are to the misguided notion that God is an inherently non-violent Being, a deeper look into the idea of violence is required in order to not only more fully understand Him and ourselves, but also to set a reasonable foundation for the violent aspect of human government, which shall be discussed in the coming and final section of the Image War.

THE ORIGINAL IMAGE

While most people won't argue with the notion that violence is not inherently good, many (if not most) will balk at the notion that violence is also not inherently evil. To dispel the notion that violence is inherently evil, we need only to look at a few Biblical examples of the use of it. The first such example is that when there was war in Heaven, Satan and his angels were cast out (Revelation 12:7-9), which was a violent act done by Heaven. The second is that God did *violence* to the Egyptian army by closing the Red Sea upon them (Exodus 14:26-28), while the third is that Jesus did *violence* to the money changers when He physically drove them from the Temple area (John 2:15).

If God (who is good) is therefore not only *capable* of violence, but has also *committed* it, we must logically conclude that violence is not an inherently evil thing. Conversely, since part of God's indictment against humanity prior to the Flood was that the planet was full of violence (Genesis 6:11), it also means that violence is also not an inherently

---

good thing. Instead, we are left to conclude that violence is a thing either appropriate or inappropriate, depending upon the context of its use. When violence is used to staunch or stop Evil, it is a thing that is good, and may be known as *appropriate violence*. When used to further Darkness, violence is a thing that is evil, and may be known as *inappropriate violence*.

THE IMAGE UNDONE

When God cast out the fallen angels of the Rebellion, it was in response to the violence stemming from the evil of the angelic revolt. When God destroyed the Egyptian army, it was done in response to the evil committed against the Hebrews. When Jesus drove the money changers from the Temple, it was in response to the evil of corruption of Temple worship.

In this way, God sets for us a necessary template in the use of violence. Regarding the *why* of it, appropriate violence is *responsive*, which means that it is committed in response to the commission of evil. This shows us that when the ungod uses violence to further the spread of Evil, violence may then be used in order to thwart or counter this spread.

Regarding the *how* of appropriate violence, the different levels of response to evil by God show us that the degree of violence used by God was commensurate with the evil done (both in measure and propriety). For instance, the money changers were not put to death, but were instead only driven out of the Temple by violence, while the Egyptian army was completely destroyed through violence. This teaches us that the lesser deeds of evil require lesser deeds of appropriate violence in response, and vice versa.

MIGHT MAKES RIGHT

The capacity for appropriate violence exists within the nature of God because He is a holy Being and therefore must within His nature contain the means by which to confront Evil. As beings created in the image of

God, humanity thus originally possessed this same capacity for violence. However, when humanity became stained by the Fall, we received the additional capacity for inappropriate violence. This capacity was made most horribly clear by Cain's brutal murder of his brother (Genesis 4:8), and is something of which we are reminded only too clearly to this very day. Since inappropriate violence is a facet of Evil, and it is the nature of Evil to spread until all that is Good is eliminated, it should come as no surprise that inappropriate human violence is a chief and preferred method by which Evil is spread upon Earth.

As Cain so ably demonstrated, those enthralled with Darkness, the Lie and Evil do not seem to hesitate to use inappropriate violence to further the agenda of Hell. But as his brother Abel demonstrated, those enthralled with Light, Truth and Good are loathe and slow to use appropriate violence to counter or forestall the purposes of Evil. We therefore see that Evil is naturally *proactive* in the use of inappropriate violence, which shows us Evil's natural place in this realm. However, God's sense of appropriate violence is by nature more a thing of judgment, which dictates that it must wait for the evil deed to occur or become inescapable before it is appropriate, making appropriate violence a *reactive* thing. In real terms, this dictates that Evil (and by extension those who are its servants) almost always lands the first blow of violence in any scenario.

In fighting terms, this natural imbalance of proactive and reactive violence favoring Darkness leaves those who are of the Light perpetually off-balance, flat-footed or just horribly unprepared for the onslaught, and history teaches us plainly enough that Evil always takes advantage of this imbalance when it has the opportunity to do so. Evil does not hold sway with kindness or through nobility of ideology – it does so with inappropriate violence.

PACIFIST OCEAN

Since the Dark One is naturally prone to the spread and hegemony of Evil through inappropriate violence, it stands to reason that he has a great and legitimate fear of appropriate violence, for it has the power to stop him and his scheming (as was demonstrated in the failure of the angelic Rebellion). He must therefore exert effort to ensure that the practitioners of appropriate violence are as few in number as possible. The ungod accomplishes this by seizing upon the decent person's natural revulsion for violence, and then pairing that revulsion with either naiveté or unbiblical theology (or a tidy combination of both), turning such people into pacifists (those who believe that violence is always wrong).

Let me make clear that I am no lover or great fan of violence; I simply understand the need for it. In heart I am with the pacifist, for I wish there were no need of violence (Isaiah 2:4), but I do not respect the thinking, for it is soft and overly wishful. People certainly have a right to believe what they may, but I must draw the line when they assert that God is a pacifist and that we should always turn the other cheek. I have already demonstrated from Scripture that God is not a pacifist. Furthermore, the same Jesus so often quoted regarding *turning the other cheek* is selectively ignored when He told His followers to carry weapons for their protection (Luke 22:36-38) or when He wages war upon His return (Revelation 19:11).

What is forgotten or missed by the selectively Bible-quoting pacifist is that when taken as a whole, the Bible paints for the world the truest and most realistic portrait of depraved, fallen humanity available. People of the Book, therefore, should above all others be people who understand the reality of human existence on this fallen planet. There are times to turn the other cheek, and there are times to crush Evil where it stands. Few things allow the spread of Evil more quickly than naïve pacifism.

PRACTICE MAKES PERFECT

Given that those who love and understand Good must reactively use appropriate violence in order to stem or reverse the tide of Evil, it is required that we endeavor to master the use of violence to make this possible. Since it is no secret that followers of Hellish ideologies train extensively in the realm of violence toward evil ends, it therefore stands to reason that those who love Good must train as (or more) extensively in the use of violence in order to thwart them. Only practice makes perfect.

For this reason our military and law enforcement personnel train extensively in the use of violence, as do many others who train with weapons or martial arts in order to defend themselves, their families and others from the practitioners of inappropriate violence. But it is an awful thing to commit violence upon another (even when needed or deserved), and it needs to be remembered well that even the practitioners of appropriate violence still possess the fallen nature, and it is natural for the fallen nature to become enamored with violence for its own sake.

For this reason the Scriptures caution us not to be enthralled with violence (Malachi 2:16). Yes, we must train (Psalm 144:1). Yes, we must fight and, yes, we must be willing to injure, kill or destroy in the fight against the evil of inappropriate violence. But we must always be the reluctant warriors, for God does not love violence, and the moment that we begin to love it we have begun the journey ending in inappropriate violence, where many once-stalwart battlers of Evil have found their paths have led. It is a dangerous and Hell-inspired thing that our society absolutely idolizes and glorifies violence outside of its appropriate context (especially in video games, television and movies). Too many – especially of our younger generation – are becoming numbed to the horrifying effects of violence and are therefore growing into unwitting disciples of inappropriate violence and its dark Master.

THE BELIEVER'S OFFENSIVE

God's people need to have God's balanced and unambiguous view of Evil and of how to respond to the inappropriate violence it spawns, for to leave inappropriate violence unchecked is to allow the world to be overrun by Darkness in the span of a generation. We should therefore comprise the vanguard of those who innovate, train and use appropriate violence in response to the relentless march of Darkness, or else strongly support those who do.

We must bear in mind, though, that we have yet to shed the fallen aspect of human nature, and so a great and searching vigilance is required lest we become enchanted with a thing so capable of leading us into the ungod's realm. For us, constant attention to the cleansing nature of the Word and the gentle but firm ministrations of the Holy Spirit are therefore our duty, for we must remember that we are called to combat Evil even while we love the human enemies who propagate it (Matthew 5:44). Appropriate violence is a grim thing, a just thing and a needed thing. But it is never to be a thing enjoyed.

BATTLEFIELD: CULTURE

Those who make them will be like them,
and so will all who trust in them
Psalm 135:18

The idea of culture goes to the heart of who a people are. It speaks of what they hold dear and what they despise, of what is important and what is unimportant, of what is right and what is wrong, and of what they pursue and what they ignore. Culture dictates how a people live, it dictates the structure of the family, and it dictates the structure of society and therefore of how they are governed. With such far-reaching implications, a synopsis of culture may seem impossible, but there is fortunately a uniting thread running through all of these facets of it, and to the study of that thread we now turn.

The Original Image

Culture has as its root *cult*, which signifies worship. Culture is therefore best expressed as the common worship of a people, and is by nature an expression and extension of the deity or deities worshipped in common by them. The nature of the deity or deities worshipped will dictate a people's sense of right and wrong, their sense of purpose and their sense of identity. In essence, a people become like – or mirror – what they worship (Psalm 135:18).

In Eden, the idea of culture would have naturally found its perfection, for it could only have entailed perfect and undiluted worship of Jehovah, which is the true calling of humanity. From the centrality of this worship by sinless human beings would have sprung a culture that likely would have mirrored Heaven itself in depth, in beauty and in wisdom, for each Image Bearer would have developed fully the Divine Reflection that defines humanity. From there each marriage, and then each family, and then all of humanity would have completely developed the Divine Image, resulting in Heaven-like conditions upon Earth.

This state of affairs (wherein the fealty of the hearts, minds, lives, gifts, talents, abilities and institutions of a people are given fully Heavenward) encompasses perfectly the idea of High Humanity, for it is the best and highest that may be achieved by us.

THE IMAGE UNDONE

In order to pollute culture into his own image, then, the ungod must simply pollute the idea of worship by making himself the center of it, dictating that the battle for culture is essentially a battle between Truth and Lie. Since God is Truth (John 14:6), any departure from a pure understanding of Jehovah will necessarily result in departure from pure worship, which in turn will lead humanity toward the Dark Image.

This departure from Truth began with human consideration of the Lie (Genesis 3:6) and ultimately resulted in the Fall, after which the degradation of human culture was so rapid and complete that Earth was destroyed by the Flood less than seventeen hundred years later (Genesis 5-7:6). During the millennia since that event the ungod has been trying to repeat such a Hellish accomplishment, but the Divine introductions of human government, of the Law and of the Church have stayed his hand. He nevertheless soldiers patiently on, for the fallen nature of humanity always comes to his aid as he attempts to sully its culture.

BLACKOUT

The ungod would ultimately prefer open and complete worship of himself in the place of the worship of God, for this would completely pollute human culture and cause Earth to resemble Hell in relatively short order. The sinful nature of humanity would willingly enough see to the accomplishment of this, but humanity is not defined merely by the sinful nature, for we still retain the Divine Image that pulls us ever upward in response to exposure to Truth.

In order, then, for the ungod to see his goal of the open and obvious worship of himself come to fruition, he needs to destroy the idea of Truth through acceptance of the Lie. At this he toils with tremendous patience, and is content to see such destruction happen in stages as he slowly but surely chips away at the resistance of the Divine Image in humanity. To the study of some of his tactics we now turn, that light may be shed upon this steady march toward Low Humanity.

PHASING OUT

Diluted worship of Jehovah is much more palatable to humanity than is the outright worship of Darkness, for it is far easier to fall for Lie mixed with Truth than for outright Lie. Here we come to the dangerous and Hellish ground of adding to (or taking from) the revealed nature of God. When this is done, the new god just formed will typically maintain some of the noble characteristics of Jehovah in order to lure followers away. However, without His complete nature intact, God is no longer God (but is only a god), for he is lacking and flawed. Those who worship such a god develop a culture that is equally lacking and flawed, and set themselves at odds with Truth, which will inevitably lead toward Low Humanity.

The Church of Jesus Christ of Latter-Day Saints (Mormons) and Islam are prime examples of such Hellish maneuvering, to name but two. Regarding the Mormons, they teach that God had once been a man and who now as God has many wives in Heaven through whom He populated the world, and so they developed a culture that prized polygyny (where a man may have more than one wife). In the case of Islam (which portrayed itself as the anointed successor to Judaism and Christianity), Jehovah was changed into the capricious and barbaric Allah of the Quran, after whom has been modeled the most regressive and oppressive major culture in world history.

Both Allah and the Mormon version of Jehovah have their noble and redeeming qualities, of course, but that is just the point – it is the honey that catches the fly. The Ammonite god Molech undoubtedly had his noble characteristics, but how long was it before he required the sacrifice of children by fire (2 Kings 23:10)? Hell cannot but eventually make itself known, for you will know a tree by its fruit (Matthew 12:33).

It is here that I would like to take the opportunity to say a few words of distinction between the Muslim and Islam itself. In my life and ministry I have had many necessary harsh words for Islam, as Islam has effectively been at war with the world virtually since its inception by Mohammed, and to this day wherever it borders something other than Islam there is inevitably a bloody border. Islam differs from Biblical faith in too many ways to detail here, but one grave difference is that the faith of Islam is commanded to be spread by the sword (as the last fourteen hundred years have shown). For Christianity and Judaism, religious bloodshed requires a gross misreading and ignoring of Scripture. For Islam, *abstaining* from religious bloodshed requires the same.

So bloodthirsty and abhorrent are the requirements of Islam in this regard that the world would by now have been put completely under the sword of Mohammed were it not for the decency of the average Muslim who (like all human beings) is an Image Bearer and for whom such requirements engender distaste and even outright horror. This fortunately leaves the bloodthirsty jihad to a small minority of Muslims, for the far greater percentage of adherents to Islam simply disregard the true nature at the heart of their faith, and we have their sense of human nobility to thank for it.

SUPER MAN

While on the subject of redefining God, we would be remiss if we didn't discuss the creation of human-like gods. Since God created humanity in His image, the ungod must certainly take a perverse delight in influencing the thinking of humanity toward creating gods in humanity's image – something for which the fallen human nature apparently has a liking (as we see from the ridiculous pantheons of India, Greece, Rome, Egypt, Scandinavia and others).

Such gods are nothing more than super-sized human beings, and are as flawed as the sinful nature of those who create and then worship them.

It tugs wonderfully at our fallen nature to think our gods are as limited and morally weak as we, and so the ability to create gods in human form is a favorite trump card of the Enemy. When we create such flawed deities, we deify flaws. When we worship these flawed deities, we develop flawed culture in which flawed behavior is the expected norm. Such a system always leads to hedonism and debauchery and the exaltation of every vice into a virtue (Romans 1:24-32), all of which to the ungod are most glorious traits.

THE FARCE BE WITH YOU

Another tack of the ungod is to influence human thinking away altogether from a personal, living deity and toward the idea of an impersonal force, much like what was depicted in the movies of the Star Wars franchise. As moviemaking and storytelling go, it's fantastic stuff. As Biblical Truth goes, though, it's horrible stuff. Yet such ideas find fertile soil in the minds of some of those who struggle with thoughts of the existence of Good and Evil upon Earth, especially regarding how the reality of Evil and its consequences relate to the idea of a Supreme Being.

The draw of such thought is that it creates a comfortable place for Evil to exist, for in this construct Evil is generally seen as a necessary balance of (and equal to) Good. If Evil is necessary, it therefore cannot be seen as inherently wrong, for it is simply a fact of existence (and a fact of existence doesn't need to be resisted). When such an idea is worshipped, a people develop a culture with a built-in fatalism toward Evil, resulting in such ideas as karma in Buddhism or reincarnation in Hinduism.

From Hell's perspective, the genius of such a system of worship is that it results in a culture that acts as an apologist for Evil, after which the trend toward Low Humanity will be as rapid as it will be complete.

NOBODY HOME

Further even than the idea of depersonalizing God is the idea of the non-existence of God. Since God exists simply because He exists, the

Enemy takes a dark delight in influencing human thought toward the idea that there is no God, from which springs the ideology of atheism.

Humanly speaking, atheism is largely the product of supposedly enlightened minds that have assumed that the need for there to be a God has been outgrown by advancements in education and philosophy. This is the natural endgame of darkened Darwinian thought, which supposes Evolution to be true while simultaneously demanding that Scripture and the idea of a Special Creation must be a lie, thereby leaving a large gap in morality once filled by worship of Jehovah. But try as they might, such arrogant thinkers cannot change the fact that all human beings are worshippers (Ecclesiastes 3:11). With a snap of their brilliant fingers they have made God disappear, but now must fill the void they have created. That void (where once dwelt loving and noble Jehovah) is now filled by ruthless, purposeless Chance, and at Chance's altar do they offer their service.

Worshippers become like the object worshipped (Psalm 135:18), and with Chance it is no different. From the worship of Chance springs the culture of Chance, and Chance is cruel, fierce and merciless. Under Chance there is no objective right or wrong, but only the strong and the weak – and Chance favors the strong. The Law of Chance is therefore the law of the jungle writ large, where what is right or appropriate is always what the strong say is right or appropriate, and where what is wrong or inappropriate is always what the strong say is wrong or inappropriate.

Such worship will generate a culture that is as harsh, cruel, fearsome and unpredictable as its god, governed only by the whims of the strong and the degrees to which they succumb to the sinful nature (whose very existence they deny). This is the worst of Hell unleashed upon us, as the scores of millions of murdered victims of communism's still-brief existence upon Earth will amply testify.

JUXTAPOSE

It should by now be evident that we have an Enemy who delights in redefining terms and ideas in order to further the dominance of the Dark Image. Toward this end he is always about the task of taking what

God calls good and renaming it evil, and taking what God calls evil and renaming it good (Isaiah 5:20). This is done not just because he must by nature be driven to undo everything of God, but also because the Divine Image in us compels us to do what is good. If we can therefore be convinced to believe that what the lying ungod says is good is actually good (although it is evil), then the Divine Reflection in us will unknowingly be bent to serve the Dark Image most remarkably.

Such juxtaposition of right and wrong and of Good and Evil is something that we would therefore expect to see in pagan or lost cultures. But the sad truth is that the same thing is happening even in our own culture, where things once recognized as a facet of Evil (such as homosexuality and fornication) are now touted as good, normal and expected behavior. For such thinking among a once-enlightened culture to occur, there must have occurred a tremendous shifting away from Biblical Truth over time. This shifting away from Biblical Truth is at the heart of how the ungod attacks those cultures that have dared to flourish Heavenward, and is something at which we shall now take a look.

High Tide

Although history is replete with cultures great and mighty, there have been but two great examples of true High Humanity upon Earth: that of ancient Israel and that of the culmination of Western Judeo-Christian culture. Both of these were built upon the foundation of Scripture, which had the effect of elevating their respective cultures to heights previously not known and without peer in the world of their times.

We shall first look toward ancient Israel, which was blessed with a cultural blueprint from the very hand of God (Genesis-Deuteronomy). After a slow and fitful start of nearly five hundred years, Israel achieved the heights of its glory and culture during the early and middle parts of the reign of Solomon, prior to his descent into folly (1 Kings 3-10; 1 Chronicles 22 - 2 Chronicles 9). During this time, the Israelites sincerely worshipped Jehovah and were obedient to His Word, thereby making them a good, moral and strong people. This led to tremendous freedom, which in turn led to tremendous prosperity. These were then followed by a remarkably high standard of living, by great architecture and by great beauty, with fantastic strides being made in the sciences. The small nation and its king became a wonder of the world, and people of all kingdoms streamed to Israel to bask in the radiance of its Light and to export its Truth.

Such a state of affairs did not last long, though, for the ungod does not sit idly by while the ideals of High Humanity threaten to suffocate his image or his influence upon Earth. And so in time Israel waned until its glory was but a faint memory (Ezra 4:19,20), fading nearly altogether from the collective consciousness of humanity – left alive for only those few who might with wonder read of her storied past in the largely-forgotten Scriptures. Humanity was then left to the drudgery of the succession of kingdom and empire, while the Dark Image slowly but surely smothered the sparks of Truth that would again try to lead the Divine Reflection upward toward Heaven's High Humanity.

But God wasn't finished with Earth, and in the due course of time the plan of Redemption was completed and the Church was born (Acts 2:1-4), bringing much needed salt and light to the world (Matthew 5:13-16). This salt and light would eventually reach critical mass when (roughly a millennium later) there were enough Christ-changed hearts and minds capable of widespread and open challenge to the Dark Image which then held sway, and who then began the long and difficult process of establishing society based upon the principles of Scripture. Though not without mistakes, from this process arose the Judeo-Christian culture of the West, and from the near-perfection of this culture centuries later came the arduous and unlikely establishment of the United States of America.

Though America's beginnings were humble and highly improbable, they would eventually result in the greatest explosion of High Humanity the world has ever known. Like ancient Israel long before her, America grew to be a free, moral and lightly-governed people at the heart of whose existence (individually and collectively) was an abiding love for Jehovah and His Word. This gave rise to a nation of such astounding national morality, character, freedom, innovation, technological achievement, prosperity and strength as had never before been seen in recorded human history.

She arose as the unlikely daughter of the then-darkening West, reviving it and then becoming its crown jewel: a template for any nation desiring to channel the upward call of the Divine Image, and a beacon of hope for all who yearned for freedom. She would eventually set millions free from bondage, beat back the tides of Evil time and again, keep numerous tyrants at bay and elevate the human condition to heights not seen since Eden. America has stayed the Enemy's hand again and again, and has literally set the cause of Darkness back thousands of years. For this she has made an implacable Enemy, and he will not rest until even the memory of her (like that of once-glorious Israel) is alive no more.

FEET FIRST

For the remainder of this Battlefield I will now shift our focus onto an observation of how the Enemy pursues the destruction of the High Humanity represented by Western culture. I could do the same by tracing the fall of Israel and Judah in Scripture, for the battle and the Enemy are the same, and High Humanity always has the same source. But I believe it to be more relevant for us to see the issue through our own times, that we might better understand the fight in which we're engaged. I don't do this because I'm an apologist for Western or American culture; I do this because I'm an apologist for Biblical culture, and the Judeo-Christian West (and America especially) is simply the finest largescale example of it available.

Our first glimpse at this Hellish challenge to Judeo-Christian culture illuminates a now quite common ploy of the ungod – the silly, relativistic notion of modern multiculturalism, which has as its basic tenet the absurd belief that all cultures are of equal value. But all cultures simply are not (nor cannot) be equal, and it doesn't require doctoral-level insight to see the truth of it, for when given the chance, people will vote with their feet for the superior culture. All that is therefore needed in order to ascertain cultural superiority or inferiority is to observe emigration patterns.

For instance, more people leave the Muslim world for the West than leave the West for the Muslim world. The West is therefore superior. More people flee communist countries for the West than flee the West for communist countries. The West is therefore superior. More people leave the countries comprising Africa and Asia for the West than leave the West for those continents. The West is therefore superior. Such a trend is seen even among the nations of the West when we look more closely at it, for more people seek to move to the United States from other Western nations than vice versa (most notable among them the millions of Central Americans who risk great hardship and death by migrating illegally to the United States). The United States therefore has the superior culture.

This superiority of American culture has everything to do with Who is at the heart of it, and is therefore due solely to the worship of Jehovah and to the degree of adherence on a large-scale basis to the principles of His Word. This means that in order to annul the superiority of American culture, the ungod must focus his attack upon the Who of American culture, and what better method of attack could there be than by the dilution of the worship of Jehovah through the acceptance of other deities upon her soil (Deuteronomy 7:3-6)? But Jehovah does not mix with other deities (Exodus 34:14), and so where Truth is concerned, multiculturalism is a ridiculous and Hellish idea. Since culture is defined by the idea of shared and common worship, its very nature dictates that it may not be shared between people who serve different deities – it simply does not and cannot work. In essence, multiculturalism proposes that all gods are equal and the same, and is therefore a preposterous notion whose sole purpose is to destroy true and high culture.

UNCOMMON GROUND

To cripple hated America, then, the ungod simply needs to divide her people culturally, which is something most naturally accomplished through the introduction within her boundaries of the large-scale worship of deities other than the Jehovah of Scripture. Since gods don't mix, this multiculturalism is by definition a unity-destroying concept, and a people without unity are not truly a people. For example, the Allah of the Quran is incompatible with the Jehovah of Scripture, and Islamic culture is therefore incompatible with Judeo-Christian culture (as history has made abundantly clear). If the widespread worship of Allah is encouraged or condoned in America (especially through immigration), the Judeo-Christian culture of America will be lost. It will not be *changed*, for these cultures are incompatible. It will be *lost*.

Yet Islam is not the only insurgency that the Enemy is using to divide and weaken the American culture, for from south of our border have streamed millions of illegal immigrants whose allegiances remain firmly rooted to their home cultures. It is understood that most illegal immigrants are decent and hard-working souls fleeing the effects of Low Humanity brought on by the cultures of their home nations. But their very flight from these cultures testifies to the differences at the core of what and in whom those cultures have believed when compared to America. Great care should be taken here, for only people who truly worship the same God (not just in name but in nature) may actually share a culture. This naturally leads us to the idea of appropriate immigration, where the Scriptures have wonderful advice for us, but this must wait until a later Battlefield for study.

To this list of insurgents must also be added the American socialist and communist. Socialists worship a god of theft and forced redistribution, which is not the Jehovah of the Judeo-Christian culture (Exodus 20:15). They are therefore cultural adversaries who openly dilute the Heavenward trend of High Humanity established upon these shores. The communist is worse, for he or she is an atheist and worships cruel Chance, who has no place at the table with Jehovah. They, too, are cultural adversaries and must be defeated or expelled (Nehemiah 13:23-27).

Such a list could be continued, of course, but my hope is that by now the ideas behind the attempt at the internal destruction of the Judeo-Christian culture of America and the Western world may be seen for what it is. High Humanity now teeters, and soon will fall if its practitioners do not protect and cleanse the worship of Jehovah that has made it possible.

SIN SPOTS

Although he has certainly tried, the ungod has so far been unable to topple America militarily. She is simply too strong, too large and too well protected by her oceans and by the blessings of Heaven to currently be conquered in such a fashion. But he is nothing if not patient; he saw ancient Israel's vaunted glory buried in the sands of time after he slowly snuffed out its Light, and he will preside over the same with America if she is not careful – and human nature dictates that over time she will let her guard down.

Since she as yet cannot be conquered from without, America must be conquered from within. We have thus far studied a number of ways that the ungod works at accomplishing this, and now we will look into one final method of attack, which is to stop America from believing in herself. To accomplish this, the ungod must tear away at the very fabric comprising the heart of the culture from which we derive our identity. If we learn to despise the deity who defines us, we will soon despise ourselves, after which we will not last long as a nation.

This is precisely what is being done through the Trojan Horse of the multiculturalism we have already been studying, for doubting one's culture is what makes the idea of multiculturalism palatable. It is necessary, however, to sharpen the focus upon this ideology a bit in order to understand the facet of multiculturalism that seeks to destroy the idea at the heart of America's original and historic worship – that of the Jehovah of Scripture.

To put it frankly, America's history (like that of any nation) has warts, and the issue of slavery is her worst example of this. Since slavery existed in America during the era of the Founders and Framers, and was not abolished by them – even being practiced by some of them – the Enemy influences multiculturalists to tear down every good thing such people accomplished, essentially throwing the baby out with the bath water.

If being wart-free were the requirement to declare a culture or a people acceptable for glorification, however, we wouldn't have a single culture or people to admire anywhere on Earth. All cultures have always been populated by fallen Image Bearers, and therefore all have their warts (including that of slavery). And what's true of individuals is certainly true of the cultures they construct: all have sinned (Romans 3:23). It is missed by the misguided multiculturalists that it is only since the rise to dominance of Western culture that the Darkness of slavery has been in retreat upon Earth like never before.

When we allow the Founders and Framers to be labeled as bigots and racists, we effectively do the same to the Jehovah that the early Americans worshipped, and thereby tarnish all that He and they have done through America. This essentially poisons the roots of her culture. If a people cultivate and harbor such distaste for the foundations of their own culture, they will not for long remain a people or retain their place among the nations – precisely what the ungod has in mind for America.

But as should be expected of multicultural thinking, it misses the glory of what was actually occurring. The tide of High Humanity was just then beginning to rise during America's founding, and though America would one day be the standard bearer and crown jewel of that tide's heights, in those days there was still much of Hell's Darkness left in the Low Humanity even then being slowly undone by Biblical thought. Such change from Low to High Humanity is a slow and painful thing, for Low Humanity is entrenched comfortably in the sinful nature of its practitioners, while High Humanity is opposed with all of the bitter power and effect that Hell can muster upon Earth.

Instead, the Founders and Framers (though fallen) should be viewed in light of their priceless contributions toward High Humanity, for they crafted a system of human government and personal responsibility that absolutely unleashed the blessings of High Humanity upon the American continent, and which would eventually spread to much of the world. If High Humanity had a Book of Acts, such individuals would most likely be considered Apostles. It is no wonder, then, that they have found such an entrenched Enemy in the ungod.

THE BELIEVER'S OFFENSIVE

The quality and beauty of life on Earth was always meant to approach and mirror the quality and beauty of Heaven. But for this to occur, the conditions of Heaven must be mirrored, and in Heaven God is the center of all things, making Heaven's culture the perfect culture. Toward such a call and a culture does the Divine Image in us naturally gravitate, spurred forward by the revelation of Scriptural Truth (something that should find a warm home in the hearts of those who love God).

This is the idea of High Humanity. It is all that we could be, is all that we should be, and is perfectly represented for us in Jesus Christ, who was God in human form (John 1:14) and about whom the volume of Scripture is written (Luke 24:44; John 5:39). Jesus was the bringer of life (John 10:10), freedom (John 8:36), love (John 13:34,35) and holiness (Hebrews 10:10), all of which are core attributes of Jehovah. The true worship of Jesus will therefore naturally bring about the highest form of culture that humanity can know.

Such a culture, however, has a sworn and mortal Enemy who seeks to enslave all of humanity in his culture of Evil, and he will not rest until it is done. This means that we are engaged in a cultural war that will know no end until God brings an end to Evil itself (Revelation 20). Through Scriptural thought and allegiance, many good and brave souls before us have managed to greatly push back Evil's despicable and oppressive Darkness in this war, establishing a remarkable degree of freedom and Light upon our shores.

We their heirs must pick up the standard of Biblical Judeo-Christian culture anew and advance the cause of Light once again, for much ground has already been lost to Hell's relentless onslaught. And let us not be timid, as we are not without Biblical warrant to forcibly establish High Humanity – especially where we are in the majority – for Jesus commanded us to *occupy until He comes* (Luke 19:13 KJV).

But let us always remember that the best and most natural course to victory is that of having people willingly worship God. To this end we must never give up praying for the lost and of seeking to see them to the salvation of Christ, for no one desires the blessings of High Humanity more than the redeemed daughters and sons of the Living God. But even as we do so, let us remember that as possessors of the Divine Image, all people have a responsibility to the ideals of High Humanity. It is a human obligation to properly reflect God's image, and so it should be demanded of and pursued by all.

THE IMAGE
WAR: HUMAN
GOVERNMENT

BATTLEFIELD: ANARCHY

In those days Israel had no king;
everyone did as he saw fit
Judges 21:25

Having discussed the ideas of violence and culture, we may now move on to the issue of human government, for it is closely connected to both of these issues. But before we proceed, we need to understand that today's notions of government have strayed dangerously far afield from their Scriptural boundaries, and so government has become quite a dangerous thing to humanity and the Divine Image we bear. It is therefore to the study of such Biblical principles of government that we dedicate this entire section of the Image War, and that study must begin with the concept of anarchy.

The Original Image

The idea of government is actually foreign to the nature of God, for He is an absolutely free Being. What this means (and what is so fundamental to our study of government) is that He has no external constraints – or *limitations* – upon His conduct. God is simply not governed, for He has only the *internal* constraints of consistency with His own nature.

As sinless beings created in the image of God, humanity was likewise never meant to be governed, for there was nothing in humanity in need of limiting. Although it has somewhat different connotations today, the state about which we are speaking (and in which the First Couple originally existed) is technically that of *anarchy*, in which people live without government or law. For the sinless this is the optimum condition of existence. For the sinful it is quite another story.

THE IMAGE UNDONE

The bliss of sinless anarchy, however, was not to last long, for the act of the Fall intervened. When it did, it brought with it the stain and stench of sin, which in turn dictated that the actions of humanity would no longer be driven by the idea of holiness, but by destructive and Hellish tendencies instead. And although anarchy was allowed most of two thousand years by Heaven to prove itself incompatible with the reality of the sinful nature, its sinless expression was now ended, resulting in harm wherever humanity found itself.

GIVE ME ANARCHY, OR GIVE ME DEATH

God would eventually reveal His principles for human government in three stages, and we shall look at these in the coming Battlefields accordingly. But His first revelation regarding the idea of human government would be to do nothing, thereby allowing humanity's sinful nature to do the revealing on its own (which in this case was to reveal the absolute need of some form of human government).

It isn't hard to imagine why God was slow to limit the freedom of Image Bearers, for limiting what was never meant to be limited cannot be an easy thing, especially for humanity's loving Creator. Thus, despite the advent of the sinful nature, humanity was allowed an age of freedom in which to prove either their ability to freely and willingly keep that nature in check, or to allow it to blossom into the fullness of its evil expression.

For example, there was essentially no punishment given to humanity's first outright murderer (Genesis 4:12). This lack of punishment had tremendous effect upon humanity, for Cain's descendant Lamech soon reveled in being an overtly violent and hostile man, and all of humanity eventually followed suit. In fact, the overthrow of the Divine Image in humanity was accomplished so quickly and thoroughly under the banner of anarchy that God had to hit the planetary reset button in less than seventeen hundred years because of it (Genesis 5-7).

Humanity had therefore made the case all on its own – it simply could not live without some form of limitation upon the expression of its freedom. God then put an exclamation point on this idea by the planetary cleansing of the Flood.

THE GOOD OL' DAYS

To the ungod, though, such Low Humanity as that found prior to the Flood represents his ideal for planet Earth. For one, it fully reflected the Dark Image (except in the family of Noah). Secondly, it resulted in the cleansing wrath of a holy God, leaving the face of Earth destroyed and essentially human-less, both of which fit well with his Hellish designs for the planet. Anarchy coupled with the sinful human nature is thus the ideal recipe for the designs of Hell upon humanity and Earth.

It is therefore incumbent upon the ungod to replicate such conditions wherever and whenever possible, giving him a stake in influencing human affairs and thinking in the direction of anarchy, libertinism and absolute libertarianism at all times. Put bluntly, the desire for anarchy (and its cousins) is an evil thing, for it either denies the existence of the sinful nature, holds to the belief that each person is policeman enough to themselves, or to a combination of the two (both of which are contrary to the clear teaching of Scripture).

At the heart of the matter is the inescapable Biblical truth that fallen humanity is simply not a perfectible creature (Genesis 6:5; Romans 1:18-32). The ungod must therefore use the Lie in order to dethrone such a truth, and here he is aided by Darwinian thought, which falsely believes humanity to be perfectible. And if humanity is perfectible, then the old-fashioned notions of government are no longer needed, for humanity simply needs to have the chance to spread its wings and fly in order to accomplish its inevitable perfection, giving us cause to throw off the outward constraints holding the worst of the sinful nature in check. This would lead, of course, into an abyss of degradation, corruption and violence (as it always has), but why spoil a good pipe dream when you don't have to?

THE BELIEVER'S OFFENSIVE

As people of the Word, more than all others we should be aware of the depth and depravity of the sinful human nature – it simply cannot be trusted, even in Believers (Romans 7:14-25). Knowing this, then, we should be as shrewd as serpents when it comes to dealing with the reality of the fallen condition of humanity (Matthew 10:16), which is not perfectible and isn't getting any better. Both Scripture and the deep scars of the Flood upon Earth testify to the necessity of human government, and so we must be those who oppose the idea of anarchy in all of its forms, for humanity must not (and cannot) be allowed absolute freedom in its fallen state. Anarchy has been tried and found wanting in the gravest degree.

Let us be thankful that we serve a God not quick to limit our freedom when perfection was lost in the Fall, but let us also pay close attention to learn the principles of how He eventually dictated such limitation should be done.

BATTLEFIELD: THE NOAHIC CHARTER

Whoever sheds the blood of man,
by man shall his blood be shed;
for in the image of God has God made man
Genesis 9:6

Since we have now seen the worse than dismal results of fallen human conduct without limitation upon its expression, we must move into the realm of actual human government, which was instituted for just such a reason. Regarding the success of government, it is really quite remarkable, for it has been the primary factor that has kept us from sinking to pre-Flood conditions of human conduct for more than forty-three hundred years now. As we embark upon this study of government, we must therefore realize that the stakes surrounding it are quite high, for its failure will once again usher in the fullness of Low Humanity (just as its absence did so long ago).

The Original Image

However erroneously humanity may think of government, it is Biblically defined by the idea of limiting human conduct. In fact, in order to make the point clear when I teach on the subject, I often speak of human government as human *limit-ment* (although I know it's poor English to do so). When we take our children to the local fun center for the day and allow them to drive the go-carts to their heart's content, we do so knowing that the go-carts are inhibited from high speeds by the use of a governor that limits the speed for safety's sake. It is this idea of *limitation* that is the sole purpose of Biblical human government.

God defined this process of limitation for us through a successive series of revelations concerning the institution of human government, and His first revelation was as simple as it was short, and may be found in Genesis 9:5b-6: *And from each man, too, I will demand an accounting for the life of his fellow man. Whoever sheds the blood of man, by man shall his blood be shed; for in the image of God has God made man.*

This basic requirement changed the course of human history, and is still today the basis for a decent and sustainable society. It contains the first (and therefore most fundamental) requirement for how human conduct was to be limited, and human conduct was to be limited simply by requiring the death of any murderer, thereby effectively limiting the freedom to murder. Simply stated, murder (in its many forms) is the worst expression of the sinful nature; humanity's freedom to murder was therefore the first freedom to be removed by God.

Yet even this first and most basic idea of government introduces to us the important principle that *government is the natural enemy of freedom*, for every ability granted to government limits a human freedom. Since God must also protect the sanctity of human freedom, he has created a framework for the exercise of government that strikes the delicate balance between limiting the expression of the sinful nature in humanity and of limiting the expression of the power and scope of government.

Moving back now into study of the command itself (Genesis 9:6), we see that this simple principle of capital punishment for murderers is the unlikely but amazing beginning of the Divine Constitution for human government, and is something I think of as the *Noahic Charter*. As the foundation for human government, this Charter is irrevocable and is absolutely required for any form of government upon planet Earth.

This Charter contains two very important factors that need to be understood for any study of human government to be done, and these factors are the *why* and *how* of government. If the *how* and (especially) the *why* of human government are understood and applied, humanity will then live under legitimate government (which is government operating within the boundaries described for it in Scripture). If this *how* and *why* are misunderstood or ignored, humanity will find itself under the oppression of illegitimate government (which is government operating outside of the boundaries described for it in Scripture). So to these two terms we must briefly turn our attention.

The *why* of government is something that will never change, and is contained in Genesis 9:6b: *for in the image of God has God made man.* This *why* is the sole purpose behind the *reason* for human government, and may be understood as follows: *Human government must honor and protect the image of God in humanity.* To be legitimate in the eyes of government's Originator, then, all government must acknowledge God, must acknowledge His nature and must acknowledge His image in humanity (which it must then be sworn to honor and protect).

The *how* of government is defined by the manner and degree to which government is directed to operate in order to accomplish government's *why*, and in terms of the Noahic Charter, this *how* is the requirement for the execution of murderers (capital punishment). As we shall see, this *how* of government may be added to by government's Originator or by applying His later principles to the changing conditions upon Earth, but it *may never be lessened.* This means that capital punishment will be the fundamental and foundational requirement of human government until the day that the sinful nature is abolished (and not a moment before).

THE IMAGE UNDONE

Since God had intervened in such a way so as to preclude humanity from existing outside of the umbrella of human government, it became necessary for the ungod to pollute or usurp the idea of human government toward his insatiable Dark Image. All that is necessary to accomplish such a task is for him to influence the *how* and *why* of Divinely-established government away from its Author, and it takes but a cursory glance (either at our world today or at Scripture) to see how wildly successful the ungod has been, for legitimate government has long been one of the rarest commodities upon Earth.

WHY NOT?

Hell's first attack must necessarily be against the *why* of government, for if this foundation can be corrupted, the entire structure of government will then be owned by the ungod. This necessitates an assault upon the idea of the image of God in humanity, especially as it pertains to the concept of life. As recipients of the Divine Image, humanity has received from God the greatest degree of life imaginable (Genesis 1:26,27; 2:7), making human life the most precious and wondrous thing in the universe.

By its very nature, then, murder is the ultimate affront to the Living God, and He has dictated that this crime must be paid for with the life of the murderer. This effectively makes the idea of human life even more sacred, for it causes humanity to always consider carefully and well the lives of others. The requirement of capital punishment for murderers therefore adds greatly to the idea of the sanctity and dignity of human life.

For this reason the ungod has much at stake in seeing the idea of government divorced from fealty to the image of God, or even from the idea of God Himself. To this end he seeks either the pollution of the idea of government through the influence of the Lie, or the complete secularization of it. In either case, human dignity and the Divine Image will suffer, and conditions upon Earth will trend toward those existing in the days prior to the Flood when murder was rampant (Genesis 6:11).

How Come?

The ungod's attack upon government must also necessarily include an assault upon the *how* of it, which in this case is the death penalty for murderers. As he did in the Garden (Genesis 3:1), here again the Serpent influences humanity toward the questioning of the Word of God, and then couples that questioning with a misguided notion of the proper place for the use of compassion – a combination that inevitably results in less than capital punishment for murderers.

The execution of murderers is a stern idea, and we are not a people accustomed to stern ideas or conduct. Nevertheless, the Divine requirement of such a death penalty has to this day never been rescinded, and so must be honored by all governments. This first Divine *how* of government therefore requires the *stern* action of government, and each successive *how* of government established through the principles of

Scripture will likewise be stern in nature. Since each and every Biblical *how* of government is a stern thing, we are therefore left to conclude that *appropriate government is not compassionate government.*

God is certainly a compassionate Being (Psalm 116:5; Matthew 9:36), but He is also a holy Being (Isaiah 6:3; Revelation 4:8). To government He has given the thankless task of representing His holiness (which to sinful beings is always a stern thing), while compassion simply remains an expectation of personal human conduct (Luke 10:37). When the ungod influences humanity to confuse human government with compassion, government then becomes illegitimate in the extreme, and Low Humanity always follows.

As for the idea of Christ opposing capital punishment, there is no Biblical basis for such a belief (as much as we may wish there were). Some may argue that He came to the defense of the woman caught in adultery (John 8:3-11), something for which the penalty in the Law of Moses was execution (Leviticus 20:10). However, this misses the point being made, for the Romans had long since removed the Jews' ability to impose the death penalty in matters regarding their Law (John 18:31). Knowing this to be true, His enemies were simply trying to entrap Jesus into teaching either against Roman law or Jewish law, which were at odds in this matter.

A far better example is how Jesus dealt with the repentant criminal being crucified with Him (Luke 23:39-43), for the man readily admitted to being guilty of crimes deserving of death. When he saw the manner and dignity of Jesus' bearing upon the Cross, this man repented of his sins, was forgiven by the Savior and was promised Heaven that very day. But Jesus (although He certainly had the power to do so) did not free the man from execution for either his sincerity or his repentance. Instead, he required that the man pay the price for what he had done on Earth. The One who had instituted capital punishment stood behind its necessity, even though it required the death of the first Believer.

Was it stern? Yes. Was it just? Absolutely. Was it compassionate? No. Compassion occurred in the forgiveness of sins (which should always be made available to the condemned). But for grievous acts committed in this life, grievous consequences must follow at the hand of government. We are never told that we must like it; we are told only that it must be done.

Murder is the ultimate affront to the Divine Image, and this affront must be paid for by the sanctioned execution of the murderer. If this is not done – and done quickly once murder is proven – the fall into wickedness in all phases of human existence will be swift (Ecclesiastes 8:11). The evildoers must simply be purged from among decent society in order for decent society to remain decent (Deuteronomy 21:21).

Human government was designed and instituted by God to ensure that the decline of the human condition into what existed prior to the Flood is slowed or never returns, which means that government was intended to enable High Humanity. Where the *how* of government is neglected, the result will therefore always be the rise of the Dark Image.

CAPITOL OFFENSE

The ungod is the original Murderer (John 8:44), and thus takes great delight in the very idea of murder and of murderers (who are his heroes). He will therefore seek to influence all expressions of government toward one of two primary ends: that government becomes the engine of murder, or that government condones the idea of murder by refusing to execute murderers.

Regarding government becoming the engine of murder, nothing more should need be said, but in these current times we have too many poor thinkers among us to leave the idea of murder loosely or not defined, or let it be confused with the idea of killing (as is often done with the Sixth Commandment). Put simply, murder is the non-sanctioned, purposeful killing of a human being by another human being.

There are Biblically-authorized times and reasons for taking a human life, and because they are sanctioned by God to deal with the reality of fallen human existence, they are not considered to be murder, but rather *killing*. As the Author of the life within humanity, God alone reserves the right to define how, when and where human life is taken, and so when He does this it by definition cannot be murder. Such sanctioned (allowed) killing of human beings includes the death penalty for murderers (Genesis 9:6; Numbers 35), the death penalty for other offenses deemed serious threats to the Divine Image in humanity (Leviticus 20), war (Exodus 17:8-13), self-defense (Luke 22:38) and accidental death (Numbers 35:11).

Such sanctioned killing does not cover, condone or allow abortion; the killing of the elderly for convenience; unjustifiable war; or killing for sport, pleasure or practice. All of these are still considered murder, and when a government participates in, funds or codifies murder, that government has become illegitimate and is serving the ungod.

Likewise, when a government fails to execute murderers, it is in direct disobedience to its Divine Charter and has become a tool of the Dark One. Any government that does not have a death penalty program for murderers has failed at its most basic and fundamental necessity, and is therefore illegitimate. Government is not called upon to study murderers, to understand murderers, to coddle murderers, to rehabilitate murderers or to show compassion to murderers. It is called upon to *execute* murderers, and a*ny* departure from this calling moves government from legitimate to illegitimate.

Giving life sentences in prison (to say nothing of less-than-life sentences) for murderers is not a legitimate practice of government, and no government ever has the right to bargain away the execution of a murderer. If someone commits murder, they simply *must be executed.* This is the basis for government as decreed by Heaven, and there is no option to it. Anything less is of Hell's making, and included in this idea of *less* is any inordinately long process (whether of appeal or otherwise) before the execution of a convicted murderer takes place.

If unsure that an individual has committed murder, there should be no conviction, for the burden of proof must necessarily be high (Deuteronomy 17:6). But if sure, convict and then execute, and execute sooner rather than later. The execution of murderers protects the image of God (Genesis 9:6) and prevents the condition of ultimate human depravity that once resulted in the Flood. The *quick* execution of murderers helps slow or even stop the spread of wickedness (Ecclesiastes 8:11), which is of much greater concern to God than mistaken human ideas concerning compassion.

The great Murderer encourages the act of murder, after which he encourages the notion that the murderer be coddled, exalted, left alive or even be set free by the very institution called to do otherwise.

THE SKY'S THE LIMIT

Another lesson to be gleaned from the Noahic Charter is the principle of *compact government.* In the approximately one hundred years between the Flood and the Dispersion from Babel (when Earth's population grew from eight to the many thousands of Nimrod's kingdom a century later), this simple *how* was all that was required of human government. It was not until the Tower of Babel that any further action or revelation on God's part was needed or given, and not until roughly a thousand years after that was the further revelation of the Law given to humanity.

The message from Heaven is here quite simple: limit no more of human freedom than is absolutely necessary. We must constantly remember that each ability granted to government comes at the cost of limiting an expression of human freedom. Since freedom is a facet of the Divine Image (and something we should rightfully and deeply cherish), it necessarily follows that freedom's limitations be as minimal as possible in order to accomplish the Divine purpose for human government. This will naturally and wonderfully leave the size and scope of government severely restricted.

The Noahic Charter teaches us that government was initially instituted by God to limit sinful humanity's freedom *only from its worst expression,* which is murder. At the time of the giving of the Charter the only *how* deemed necessary by God was the death penalty for murderers. Since nothing else was needed, nothing else was demanded, leaving government as small as practicable. And because government is God's idea, it may only legitimately limit in humanity what God has sanctioned that it may. Government limits humanity; God therefore limits government.

But the Evil One delights in the limitation of human freedom, for it is a form of slavery and therefore bears his Hellish image. Since God has imposed the idea of government upon humanity and will not allow us to exist without it, the ungod must therefore hijack government and move it past the boundaries God has set for it. To this end he influences the philosophies of government to become large and dreadful and the master of its people, rather than the small but stern protector of the Image that gives them dignity. Both history and our current state of affairs testify to the success of this endeavor, for it is the well-known march of totalitarianism.

THE SHORT ARM OF THE LAW

Finally, there is the idea of how much government is needed in order to accomplish the Divine requirements upon it. Regarding the Noahic Charter, it was only necessary to have the means by which to establish that murder had occurred and to investigate the murder; to have the means of detaining the suspected murderer and of establishing the guilt or innocence of him or her; and to have the means of executing the murderer if found guilty.

We thus have the minimal requirements necessary to fuel the machinery of human government originally deemed appropriate by God, thereby constituting the *what* of government (that machinery of government necessary to fulfill its *how*). Here, by Divine origin, begins the noble profession of law enforcement (being represented by those individuals necessary for the investigation, arrest, detention and execution of someone who has committed murder). Here also (again by Divine origin) necessarily begin the noble professions of judge and advocate, for Divine justice (though a stern thing) must always and ever be a fair and reasonable thing.

But if a compact machinery of government is the design of Heaven, it stands to reason that the ungod desires to see governmental machinery grow larger than the restraints of its Charter, for this machinery can then begin to be used to exercise more influence than necessary upon a population. This will lead a people down the path of slavery at the hand of its government, and is the great lesson of Babel (at which we will look in the next Battlefield).

THE BELIEVER'S OFFENSIVE

Human government is an idea that belongs solely to God, and so to Him every good facet of government owes its allegiance. And since the idea of human government is a mandate originating from Heaven, we who are Heaven's servants therefore owe an allegiance to the very idea of Biblical government (and to the Divine Nature which dictated its necessity).

This requires (however uncomfortable it may seem) an absolute commitment on our part to the Charter's mandate to secure the death of each and every murderer of a fellow Image Bearer, regardless of how it may affect us personally or professionally. Furthermore, we must demand this same commitment of our own systems of government, for it is not an option given by Heaven – it is a requirement, and this requirement is the foundation of how the image of God in humanity may be honored and protected upon Earth.

To this foundation of all human government we must press our understanding, our teaching, our allegiance, our legislation, our votes and our efforts, for humanity cannot last long without it. If true understanding of the Noahic Charter is lost, understanding of the *why* and *how* of government is likewise lost, which will lead inevitably and swiftly to the degeneracy of Low Humanity. As the salt and light of the world (Matthew 5:13-16), we have an obligation against such a thing.

BATTLEFIELD: THE BABEL AMENDMENT

The Divine revelation of human government had begun with great simplicity through the Noahic Charter, and as the population of humanity again exploded, this simplicity would serve the Divine Image admirably and well until the time would come when the complete Law was necessary. But in the interim there arose such a grievous threat to High Humanity that the hand of Heaven was prompted to act yet again, resulting in the forced dispersion of humanity across the face of Earth.

In the course of roughly one hundred years, humanity had taken the principle of human government from a compact system of maximum human freedom to a single, centrally-planned, heavy-handed governmental system under the leadership of Nimrod (Genesis 10:8-12). Humanity has the natural and unfortunate tendency to corrupt everything it touches (eventually corrupting it completely), and the idea of human government was no exception to this, for humanity soon found itself in near-complete bondage to totalitarianism. If a little government is good, a lot of government must be great (or so one would think).

THE ORIGINAL IMAGE

God had promised that He would not again destroy the earth as He had done (Genesis 8:21b), and inherent in this promise was the idea that humanity not be allowed the degree of Evil it had obtained prior to the Flood. That God so soon and drastically intervened in human affairs at Nimrod's Babel can therefore only mean that the Divine Image was once again in danger of extinction, only this time that extinction was threatened at the hand of government, and not at the hand of anarchy.

God therefore confused the language of humanity, forcing them to separate into smaller groups and to spread out upon Earth.

In Scripture, this is widely known as the incident regarding the Tower of Babel and the resulting Dispersion (Genesis 11:1-9). In terms of the principles of God's revelation concerning human government, I refer to it as the *Babel Amendment*, for it amends the Noahic Charter in an important manner. But before we proceed, it's important to understand that the *why* of government was not changed (for it never can be), but rather it was the *how* of government that received an addendum. This addendum was the requirement of maintaining *several separate and sovereign peoples or nations* with their associated governments upon Earth, rather than a single government for all of humanity, and this requirement has never been rescinded by God.

THE IMAGE UNDONE

God would naturally and fully have understood that the confusion of tongues at Babel would result in the establishment of many separate and sovereign nations (Genesis 10:5,20,31,32). It therefore stands to reason that in such a separated state of affairs, both human freedom and High Humanity have the greatest potential to survive and thrive. This dictates that the ungod has a vested interest in seeing just the opposite occur, and so he seeks to influence the thinking of humanity toward embracing the ideology of a single, central government, for in such a system the Dark Image will flourish through the heavy-handedness of it.

UNLAWFUL ASSEMBLY

Among the few commandments that God had given to the sons of Noah was the command to fill the earth (Genesis 9:1,7). Their descendants refused to do so, however, and chose instead to stay as close together as they could. This resulted in the vast majority of the human population staying in large cities centered in the area of the Tigris and Euphrates Rivers, leaving Earth largely uninhabited. This ignoring of the command of God eventually developed into outright rebellion against Him (the name *Nimrod* means *let us rebel*), resulting in the events of the tenth and eleventh chapters of Genesis.

The sinful nature essentially exists in order to defy God, and so when the nature of God dictates something for humanity, the sinful nature is inclined to do just the opposite. It was this defiance that led to the lack of the spreading of humanity, which in turn gave rise to the large urban complex. Such complexes required the idea of central planning in order to function, and as the need for central planning increased, government would naturally arise to take the reins of such planning, for such planning necessitated the giving up of personal freedoms to the common interest (the collective). By the time God intervened at Babel, collectivism under Nimrod was nearly complete, and all of humanity was united in rebellion under their leader and was engaged in the outright worship of Darkness.

One of the things this teaches us is that the worst primer for the sinful human nature is simply more of it, and so the more compactly that humanity is crammed together, the worse will be the development of that sinful nature in its midst. Simply put, the sinful nature feeds off of itself and encourages itself toward ever-increasing depravity. From observation of this phenomenon comes the phrase *clean country living*, and law enforcement officers will readily testify to the reality of the increasing rates of crime and depravity as the density of the human population increases in any area. It is not that the folk of the country are any better than their counterparts in the metropolis; it is simply that they lack the magnitude of sinful catalyst found there.

This brings to us the idea of *metropolitan critical mass*, in which the sheer density of the sinful nature creates a dark life all its own – a life that feeds and grows upon itself until it no longer sees the wrongness of open rebellion against God. This critical mass is music to the ungod's ears, for it accelerates the decline into Low Humanity, and gives to the wicked the sheer power of numbers they would otherwise not have, resulting in the forced feeding of their dark ideologies upon all others.

This is not to say that the city cannot be a catalyst for many fine and noble things due to this same reason of compactness, since it can bring together great minds, talents and resources that may be used in the direction of High Humanity. Yet for all of the advances the metropolis may bring, caution is warranted, for history is history (and we ignore the tendencies of the sinful nature at our own peril).

THE MORE, THE MERRIER

By confusing human speech into several languages, God forced humanity to separate, thereby causing them to scatter to the far reaches of the globe. Through this Divine act of the Dispersion at Babel, God essentially thrust the dagger of Heaven through the heart of human unification – something that the ungod has been trying to resurrect ever since. But God's message is clear: Many smaller governments are better than a single, central government, and for good reason. Government is a necessary beast that feeds off of human freedom in order to exist. It therefore needs to be kept in as small a cage as possible, for if it is allowed unfettered growth it will eventually devour all human freedom.

A myriad of separated peoples with separate governments is therefore the Divine method of ensuring that a maximum degree of human freedom survives upon Earth. With a single government, all of humanity will eventually be enslaved. But with many governments this will be much harder for the ungod to accomplish, for nations may hold others to account for tyranny or enslavement. This gives birth to the idea of what we now think of as the separation of powers, and also shows that local expressions of government are preferred by Heaven to centralized expressions of it.

The Babel Dispersion was therefore no minor thing for planet Earth, but was rather a drastic and large-scale change. Since at least seventy descendants of Noah's sons are listed in the tenth chapter of Genesis regarding the dispersal by languages, this means that humanity went from being a single people with a single language to being at least seventy peoples with seventy languages overnight! Such a phenomenal overhaul of the affairs of humanity by Heaven shows how deep a danger the idea of centralized government is to dignified human existence, and why such an idea of government must always be resisted.

The ungod, however, is one who has no taste for dignified human existence, and so he has a marked stake in seeing humanity move toward strong, centralized governments (and eventually toward a one-world government). Since smaller, sovereign states and peoples are the bedrock of human freedom upon Earth, the great Enslaver must influence sovereign states and peoples to cede their sovereignty to ever-increasing national, regional, hemispheric and international governmental movements.

The Enemy does this by appealing to the naïve but attractive belief among humanity that a lack of nations will end conflict in the world. It will not end conflict, of course, but it will end freedom.

THIS LAND IS MY LAND

The question of national land ownership must now be discussed, for it is an idea inherent to the Babel Amendment, and the answer to it is a simple one (though it may not be music to many ears). In Genesis 9:1, God commanded Noah and his sons to fill the earth. Shem was not told to go eastward, nor Japheth westward, nor Ham southward, nor did the Dispersion see the language groups spreading out with maps and property deeds in hand. They went where they willed. They moved, explored and settled.

This essentially meant that the earth was up for grabs, for no one was given a title deed to any part of it. The harsh Biblical and historical truth of the matter is simply this: The only people who may call a particular land their own are those who occupy it and who can hold it by their strength. In fact, the only people or nation ever given a deed to any part of planet Earth is Israel (Genesis 13:14-17; 26:3-5; 35:12), and even they were (and are) subject to this reality (Deuteronomy 28). It must also be understood that Israel was not the first to inhabit the Promised Land (Exodus 23:23), proving that the notion of *finders, keepers* does not determine final ownership of any part of Earth.

This is not said in order to facilitate a new land war among the peoples of this marvelous sphere, but is said, rather, to simply comment on Biblical reality. Israel occupied her land and called it her own as long as she was strong, and she was strong as long as God blessed her, and God blessed her as long as she was a good nation. God owns this planet (Psalm 24:1); we peoples and nations are but tenants and stewards, and may be removed for cause as Heaven sees fit – an idea that should breathe sobriety into the thinking of any people who love their portion of Earth.

But because we are ultimately just tenants and stewards, however, does not mean that we are not meant to be connected to the land of our people or nation, for good stewardship demands that we be connected to the land that sustains and nourishes us. We are therefore meant to have a stake in the land and to think of it as our own, for if we are vested in our land, we will naturally want to hold onto the ownership of it. If we want to hold onto it, we will need to be strong enough to do so. If we want to be strong, we will need to seek the blessings of God. If we want the blessings of God, we will need to be a people of righteous conduct. And if we want to be a people of righteous conduct, we will need to be a people of the Word and of Truth (Deuteronomy 28:1-14).

There are probably few things that are more delightful to the ungod than the incessant number of land wars that he has inspired over the millennia of human habitation upon Earth. In this direction he has but to unleash the sinful nature upon national existence, for people who embrace the ideals of Evil will either covet the land of others or will be too weak to hold their own when others come knocking. And the seeds of upheaval and dispossession that are sown in the aftermath of such activity will long be reaped in the undying hatred and enmity between peoples afterward.

GOOD FENCES

Continued study of the Babel Amendment now leads us naturally into a discussion of borders, and so we must now set ourselves to the tackling of such a contentious issue. A border is simply a boundary between two differing things, and an international border is simply a boundary between two different nations or peoples. After the Dispersion there were natural dividing lines between all peoples, and those dividing lines were the languages that God had used to separate them. In a very real sense, then, languages were the first borders, and God was the inventor of those borders. An argument with the idea of borders, then, is actually an argument with God.

This idea of international borders was later more fully developed by God via His blueprint for the nation of Israel, to whom He gave very clear and specific borders (Numbers 34:1-12). Since a border is a boundary between two differing things, we must look at what was different when one would cross a border into ancient Israel, and the first difference we already know, for it was language, and the Israelite language was Hebrew (2 Kings 18:26).

The second difference would be that of law, for Israel had a distinct system of national law (the Law of Moses), to which God did not hold those outside of Israel accountable (Exodus 12:49; 13:7; Numbers 15:29). The final difference was the culture, for in Israel Jehovah was to be worshipped to the exclusion of all others (Exodus 20:2-4). When we put all of this together, the idea of an international border becomes a boundary between two peoples and their separate languages, systems of law and cultures. Since God has dictated that people separate themselves into many nations – and these three issues are what cause a people to be a separate nation – this sanctifies the idea of borders and of what those borders protect.

Borders are therefore something that must be guarded with the utmost care. Inside of a nation's borders there should be a common language, a common law and a common culture, and these things must be guarded as if they were the very life of the nation, for indeed they are. If you lived in ancient Israel, you spoke Hebrew, you were subject to the Law of Moses, and you worshipped Jehovah. If not, you were deported (Numbers 15:30,31) or put to death (Leviticus 24:14), for any compromise to the language, law and culture was seen as inappropriate and a capitulation of national sovereignty and identity.

The ungod understands this arrangement well enough, for we see how jealously he guards the borders of the nations controlled by his dark ideologies. Saudi Arabia, for instance, has an official language (Arabic), system of law (Islamic Sharia) and culture (worship of Allah), and Heaven help the person who crosses swords with any of these ideas while in that nation, for it will not go well with them.

Yet while he so jealously guards his own domain according to the principles of the Babel Amendment, the ungod at the same time organizes the dismantling of the languages, laws and cultures most representing High Humanity in the many nations of the West. He is therefore behind the cry for open borders and multiculturalism, both of which will always spell national suicide for any people. For once enough people of foreign speech, law and culture have infiltrated a nation, that nation will fall, no matter what heights it may have reached.

WAVING THE FLAG

The Babel Amendment now brings us to the question of patriotism, and simple logic will direct us to the appropriate conclusion regarding whether the idea of patriotism is proper or not. We've already seen how God has instituted the idea of many smaller, sovereign nations as being necessary for the preservation of freedom and the Divine Image upon Earth. For such an idea to work, it necessarily requires that each person has a stake in his or her nation, which in turn means that they speak its language; that they abide by its system of laws; that they love, admire and participate in its culture; and that they support its sovereignty. It is hard to think of a better definition of patriotism than that.

There are two fine Biblical examples of patriots, and both were followers of Jehovah (though only one was an Israelite). David was wronged time and time again by the king and nation he loved, yet he was always faithful to Israel, as may be seen throughout the latter chapters of First Samuel. The Scriptures also introduce us to Naaman the Syrian, who became a convert to Jehovah after being healed of his leprosy in the Jordan River. Yet Naaman remained a loyal patriot to his king and to his nation with Jehovah's blessing (2 Kings 5).

When we couple this necessity for patriotism with the nature of what the idea of culture truly represents, we see that it is the required duty of a nation to winnow the non-patriotic from its midst. But it is just as important that a nation strongly sift those of foreign citizenship who desire entrance across its borders, especially those who come for the purpose of making the potential host nation a long-term or permanent home (for they have the potential to destroy a nation). Regarding Israel, this meant that she was only allowed to confer citizenship upon someone if that person *converted* to Israel's language, law and culture (Joshua 2:8-13; 6:23,25).

There is an excellent example of this in the Book of Ruth, where the Moabitess pledges to Naomi: *Where you go I will go, and where you stay I will stay. Your people will be my people and your God my God. Where you die I will die, and there I will be buried. May the Lord deal with me, be it ever so severely, if anything but death separates you and me* (Ruth 1:16,17). This is probably the most eloquent and touching case of national conversion ever known, and Ruth is listed proudly in the genealogy of the Savior (Matthew 1:5).

If someone forsakes their native country for another, they must change their loyalty as well. If unwilling to do so, the Biblical example is clear – they should stay on their native soil. Additionally, if a people or nation have lost sovereignty (or if national boundaries have shrunk or changed to exclude someone), it must be recognized that this is most likely due to weakness or national sin, and every effort to live loyally under the newer, stronger or more righteous system must be made.

It is the ungod who is behind the idea of a borderless global citizenry, for such a sentiment weakens national resolve and character, leading to larger and larger expressions of human government. This will eventually result in Hell's desired one-world government, through which he will once again enslave all of humanity. We must tread thoughtfully here.

ADD-ONS

There remains now one important facet of the Babel Amendment to be discussed, for we have yet to speak of how it legitimately adds to the machinery (the *what*) of human government. It does so in but two ways, and these are easy to define and understand. The first is the simple requirement to maintain secure borders (however that may best be accomplished), and the second is the eventual necessity of establishing a guardian for the official, national language. Only these two things were now added to the previous necessities of law enforcement and the judicial system, and this small model of government would serve humanity well over the course of the next thousand years.

THE BELIEVER'S OFFENSIVE

The idea of many separate and sovereign nations is a necessity decreed and codified for humanity by God through the Babel Amendment, and this Amendment was given in order to prevent the Hellish and enslaving idea of one-world, overly-centralized government from institution upon planet Earth. As those who deeply love both God and His image, we must therefore be this world's staunchest foes of strong, centralized government, for it is freedom's greatest enemy.

We are thus to be patriotic citizens of our nation, and must be deeply tied to its language, law and culture, and also be those who are committed to its health, survival and national sovereignty. In so doing we will make every effort to see to our nation's goodness, and so to the spread of dignified human existence upon Earth.

BATTLEFIELD: THE MOSAIC AMENDMENT

*And what other nation is so great as to have
such righteous decrees and laws as this body of laws
I am setting before you today?*
Deuteronomy 4:8

The Noahic Charter and the Babel Amendment ably served the Divine Image for roughly one thousand years after the Dispersion, ensuring the spread of humanity upon Earth and keeping alive the ideals of High Humanity. The specter of the totalitarianism of one-world government had not again risen, and the God-ordained border of language differences had seen large portions of the world now populated. But as the various peoples established their separate cultures wherever they had spread, it eventually came time for God to complete His revelation to humanity regarding the institution of human government. This was done through the Law of Moses, and is something I call the *Mosaic Amendment* to the Noahic Charter.

THE ORIGINAL IMAGE

In the Divine course of time, God called a people to Himself, gave them His Name, delivered to them His blueprint for society and then settled them into the land promised by Him to their forefathers. The people of whom I speak are (of course) Israel, and the blueprint of which I speak is Israel's Law, which consisted of the Ten Commandments, Israel's religious laws and Israel's civil laws (Exodus 18 - Deuteronomy 34). This body of law was known collectively as the Law of Moses, and would eventually be referred to simply as the *Law*.

The land into which God settled them was formerly known as Canaan (Genesis 12:5), but would afterward be known as Israel, and was uniquely situated in the crossroads of the world at that time. To Israel were promised the heights of culture, honor, prosperity and freedom if they would honor the Law and the God who authored it (Deuteronomy 28:1-14), but to them also were promised the depths of despair, reproach, poverty and slavery if they neglected the Law and its Giver (Deuteronomy 28:15-68). In essence, God would honor them if they honored His Word, and would dishonor them if they did not honor His Word.

The idea in Scripture is clear: Israel was designed to be a lighthouse nation that would shine the Light of the Law to all peoples (Deuteronomy 4:6). This meant that the Law was not just for Israel, but was meant to *influence* the governing of all peoples (as recognized by an astonished Queen of Sheba in 2 Chronicles 9:5-8). The requirements of the Law were demanded of Israel as the covenant nation; the Law was (and is) voluntary for all others. However, because it is an extension of the Divine nature, the Law is perfectly designed for the governing of humanity wherever it finds itself upon Earth (Deuteronomy 4:8). To the degree that God's Law is adopted by any people, they will therefore be a blessed people, a moral people, a free people, a prosperous people of great delight in life, and a people among (and in) whom the Divine Image will naturally flourish.

For this reason the Law is – apart from the Savior – God's greatest gift to humanity, and why Israel should be loved and venerated by all. That she is largely detested by humanity testifies to the Dark One's intense hatred of the Law and the people through whom it was revealed.

THE IMAGE UNDONE

Because of what the Law represents, it is therefore imperative that the Enemy in every way oppose the dissemination, understanding and implementation of the Law upon Earth, and the best way to accomplish such a desired end would be to utterly destroy the people of Israel. But throughout the ages and despite the overwhelming odds against them, God has protected the covenant people from annihilation (Jeremiah 31:35,36), and the very existence of Israel and the Jewish people today is perhaps the greatest testimony we have to the greatness of the Law and of its Giver.

Being unable to destroy the Israelites, then, the ungod would naturally turn to the idea of polluting the transmission of the Law. But here we must thank both the stalwart Israelite scribes of antiquity and the mighty hand of Divine protection, for we can today with absolute certainty read the very words of Moses as if he had just put them to skin and scroll. God did not deliver the Light of the Law just to have future generations and peoples left in the Darkness, and He is far stronger than His foe. The Law survives intact.

With both Israel and the Law supernaturally protected from extermination, the ungod is left with influencing the affairs of humanity toward seeing that the Law is ignored, forgotten or simply not implemented. Israel's painful history from Moses to David may be viewed in this light, for it is the history of struggle between the ideals of the Law and of fallen sinful nature, which fought one another every step of the way. Not until roughly five hundred years had passed would Israel's great summit of High Humanity be reached, and then all-too-brief would be its stay at that height, after which humanity was largely bereft of Heaven's Light until the rise of the Biblical West many, many centuries later.

THOU SHALT NOT

A great starting lesson of the Law is that it is the imposition of a Divine moral code, for the giving of the Law begins with the phrase *I am the Lord your God* (Exodus 20:2), and what then follows is a revelation of expected human conduct by a holy God. Since government is the instrument of law, this essentially means that it is not possible to separate the ideas of God and government. Simply put, true morality is defined as *thought and conduct in keeping with the nature of God*, for the Being that creates the universe gets to set the rules (Isaiah 45:9; 64:8). By definition, then, what that Being *is* defines what is right; what that Being *is not* defines what is wrong. Good law (and thus good government) is simply an extension of this idea, and dictates that good law and government cannot be divorced from God's nature. The Ten Commandments are simply God's way of making His expectations perfectly clear to humanity.

Good law therefore has the ability to reign in the influence of the sinful human nature – a state of affairs that slows the dominance of the Dark Image. Because of this, the ungod must oppose good law, and he does so in two primary manners. The first is by redefining the nature of God in Hell's image, and then basing law upon this false idea of God. The second method is by divorcing the idea of law from the idea of God completely.

By far the most successful example of this first method employed by the ungod today is his having redefined the orderly, transcendent, loving and knowable Jehovah of Scripture into the far different Allah of the Quran, for the sense of law (Shariah) that has followed Allah is one of the greatest blights of human history. At the other end of the spectrum are the secularists who seek to divorce the idea of government from the idea of God, (perhaps) not knowing that to truly divorce government from God would require making things like murder, adultery and theft both legal and acceptable. And strangely enough, under the Hell-inspired guidance of atheist and Marxist ideologies, just such a trend is at a full gallop in our midst today.

The influence of Hell dictates that any law that honors the nature of God must simply be cast aside, while every law that does violence to the nature of the Lawgiver must be exalted. This results in the twisting of the very idea of law, which in turn results in illegitimate government of every kind.

GOOD FOR THE GOOSE

A fantastic tactic employed by the ungod in his war against the Law is to spread the idea that the Law was meant only for Israel. To be sure, the Law was a covenant between God and Israel, for the Ten Commandments are preceded by Exodus 20:2, which reads: *I am the Lord your God, who brought you out of Egypt, out of the land of slavery.* Clearly, God brought only Israel out of Egypt, and so the Law has a unique relationship to Israel – something it shares with no other nation or people.

Yet when (by the express command of God) Joshua had the Israelites march in silence around Jericho thirteen times in seven days, the Ark of the Covenant was for the only time ordered into battle (Joshua 6), and the Ark contained the Ten Commandments. In this way, God used the opportunity of the first and seminal battle for the Promised Land to have the Law testify against the conduct of the people inhabiting that land, and they had been found wanting (just as God had predicted they would be to Abraham over four hundred years earlier in Genesis 15:16).

The Scriptural message is therefore quite clear: all nations will be judged by adherence to the Law. When God wrote the Ten Commandments on stone, He essentially had them bolded, italicized, underlined and capitalized in order to gain the world's attention. This means that while the Law is specific to Israel, it may be generally adopted by any nation – something the Queen of Sheba would one day understand (1 Kings 10:1-13; 2 Chronicles 9:5-8).

To be sure, only Israel would (and could) have the Tabernacle, the Temple and the Levitical priesthood. And only among Israel would God uniquely dwell in the Holy of Holies (Exodus 40:34,35; 1 Kings 8:10,11), making Israel's relationship with God a unique and singular thing among the nations. Yet it must be remembered that Israel was designed as the Law's lighthouse nation, which meant that she was designed to *export Truth*. The nations were to see her Law and want it for themselves, that they might appropriate its blessings of High Humanity. This, in turn, means that while those things specific to Israel were not exportable, the Law in the form of the Ten Commandments certainly was, and could easily form the basis of a marvelous system of law, as even my crude attempt at a Gentile paraphrase shows:

> *There is but one God and Creator. He is holy and has revealed Himself to the people of Israel, granting to them His expectations of human conduct through the Ten Commandments. We shall honor Him to the exclusion of all other gods, created things and man-made objects, and shall speak of Him with reverence at all times. We shall set aside one day per week for the purpose of rest and remembrance of Him and His six-day act of Creation. We shall honor the ideas of family and of marriage until death. We shall be people of honest and honorable speech, conduct and intent, and shall honor each person's life, freedom, property and good name.*

Such an adoption of the Divine principles of Israel's Law by any people can easily set the cause of Darkness back hundreds (if not thousands) of years in their midst, as we have seen upon our own fair shores. It is therefore imperative that the ungod convince humanity that the Law is either obsolete or meant solely for the people of Israel.

WE THE PEOPLE

A noteworthy facet of the Law is that although it was not a form of democracy, it was actually an expression of self-government, for there were no nobles or commoners in Israel, and there was no ruling elite. Instead, ordinary people were chosen to carry out the non-priestly and non-Levitical aspects of the Law. Such officials were called *judges*, and they formed an appellate court system that saw Moses (and later the High Priest ministering with the Urim and Thummim) as the final arbiter for the most difficult cases (Exodus 18:13-26).

Remarkable to this passage of Scripture – and something absolutely necessary to the idea of legitimate government – are the requirements for filling such a position. Simply stated, judges were to be the most demonstrably *capable* and *moral* people in Israel. A capable person is someone who generally succeeds at whatever task they attempt, and is someone who demonstrates intelligence, hard work, indomitability, ingenuity, thoughtfulness and levelheaded-ness. A moral person is simply someone who has committed his or her life to honoring the image and nature of God. According to the Law, then, government is best when entrusted to those who have *already clearly demonstrated* that they are the very best of us – and to no others – for government is by nature a dangerous thing.

Our Enemy must therefore see to it that the ranks of government officials are populated with the most incapable and immoral people imaginable, and one has but to look at the ranks of our modern politicians and governmental bureaucrats to see to what a deep degree this has already been accomplished. We do well to remember that since every law or regulation enacted limits a human freedom while simultaneously granting a power to government, if government is peopled by the mediocre and immoral, it will quickly become a tool by which the ungod moves humanity toward the Dark Image. To this end he actively encourages the incompetent, the lazy, the immoral, the greedy and the power-hungry into governmental service.

WEAK MIDSECTION

The same passage of Scripture we have just studied (Exodus 18:13-26) also reinforces another lesson already brought to us by the Babel Amendment – that of localized and decentralized government. Apart from a centralized worship (which ensured a common culture), all government in Israel was originally *local*. Although a weak central monarchy would one day be established in Israel, there was originally no central government to be found in her midst. Instead, the twelve tribes were each given a portion of the Promised Land, in which the people were answerable to their tribal leaders.

Yet even within these tribal areas, issues of the Law, courts and justice were first handled by the judges of ten (Exodus 18:21), which was the most local expression of government possible. From there the issues were handled by the next level of judge, and so on and upward until the issues reached the tribal level of leadership (comparable to the level of our state government). From there it is likely that any difficult issue was looked at by regional leaders in the Cities of Refuge, after which it would be resolved at the federal level (which consisted only of the High Priest ministering with the Urim and the Thummim).

Under such a system the Israelite knew the maximum amount of freedom possible, but the decline of Israel into anarchy by the end of the Book of Judges (Judges 19-21) must be allowed to teach us something. Since government is designed to (among other things) stave off anarchy, the existence of anarchy means that the government has failed in its purpose. In Israel's case, this was not due to the inadequacy of its Law (Deuteronomy 4:8), but rather to the idea that its government was too decentralized to be effective against the sinful nature. This would be corrected by God through the eventual establishment of the Davidic monarchy (2 Samuel 5:1-5), but it brings us to discussion of an interesting and necessary concept.

As we follow the establishment of a stronger central government in Israel, we see that it would not be long before it would pose its own problems, for by the third generation of the monarchy it had become large, odious and controlling to its people, and bore the familiar stench of totalitarianism (1 Kings 12:1-19). But the order in which God established Israel's government serves to reinforce this very lesson of the Babel Amendment, for decentralized government was instituted first, followed much later by a cautious and limited centralized form of government. Government is mandated for humanity; however, this mandated government is preferably decentralized, and where centralization is needed, it should be as limited as possible.

One of the lessons we should learn from this Divine instruction is that there is an appropriate and delicate balance to the idea of human government. If it swings too far in the direction of human freedom, anarchy will result. If it swings too far toward centralization, totalitarianism will result. Either of these is acceptable to the ungod, for both lead to the finish line of Low Humanity, and so Hell works tirelessly to tip the balance of government in either direction.

WHAT'S YOURS IS MINE

The Sixth Commandment prohibits a person from violating another person's life. The Seventh Commandment prohibits a person from violating another person's marriage. The Eighth Commandment prohibits a person from violating another person's goods, and the Ninth Commandment prohibits a person from violating another person's good name. Since these Commandments show us that each person has an inherent right to possession of their own life, marriage, goods and good name, it means that each person naturally owns these things, which make them their private (or personal) property. As the servant of the idea of law, it is therefore government's sworn duty to protect the idea of private property.

For the ungod, then, the Dark Image must necessarily include the idea that government is the opponent of private property, and that no person's life, marriage, goods or character is safe from violation or theft. This may be accomplished by the existence of an overly weak government (Judges 19), by a corrupt government (2 Samuel 11) or by a confiscatory government such as existed under Queen Jezebel and King Ahab (1 Kings 21), and which is so ably represented by the intense thievery of today's redistributive socialism.

The protection of private property is the fundamental basis of the *how* of government. Without it there is no stability. With no stability, there is no order. Without order, there is no freedom. And without freedom, there is no High Humanity, which is precisely the point desired by the Enemy.

SIMPLETON

One of the most refreshing aspects of the Law of Moses is its brevity and simplicity, for at pulpit reading speed I can read through the entire Law in less than a day, and understand everything that I read. There are some important lessons to be learned from this brevity and simplicity, so let us briefly look at what they teach us.

The first lesson is that the Law – while deep and penetrating and serious – is not so complex that it could not be readily understood by the average Israelite. The language is plain, and the ideas are plain. Secondly, the Law is short enough to be memorized if one were to put forth the effort to do so, meaning that the sheer size and volume of it were not enough to overwhelm the intellect of the common Israelite. It could be memorized, and was therefore portable. One needed not worry whether or not they were in violation of the Law, for the brevity and simplicity of it made it obvious where a person stood in relation to it.

Sadly, we have travelled far past that point today, for the sheer volume of law overwhelms even the most decent citizen. For instance, here in California we are held liable to the federal laws and statutes, the state penal code, the state vehicle code, the health and safety code, state and federal taxation laws and an ever-increasing burden of environmental regulations (to say nothing of the necessity of keeping up with the ever-growing standard of judicial case law). There is a law, statute or regulation handcuffing virtually every single thing we do, and it is *impossible* to fully know the depth of law arrayed against us.

Regarding the idea of simplicity of law, our federal government recently passed a single healthcare regulation bill that is half as long as the Bible! Added to this idea of ridiculous length is also the issue of understandability, for the truth of the matter is that most modern law cannot be understood without the aid of a specialist who can translate it from legal-speak into the language of reasonable human beings. The beauty and necessity of the simplicity of law is now effectively destroyed.

Such volume and complexity are contrary to the spirit and purpose of the Law, which was meant to be memorized, understood and appreciated by its citizens. By drastically increasing governmental regulation, the ungod encourages fear of law where it is not understood and the breaking of law where it is not known, which lead into either anarchy or the heavy hand of totalitarianism.

FIXATION

A most important trait of the Law is its finality, for the Israelites were forbidden to add to it or take away from it (Deuteronomy 4:2; 12:32). The Divine reasoning behind not adding to the Law is not hard to fathom, for if no limit is placed upon law, there is no limit placed upon the removal of human freedoms – a condition that will lead to complete human enslavement and the loss of the Divine Image. Knowing how and where to draw the line of finality for law is therefore the genius of good and legitimate government. *Genius* and *government*, however, are not terms generally associated with one another, and so we must look to the great Lawgiver for guidance in this regard.

God's successive revelations regarding human government imposed a successive and increasing set of limits upon human conduct, which beforehand knew no limits whatsoever. The Noahic Charter imposed the barest of limitations upon a sparsely populated planet, and was eventually followed by the Babel Amendment, which imposed more limitations by requiring the separation and sovereignty of nations and peoples. These were in time followed by the limitations of the Mosaic Amendment (the Law), after which God deemed the people of His model nation sufficiently limited in order to honor and protect His image. Heaven's limitation of human conduct therefore stopped with the conclusion of Deuteronomy, for God had struck the balance He desired between necessary law and human freedom.

Such a Divine balance is the point of greatness in human government. Wise is the government that studies and emulates that Divinely-balanced point; foolish is the government that ignores or strays from it. For Israel, this balance meant that there was no regulation of travel, no regulation of the marketplace, no regulation of land use, no regulation of labor, no regulation of food production, no regulation of the environment, no regulation of medical care, and no regulation of education or anything else not specifically enumerated in the Law. Adding such regulations – or any like them – would have been then (and is now) governmental tyranny in the eyes of Heaven, for such regulations overstep the small and confining box built by God to restrain human government. Everything not specifically restrained by God was to be left to the idea of human freedom.

This is not to say that law may not be changed or given additions as human conditions and technologies change, for the successive revelations of human government by God speak otherwise. The trick is to know how and when such an addition to God's finalized list of human limitations may legitimately be made.

There is but one example of challenge and change to the given Law, and it is regarding the plight of the five daughters of Zelophehad (Numbers 27:1-11; 36:1-12). Their father had no sons, and so according to the Law their family would lose their inherited portion of the Promised Land – something contrary to the spirit of the Law (Numbers 27:4). Consequently, at the Lord's direction it was made law that if a man had no sons, his daughters could inherit his land, or if he had no daughters, then his nearest relative could inherit it.

God could have placed such a requirement in the Law originally, but He did not, knowing that Zelophehad's daughters would rightly raise the issue, thereby giving both Israel and us an indication of how changing conditions may potentially affect the practical observance of law. Through this issue we see that no new *rights* were created in God's decision, and no new limitations upon human freedom were made. The only *right* involved here was the right of the land to remain in the control of its given tribe, and this was not changed. Israel therefore knew no further limitation upon its conduct after the issue was clarified.

But since God commands that we neither take from nor add to His Law, the Lawless One influences the philosophies of human government to do either or both, which will again tip the scales in either the direction of anarchy or totalitarianism. To the degree that such thought is embraced, governments and their citizens trend quickly toward Low Humanity, and Hell's image again waxes in strength.

ONE FOR ALL

Another noteworthy facet of the Law is its homogenous applicability. It may seem strange to need to remark upon the idea that law is equally applied to all people within a nation's borders, but it unfortunately does merit some review and discussion in these times. The rich in Israel were subjected to the Law the same as the poor (Leviticus 19:15), and the alien was subjected to the Law the same as the native-born Israelite (Leviticus 24:22). Israel's delivered Law was therefore blind to race and social status, and this blind implementation of the Law was essential to the Divine idea of justice and to the idea of the equality of all human beings.

Such a system of law – where the rich are not favored in court because they are rich, nor the poor favored in court because they are poor, nor the native-born favored in court over the alien or vice versa – naturally lent itself to the ideas of human dignity and worthiness, which in turn would lead a people to High Humanity, for this is how God treats all people (Romans 2:11). Against such a development in the realms of human dignity and worthiness the ungod must battle most strenuously, giving us Israel's subsequent downward spiral of unequal application of the Law throughout the Book of Judges, whose anarchist ending is a dream come true for Hell.

When the wealthy or powerful are able to circumvent the requirements of the law through bribery or undo influence, the law then becomes a tool by which the poor and non-influential are browbeat into submission to the will of those deemed their betters. Such an unequal legal system will ultimately result in dividing a society into one in which some people have rights and others do not, causing the one group to use the idea of law for their own enrichment, while those in the lesser group are forced into an undo fear of it. In this case the law has been used to create nobles and serfs, something contrary to the very nature of the Lawgiver.

Conversely, when a judge or jury awards the wealth of another to a person or group simply because they seem poor or disenfranchised, they have committed an equally grievous offense against the idea of good law (Exodus 23:3). True Biblical justice is indeed blind, for it doesn't see whether a person is a person of means or not, but rather that a law has been aggrieved and must therefore be righted. Despite how loudly the Marxist may complain, being wealthier than another is not a sin (or even wrong). In the end, awarding judgments against the wealthy or powerful simply because they are wealthy or powerful is merely a method to reward covetousness, and is a form of theft. When such an attitude is pervasive, the court system becomes the weapon that destroys the idea of law, and when law is destroyed, anarchy soon follows.

Finally, we must discuss the idea of a nation's laws and the aliens (whether legal or illegal) within its borders. As discussed previously, an international border protects the sovereignty and sanctity of a nation's language, law and culture. When someone crosses a border, they therefore become subject to the law of the nation they enter (Numbers 15:16), and they have neither right nor expectation to the law of the land they exited. If it is against the law of a nation to enter that nation without its permission, then entry without permission makes a person a lawbreaker.

The offended nation must then deal with such lawbreakers according to the laws that they have broken. If a nation does not do so, it lets its citizens know that there is a group of people not required to obey the law of the land, and once such a principle has been established, the nation's law has lost its moral authority. And where one exception has been made to accommodate one group of lawbreakers, more exceptions will necessarily follow. The end result will be a weakened, pathetic idea of law disregarded by all, leading inevitably to anarchy and its consequences.

WHAT MORE?

The Law proved applicable not just to the original theocracy of Israel, but also to the later addition of the monarchy, which found its fulfillment in the House of David. And although the Mosaic Amendment did substantially add to the Divine limitations upon human conduct already established through the Noahic Charter and the Babel Amendment, it added very little to the machinery of necessary government (even when the history of Israel is followed until the heights of Solomon's glory and splendor are reached).

The Noahic Charter and the Babel Amendment had thus far shown to us the need for law enforcement, a fair judicial system, secure borders and a national language monitor as the only Divinely-established machinery of legitimate government. To these the Law has merely added in degree, and not in principle, except for the necessity of quarantining those with dangerous, infectious diseases (Leviticus 13). But as the under-centralized theocracy eventually proved inadequate for national well-being (Judges 21:25), the slight degree of centralization added by the monarchy proved the necessity of slightly more governmental machinery. These were the annexation and establishment of a capital city (2 Samuel 5:6-10); a centralized, professional military with regional military centers (1 Kings 9:15-19); and the taxation necessary to support these functions (1 Kings 4:7-28).

The close of God's series of revelations regarding the establishment of human government therefore finds us with the idea of an extremely limited and bound model of it, for human government is called upon only to do very few things, with all else being left to the idea of human freedom. Those very few things require very limited governmental expression to be achieved, illustrating that the size and scope of human government should be dwarfed by the freedom and strength of its citizens.

THE BELIEVER'S OFFENSIVE

As Believers, our relationship with God is not based upon compliance to the Law, but upon His loving grace (Ephesians 2:8). Yet let us beware, for we must not allow this wonderful truth to cause us to be cavalier regarding the Law or to dismiss it, for such an attitude is nowhere permitted in Scripture. Jesus taught that the Law will outlive the universe (Matthew 5:18), while Paul taught that the Law is holy, righteous and good (Romans 7:12), and that it is rightly the delight of our inner being (Romans 7:22).

Our God is the Lawgiver. As humanity's Creator, He alone knows best why and how to limit human freedom, and that why and how is finalized through the giving of the Law, which simultaneously establishes appropriate human conduct and the appropriate limitation of human government. The Law does not bind us to Heaven (for grace binds us there), *but the Law does bind all human conduct upon Earth*, and therefore requires our respect, admiration and complicity.

As adopted sons and daughters of God, we can (and should) have no qualms about the imposition of a Divine moral code. Rather, we should fully embrace and submit to this idea, knowing that there is never a need to apologize for the Law, since it springs from the Divine Nature. We should therefore seek to see it implemented as fully as possible and wherever possible. We should exert all due influence to see that our nation's laws are in concert with God's laws, and that our government is in concert with God's idea of government. Anything more or anything less is done at our personal and national peril.

There can be no greater blessing for a people than to live in willing submission to the Law, for it will bring the manifold blessings of Heaven upon that people. Let us be that people, and let us seek to see the influence of the Law spread upon Earth.

BATTLEFIELD: THE NATURE OF GOVERNMENT

Because of the LORD's eternal love for Israel,
he has made you king, to maintain justice and righteousness.
1 Kings 10:9b

Having discussed the Noahic Charter, the Babel Amendment and the Mosaic Amendment (which together form the wonderful and compact Divine Constitution for human government), we are now equipped to move into a more detailed discussion of the very nature of government, for few things today are more in need of Scriptural insight than is this idea.

THE ORIGINAL IMAGE

We are perhaps forever indebted to the Queen of Sheba for her simple and beautiful proclamation of amazement at Solomon's government, in which she so succinctly summarized the whole of appropriate human government, which is *to maintain justice and righteousness* (1 Kings 10:9b). This simple phrase from a stunned Gentile monarch neatly encapsulates both the *why* and *how* of government, and all peoples should heed the wisdom of her words.

Maintaining justice means that all true wrongs are righted, and *maintaining righteousness* means that godly conduct is encouraged, expected and protected. Both of these ideas are stern things and run contrary to the sinful human nature, which leads us to the necessary conclusion that appropriate government is stern in every facet of its existence.

THE IMAGE UNDONE

In order for the ungod to destroy the good exercise of government, then, it's only necessary for him to introduce the concept of compassion into it. Since we have already discussed the issue of the sternness of government in the previous three Battlefields, we now only need to discuss some of the more fearsome roles of government from a Biblical perspective.

JAIL BREAK

Under the Divine Constitution, every aspect of human government is stern in nature. Government is not authorized to forgive; government is not authorized to make life more comfortable; government is not authorized to administer charity; government is not authorized to look the other way; and government is not authorized to turn the other cheek. Government was designed to be stern to lawbreakers, stern in the maintenance of its borders, stern in its sovereignty and protection of its people, and stern in its protection of the Divine Image.

A great example of this sternness is that under the cultural blueprint of the Law of Moses there were no Israelite prisons. Under this Divine system of law, all serious criminal offenses resulted in the death penalty (Leviticus 20), while all minor criminal offenses resulted in swift, stern physical punishment or financial fining, followed by release (Exodus 22; Deuteronomy 25:2,3). If a person regularly committed minor offenses, this was considered a serious offense and also resulted in the death penalty (Deuteronomy 21:20,21). Israelites were given one opportunity at life – if they abused that opportunity by serious or serial law breaking, the government was to sternly see that such people paid for their conduct with their lives.

Since these core requirements of an appropriate criminal justice system are always stern, the ungod will necessarily influence the idea of criminal justice toward compassion, and nowhere is this more evident than in our own criminal justice systems today. It stands to reason that stern punishment of criminals (especially capital punishment) is difficult for compassionate people to stomach, for we would rather rehabilitate and redeem. But Scripture teaches us that if criminals are shown compassion by government, then all of society will soon be overrun by criminal activity (Ecclesiastes 8:11; Deuteronomy 19:19,20).

This is an important and fundamental truth for dealing with the sinful human nature when it turns criminal: Fear of stern and final punishment is the greatest deterrent to criminal behavior in existence, and we ignore such truth to our own peril. Our modern system of criminal justice – with its light sentencing and reasonable, compassionate prison system in which nary an execution occurs for even the most heinous criminals – only serves to destroy all decency in society, for it engenders no fear of law or punishment. Such a system encourages lawlessness, and for this we are truly reaping the whirlwind.

It may pain us to admit it, but the Biblical model is plain: we would quite likely be better off if there were no prison system. Jails may be used to temporarily house those on or awaiting trial, or for the condemned awaiting their execution (which is something that should be carried out quickly once convicted). Those found guilty of minor offenses should be punished and released, while those awaiting execution may be shown only the compassion of the opportunity to repent before God (Luke 23:41-43).

Border Patrol

The sternness of government isn't limited to its own populace, however, but extends to the very idea of its borders, and thereby to its relationship with those of all other nations. Since an international border is the difference between a unique and sovereign nation and all that is outside of it, one purpose of the Biblical idea of borders is that a government might know where its responsibility stops, for nowhere in Scripture is a government tasked with responsibility for a people outside of its borders.

The Israelites were not responsible for the Sidonians, the Syrians, the Ammonites, the Moabites, the Edomites, the Amalekites, the Philistines or the Egyptians. Israel and its government were responsible only for Israel, and for no one outside of its borders. There was *Israel*, and there were the *others*. There was the *us*, and there was the *them*. So must a government's view of its responsibilities be.

Since a government is charged with the safeguarding of the lives, freedom and property of its citizens to the exclusion of all others, this makes the borders of a nation a thing of tremendous importance. From those borders the stern face of a nation's government should therefore stare outward and imposingly at a world of *others*. All such *others* must know that any attempt to cross those borders without permission or with ill intent will be rebuffed, and so too that any severe threat or the actual taking of a nation's citizen's life, freedom or property will be met with the stern fist of justice (however far it may have to travel to impose itself).

The Hellish idea of compassionate government will therefore seek to influence a government into believing that it is somehow responsible for the inhabitants of other nations. When such thinking is embraced, it results in a weakened idea of borders, which will in turn invite challenge from outside of those borders. The Biblical definition of a border, however, tells all outsiders to fear and honor what lies within, for borders maintain national sovereignty, and national sovereignty is necessary in order to promote a higher degree of freedom upon Earth.

WAR FAIR

A government's international responsibility goes no further than protecting the life, freedom and property of its populace from international harm. When there is a severe threat or the actual taking of life, freedom or property committed by the *others*, then, a government is demanded to seek justice on behalf of its populace, for that is government's charter. If such justice is thwarted, it may have to be rectified through the use of appropriate violence by the government of those offended (Judges 3:12-30). If the threat or injustice is severe enough, it may require a government to wage war upon the *others*.

War is not a dirty word any more than is *violence*, for like violence, war may be either appropriate or inappropriate depending upon the context of its use. When war is used to further Evil, it is inappropriate.

When war is used to combat Evil, it is appropriate, and the Scriptures give us clear guidelines in its use.

One manner in which war may be appropriately waged by a nation is simply to protect its people, and is something that may be done either preemptively or reactively. A Biblical example of preemptive national violence is when the Jews rose up and challenged those who would annihilate them on the following day (Esther 8:11,12). An example of reactive national violence is when David was ordered by God into battle against the Philistines, who were attacking the Israelite city of Keilah (1 Samuel 23:1-5).

Justice for the slaying of its people is also an appropriate reason for war. In First Samuel 15, God commanded Saul to exterminate the wicked Amalekites, who had been slaughtering Israelites ever since their flight from Egypt (Exodus 17:8). It is of tremendous importance to note that there is no issue of forgiveness being offered to the Amalekites, for governments cannot forgive or show compassion. The command to *turn the other cheek* (Matthew 5:39) is a personal command, not a national command. Likewise, the command to *love your enemies* (Matthew 5:44) is personal and not national, as governments are not capable of love.

Since no people is responsible for the government of another people, when an unjust system of government arises, the responsibility for that unjust system lies primarily with the people who allowed it to arise in their midst, and they should be left to deal with the consequences of their actions. When the Darkness of that unjust system grows to be problematic to a people's national neighbors, it then becomes appropriate for the national neighbors to put down the threat to their respective populaces. If these national neighbors fall prey to the unjust system themselves (making regional or hemispheric subjugation to Darkness likely), then stern international measures may need to be taken.

The why of government is to protect and honor the image of God, and so when the international spread of Darkness (if left unchecked) threatens the eventual extinction of the Divine Image, this Darkness must then be halted by stern international action, which is something usually accomplished through warfare. All governments that may – and all men that may – must at times stand and be counted lest the Divine Image (which is common to all men) be lost, and all that is good be lost with it.

ROCK 'EM, SOCK 'EM

Having now justified the appropriate use of war, we must tackle the thorny issue of how war should be waged when it becomes a necessity. Since government is stern, warfare must likewise be a stern and awful thing – devoid of the compassion that would make government illegitimate.

There are two very important points that must be understood regarding this deeply sobering subject of study. The first has just been made, but certainly bears repeating: people are responsible for the government they allow to arise over them. If they allow a tyrannical and evil system of government to rule over them (and do not overthrow it), the people of that nation are responsible for the evil that is among them – their hands are not clean. And if that evil should spread to affect or infect the peoples or region around them, their hands are not considered clean either, for they have allowed their borders to fail them. There were wonderful Germans in Germany in the 1930's, but the hands of the German people were not clean, for Hitler arose with their acquiescence. The same is true for many European nations of that time, for they failed to have the strength to repel their neighbor.

The second point to be made is that a government is only responsible for the lives of its people; it owes nothing to the lives of people abroad. When, therefore, a government must take the unenviable step of waging war, it must do so under the firm understanding that the lives of its people are worth more to it than the lives of the people on the other side. This leads us to conclude that the lives of a nation's combatants are worth more even than the lives of the non-combatants of the declared enemy. The combatants' lives should therefore not be put at risk even to save the lives of the enemy's non-combatants.

War is not for the limp-wristed, nor can it ever be a palatable thing of precision and compassion. A war is waged to right a national wrong or to protect the Divine Image from extinction, and it must be done fiercely, quickly and sternly. It is not done to win hearts and minds or to build nations in your image. You wage a fierce war, you devastate your enemy, you make them understand that they never want to have your national blood on their hands again, and that if you have to return it will be worse the next time. Such war is therefore only to be waged when a people, nation or region have it coming to them. When you let them have it, then, make them deathly afraid of crossing you in the future. Then bring your military home. The devastated nation or region can rebuild itself.

After David defeated the Moabites (who were his distant relatives), he put two out of every three captives to death (2 Samuel 8:2) because he knew they would again wage war upon Israel if left alive, as they always had. He was not concerned about winning hearts and minds. And when the national animosity of Moab arose again and continued for hundreds of years more, God ordered that they be overthrown and their land environmentally destroyed (2 Kings 3:19). He did not order Israel to be concerned about winning Moabite hearts and minds, or of rebuilding their nation. They had it coming, and lost their place in the world because of it.

It is insanity to wage palatable, politically-correct warfare, which unnaturally and painfully extends the length of wars, and unnecessarily costs the lives of valiant men while simultaneously imposing a devastating financial burden upon a nation – both of which are demoralizing and sap national heart and resolve. The end result will be a nation that has no stomach for the brutal necessities of war, making it ripe for eventual military conquest by those who do.

THE BELIEVER'S OFFENSIVE

The Divine Constitution not only outlines the limits of human government, but also dictates the nature of it, and human government is fashioned by its Designer to be a thing that is stern from start to finish. As the people of the Word, we need to understand that the idea of compassionate government is Hellish government and must therefore seek to keep compassion and government forever separate.

But without compassion in government, what then of caring for the poor and needy? Simply put, the answer is humanity. Individuals are to show compassion (Luke 10:37), families are to show compassion (1 Timothy 5:8), and churches are to show compassion (2 Corinthians 8:1-15). There is more than enough compassion to go around – especially where Christ has touched the hearts of His followers. We must let government do its stern business, and let compassion rest upon our shoulders.

Religion (not government!) *that God our Father accepts as pure and faultless is this: to look after orphans and widows in their distress...* (James 1:27a).

BATTLEFIELD: THE FORM OF GOVERNMENT

Appoint a king to lead us, such as all the other nations have
1 Samuel 8:5b

No study of government would be complete without remarking upon what form of it is best for humanity, and we shall do that now. But since we have already seen much of anarchy and totalitarianism in previous Battlefields, we will in this Battlefield isolate our focus upon that hideous form of government commonly known as *socialism*, for it is a vampire in desperate need of a stake through its heart. Once that is done, we will have the pleasure of viewing that wonderful form of government best suited to humanity.

THE ORIGINAL IMAGE

As we know only too well by now, the genius of great government is that elusive point of balance where human freedom is limited only to the degree necessary that it will most allow the Divine Image to flourish among a people. This point of balance may be found through study of the Divine Constitution, and so when that Constitution is used by a people as their model for government, there is a tremendous chance that an explosion of High Humanity will occur in their midst.

THE IMAGE UNDONE

The course for the ungod is therefore simple and clear: he must influence the ideologies of human government away from its Divine point of balance and toward either anarchy or totalitarianism. As we are concerning ourselves now with the study of socialism, we'll begin with a look at communism, which is the ungod's perfect example of human government.

WORST CASE SCENARIO

Since the nature of God is central and key to true and good government, the ungod's most obvious and complete success at Hellish government is communism, which is the logical outcome of the institution of government in the hands of atheists. Since atheists reject the existence of God, they believe they are neither beholden to His image nor answerable to Him in either this life or the next. Such utter lack of Divine accountability for human government is a dream-come-true for Hell, and it is therefore no surprise that communism's brief history upon Earth is as brutal and bloody as any that the planet has ever seen, for under communism's iron fist, human freedom is obliterated, and the Divine Image is nowhere to be seen.

GATEWAY DRUG

When the Enemy sees how the Divine Image has flourished in the democratic West, he must find a way to entice such free people into the slavery of his communism, for freedom and dignity gall him to his very core. He does this enticing through the gateway drug of *socialism*, which is typically used as a means of combatting the issue of social inequality (where one person has more than another person). This socialism inevitably leads to economic collapse, after which military conquest or totalitarianism follows, and the brand of totalitarianism most likely to follow is that of communism.

All free people must deal with the reality of social inequality. If they do so apart from an understanding of the limitations imposed upon human government by the Divine Constitution, they will most likely become ensnared by the enticing and Hellish tentacles of socialism, which operate under the guise of *social justice* (where it is attempted to have everyone own the same amount as everyone else). Here we see the idea of compassionate government on steroids, and once that door to compassionate government is opened (even for the noblest of social causes), every seemingly noble cause will follow through that door until every perceived social injustice is righted (by which time either the government will be the owner of all, or all will be equally destitute).

If my neighbor's family of four has three automobiles while my family of four has but one automobile, there is an inequality that exists between our two families. If I (in order to right this inequality) went to my neighbor's home and took one of his cars by force, I would be considered a good socialist by virtue of having cured the social inequality. Yet I would also be expecting a visit from the Sheriff's Department, for although I have equalized things between our two families, I am guilty of theft.

However, if the government passes the Automobile Equalization Act (which taxes those families with three automobiles the amount of one automobile and then deeds that automobile to a family with only one), the same outcome is achieved – both families now have two automobiles. Had I done this deed, I would rightly be guilty of theft. But when the government does this deed, we call it the *redistribution of wealth* or *progressive taxation*, and decree that the government is guilty only of fairness and compassion.

But theft is theft is theft. We may hold Robin Hood up as a hero, yet the truth is that if such a person as he ever existed as we now lionize him, he was a thief then and would still be a thief today. What the principles of Scripture teach us is that any forced redistribution of wealth is wrong and immoral (for theft is wrong and immoral), and is especially reprehensible when committed by or through government, which is the entity created by Heaven to ensure the protection of private property.

VIRTUE TAX

Such a policy of forced redistribution from the have's to the have-not's has the additional effect of elevating poverty into a virtue – an idea that will spell doom for any people. If a group of people is told that they deserve what another group has, it effectively tells them that they are the more virtuous of the two groups. Regarding the poor, when the redistribution of wealth and progressive taxation are instituted, the poor have now been legally proclaimed more virtuous (and therefore more deserving) than the wealthy, and because of this are owed the property and goods of the wealthy.

Since the sinful nature of humanity is lazy and self-serving in the extreme, it will not be long before a large and overwhelming percentage of a nation's citizens rush to become the virtuous poor, causing the non-virtuous wealthy to eventually buckle under the weight of supporting them. This moral collapse into the culture of entitlement will then shortly be followed by economic collapse, for the producers will tire of producing for the sake of the *virtuous* masses. Into such a collapse communism will typically march, for socialism has already done all of the heavy lifting required for communism to comfortably exist.

FAIR AND SQUARE

To prevent this slide into socialism, a government must draw a line between itself and the idea of compassion, and then vow to never cross that line (no matter how compelling the cause may seem). Government is not authorized to provide welfare to its populace, food or housing to its populace, education at any level to its populace, healthcare or retirement to its populace, criminal rehabilitation to its populace, psychiatric care to its populace, foster or special needs care to its populace, disaster relief to its populace, or disaster relief or foreign aid to citizens of other lands. No matter how noble the need, it cannot – and must not – be met by government, for this represents the forced redistribution of wealth (which is simply the pig of theft wearing lipstick).

In order to keep from crossing the line leading to socialism, government must be limited to those few things specifically allowed to it by the Divine Constitution, and must raise the revenue required to do these things in a manner consistent with the nature of God. Here again, the Scriptures come to our aid, for in them we see that each Israelite was required to pay the same percentage on his or her income, regardless of whether they made much or little (Leviticus 27:30), introducing us to the idea of the tithe (ten percent).

Although it is true that the Israelite tithe was not a governmental tax (for it was a cultural tax meant to sustain the Tabernacle and Temple worship), the principle for taxation that it establishes is absolutely undeniable: all are taxed an equal part of their income. No one is taxed less, and no one is taxed more, for all have an equal stake in human freedom and dignity.

High Ground

We now have the pleasure of remarking upon those manifestations of human government that may be considered successful in a Biblical sense, which are the early Israelite theocracy (under which Israel conquered the Promised Land) and the monarchies of David and Solomon. Apart from these we have the dictatorial and democratic forms of government left for study, but before we proceed to those forms of government, we must peer a bit more closely at the success stories we have just mentioned, for the thing they have in common is the key to successful government of any kind.

The commonality between the Israelite theocracy and the Israelite monarchy is the fact that they were both based upon the Law of Moses. This means that regardless of the form of government, they were both effectively *theocracies*, since the nature of God was the basis for their system of law and existence. If any form of government for any people is to be truly successful, then it must likewise be a theocracy *at heart*, and the core of that theocracy must be the Jehovah of Scripture, for only He knows how to appropriately limit the fallen humanity that bears His image.

This theocracy need not (and should not!) be heavy or heavy-handed in nature, such as the kind we now see at the hands of the mullahs in Iran, or once saw at the hands of the papacy in Rome, where individuals claim to rule as God's appointed and inspired stewards. It should, rather, be a *feather-touch theocracy*, where the only theocracy required in that of acknowledging the existence of the God of the Bible, acknowledging that humanity is created in His image, and acknowledging that the purpose of government is to protect that Image among its people. This feather-touch theocracy was, in fact, part of the genius of the founding of the United States.

Regarding the idea of a dictatorship, since there is no significant difference between it and a monarchy (except for the issue of royal blood), it is quite possible for such a form of government to accomplish what God demands of government. All that is necessary is for the dictatorship to be a *theocratic* dictatorship with the nature of Jehovah as the basis for its law and existence. The same is true for any form of democracy, as it needs to be a *theocratic* democracy based upon the nature of Jehovah in order to flourish.

The only forms of government that are never appropriate are therefore those that will not allow the nature of Jehovah to be their basis for existence. In this regard, *theocratic communism* is an oxymoron of the highest order, *theocratic totalitarianism* is not possible, and *theocratic socialism* is laughable. All other forms of government at least have a fighting chance at being appropriate, but these three never will.

THE BELIEVER'S OFFENSIVE

Few things have the potential to elevate the human condition more than does true and good government, and so we must concern ourselves greatly with its form. This means that we must firmly oppose in government all that is outside the boundaries of the Divine Constitution, requiring our opposition to every social program that entails the redistribution of wealth, for we cannot worship God and at the same time condone theft. We must then fill the vacuum of compassion left by government with individual and corporate good deeds and giving.

We are to be the world's greatest proponents of good government, just as we are to be its greatest opponents of poor government. And the nature of our magnificent God is to be the sole criterion by which we judge such things, for theocratic government is the only decent expression of government possible upon Earth.

BATTLEFIELD: RESETTING GOVERNMENT

In the seventh year Jehoiada showed his strength
2 Chronicles 23:1a

The sinful nature corrupts everything with which it comes in contact, eventually corrupting it completely. For this reason, every institution of humanity – no matter how well or nobly begun – must eventually be reset, and human government is no exception to this rule. This brings us (at long last) to the final Battlefield of the Image War, in which we will study how such a resetting of government may be properly undertaken. For if this resetting is never done, the Divine Image and High Humanity will become extinct upon Earth.

THE ORIGINAL IMAGE

Because God is holy, He opposes Evil in all its forms. Opposition to Evil is therefore a requirement imposed upon all Image Bearers, and to oppose Evil in the institution of government is no exception to this requirement. Since a government becomes a tool of Evil when it steps outside the boundaries of the Divine Constitution, it necessarily falls to its populace to rein it back within those boundaries. And if government will not be reined in, then it is to be replaced by whatever means are necessary.

THE IMAGE UNDONE

The Enemy is diametrically opposed to the idea of government existing within the bounds of its Divine Constitution. Because of this, every effort is made by Hell to influence human government into existing apart from this Constitution – something at which the ungod has been only too successful (as we have already abundantly seen). When the reins

---

of governmental tyranny rest in his hands, he will therefore be tenacious and vicious is his opposition to any attempt at reformation, requiring that any movement aimed at resetting government to within Scriptural confines be led with bravery, commitment, strength, wisdom, cunning, planning and the blessing of Heaven.

STOP EARLY, STOP OFTEN

When government oversteps the bounds of its Divine Constitution (and it always will), the response of the governed must be swift, thorough and Biblical in its opposition. If it is not swift or thorough, the tyranny will be emboldened and grow quickly. If the response is not Biblical, the form taken by the new government will likely be worse than the original (1 Kings 12:26-33). Toward the slow or half-hearted response is allied the apathy of the sinful nature, which always wishes someone else will do all things difficult, while toward the non-Biblical response is allied the Lie. Since poor Biblical theology is a facet of this Lie, we must take a closer look at the subject through the lens of Scripture.

When the Bible states that no authority is established but by God (Romans 13:1,2), it doesn't mean that God has *ordained* every specific government or the form it takes. Were this so, such an idea would place the blame for every tyrannical government that has ever existed at the feet of God, who went to great lengths to outline for humanity governmental boundaries that would ensure freedom and blessing. It would also leave us as perpetual slaves to bad and tyrannical government.

It is certainly true that the *idea* of government is God's (as is the mandate that all people be governed), but that they be governed well and according to His blueprint is a choice left up to them. Furthermore, while it is true that submission to authority makes an orderly society possible, not all authority is equally deserving of submission. For instance, God led Israel away from submission to Pharaoh (Egypt's authority) because Pharoah's treatment of the Hebrews was evil (Exodus 1:11-14).

What is required by God is that we submit to governmental authority when it is in keeping with appropriate government (Romans 13:1-7), while we must oppose governmental authority that is a manifestation of inappropriate government (Exodus 1:17; Acts 5:29). Governmental fatalism based upon the first two verses of the thirteenth chapter of Romans plays directly into the hands of the ungod, who has cornered the market on inappropriate government, and who would love to see it emboldened and enshrined by such fatalism (especially at the hands of those who profess allegiance to the Scriptures).

Everyone must submit himself to the governing authorities, for there is no authority except that which God has established. The authorities that exist have been established by God. Consequently, he who rebels against the authority is rebelling against what God has instituted, and those who do so will bring judgment on themselves (Romans 13:1,2) is not the sum total of God's revelation in Scripture regarding the issue of human government. Being salt and light means that we submit to appropriate government and seek to change inappropriate government.

REFORM SCHOOL

Since apathy and fatalism are not allowed by Scripture, the next logical step in the process of resetting government is to seek to reform a current government back to within its Divine Constitution. Of this there are two great examples in Scripture: the Year of Jubilee (Leviticus 25:8-55) and the office of *prophet* in the Old Testament. There is probably no greater practical lesson regarding the resetting of government than the Year of Jubilee, and so we shall study it first.

It must be remembered that as originally designed, Israel had no true central government, and therefore had little chance of being enslaved by it. Yet due to the Fall, life on Earth is tragic and has tragic consequences, and Israel was not excepted from such tragedy. Some Israelites would become impoverished and would either lose their land or become indebted to others – some even to the point of selling themselves and their families into indentured servitude.

But every fiftieth year in Israel the ram's horn would be sounded, and *liberty* was proclaimed throughout the land. At this time every parcel of land was returned to its owner, every debt was cancelled and every servant was set free. In this manner, God codified into Israel's blueprint that there must be an automatic reformation in their nation every fifty years, and this reformation would return Israel to its original state of formation. In effect, everything that enslaved or oppressed the Israelites was automatically reset twice a century.

The lesson taught here is that the tyranny of life's harshness is inevitable even in God's Israel, and government is no exception to this inevitability. Since this is true, there needs to exist the idea of the reformation of government in order for freedom and dignity to survive – something a people disregard at their own peril. Our own nation would be an unfathomably more free nation if every government institution and social program not expressly found in its Constitution were reset to zero every fifty years (or sooner). The wisdom of Scripture is most profound regarding this issue, and the ungod would keep humanity from that wisdom, for the corruption of government is inevitable, and he would not have it reformed or reset back to God's plan.

As a necessary thing, then, reformation is best when frequent and ongoing, and best also when accomplished by non-violent means, for the Year of Jubilee was a fantastically festive time. This preferred non-violence is also taught to us by the prophets of Israel and Judah, who time and time again peacefully pointed out the vast differences between what was represented in Scripture as opposed to what was represented in their cultures and governments. They did this by speaking to the people in order to reform their cultures, and by speaking to their monarchs in order to reform their governments. Both of these illustrate for us that the concept of true reformation necessarily begins with the hearts of all involved.

UNDER THE INFLUENCE

Government is never static, for human nature and the ungod dictate that if left alone, government will automatically trend toward Darkness and become the engine of tyranny. This means that government moves toward the Divine Image only if careful and serious pressure is brought to bear upon the idea of it, mandating Christian involvement in government (for we possess the Scriptures that outline its Divine Constitution).

Nevertheless, Believers have for long been cowed from strenuous involvement in government by the secularists among us, and so a brief discussion on Biblical reformation of government must be undertaken. This process of reformation should begin personally and Scripturally – by which I mean that Biblical change must begin with us before it moves outward. We must first develop Scriptural thinking (Romans 12:2; 1 Corinthians 2:16), and then follow that with aligning our lives with Scripture (James 1:22). We are then to pray for those in government (1 Timothy 2:2) while we personally and corporately repent and pray for our nation (2 Chronicles 7:14; Daniel 9:4-19). After this is done we may then begin to put our government in line with Scripture by imposing the Divine Constitution upon it.

The affairs of Earth are human affairs (Genesis 1:26,28; Psalm 115:16), and since we qualify as human, the affairs of Earth are our affairs. This gives us as much right as anyone to impose our system of values (morality) upon government, for all legislation is an expression of someone's morality. Ours just happens to be the best there is. In light of this we are commanded by Jesus to be *salt* and *light* to a rancid and dark world (Matthew 5:13-16), and to *occupy* until He returns (Luke 19:13 KJV). We must therefore not allow either the world or the ungod to tell us otherwise.

SECESS-FUL

If reformation is unsuccessful, the more serious ideas of secession and revolt may need to be tried, since the tyranny of non-Biblical government can become so entrenched that either a significant portion of the populace or of the government itself refuses reformation toward Biblical principles through peaceful means. When this occurs, sterner and possibly violent action will have to be taken in order to protect and sustain the Divine Image.

When the national government of Israel under Solomon's son

Rehoboam threatened greater tyranny to the people than that experienced under Solomon's latter years, Jeroboam led the ten northern tribes to secede from the nation (1 Kings 12). This was successfully accomplished because the northern faction was numerically far superior than the remnant from which they seceded, and also because their plight was aided by God (who ordered Rehoboam's army to stand down when they wanted to wage war over the issue).

However poorly the Northern Kingdom may have managed its subsequent affairs does not detract from the fact that their cause was just, or that they had Heaven's support. It is also worth noting that the northern faction was able and successful at secession because they had military might, which means that the populace was armed and therefore dangerous to the previous national government. This teaches us the important Biblical principles that a free people in a fallen world must be an armed people in order to remain free (Judges 18:27), and that to secede from a government the secessionists must be well armed.

Tyrants rule by fear and superior force, and superior force is guaranteed for a tyrannical government when it disarms those it governs. When Philistia enslaved Israel, for example, they had so disarmed the Israelite populace that by the time of Jonathan and his armor bearer's famous two-man stand against the Philistine outpost (1 Samuel 14), only Jonathan and his father Saul possessed weapons (1 Samuel 13:22). This allowed a numerically inferior people to rule forcibly and cruelly over a numerically superior people.

Since government tends naturally toward tyranny, it needs to exist in constant fear of the ability of its populace to be done with it – something that can only be done when its populace is stronger and better-armed than the government itself. Superior firepower always makes for a better secession.

How Revolting

Revolution differs slightly from secession in that it is characterized by the actual or attempted overthrow of the current government by force, rather than by divorcing from it. The same elements required for secession are also required here, and so can result in a tremendous amount of bloodshed and loss of life. Revolt (like secession) should therefore not be done for light and transient reasons, but rather should be undertaken only when all attempts at reformation have failed, and when the Divine Image is in danger of extinction within a people due to tyrannical rule.

After being anointed by God as king of the Northern Kingdom, Jehu revolted against the remnants of the House of Ahab (2 Kings 9-10), and although it did not come to outright civil war, it was nonetheless a costly and bloody affair. From the Southern Kingdom comes the revolt of the High Priest Jehoiada, who overthrew the tyrant Athaliah and restored the throne to the rightful House of David (2 Kings 11), costing the tyrant her life.

Revolution thus has Biblical basis, but like secession it is deathly serious business, for tyranny will not go quietly into that dark night (2 Kings 11:13-16). It is a much better thing that a people always keep themselves and their government in check, rather than need to resort to such drastic and terrible measures. But let it be understood that the ungod will not hesitate to use inappropriate violence to overthrow legitimate government or to install illegitimate government, and so those who understand Good must therefore be poised to use appropriate violence in order to return the favor.

THE BELIEVER'S OFFENSIVE

The resetting of human government is a Biblical necessity and reality, for Evil will never rest until all that is Good is gone, and this is as true of government as it is of anything else. Of all people, then, we should be those who keep the closest and most critical eye upon the natural and Hellish trend of government toward tyranny.

But government is also an extension of who we are as a people, and so we must understand that we are as responsible for the form, system and degree of our government as is any other people. Its deficiencies are thus reflections of our own, and so great introspection is needed on our part.

Let us therefore tend first to the Biblical fealty of our own thinking and lives, and then to the reformation of government toward Biblical standards.

When we do so, let us be bold and sure in our efforts, and not cower as our cultural adversaries insist we must. For we are the purveyors of Truth and are the possessors of the Divine Constitution, which is Heaven's blueprint for perfect government, and which needs to be proclaimed and pursued with all of the power we can muster.

Finally, we must understand that in our fallen world a people's freedom is secured when government duly fears the might of its populace. We should therefore be armed and proficient in the use of our weapons, for there is no Divine promise that a people's attempts at peaceful reformation will be successful, or that government will not grow tyrannical if unchallenged. And though it is never to be desired, we must be (as were the Founders before us) prepared with plans of Biblical secession and revolt should governmental tyranny threaten the extinction of the Divine Image in our midst.

V-DAY

PLANTING THE FLAG OF VICTORY

I have fought the good fight...
2 Timothy 4:7a

The end of a war is a joyous occasion for its combatants, but it is also a melancholy thing, for there is no camaraderie upon Earth as deep and moving as that developed by brothers-in-arms through the protracted struggle of war's grievous necessities. When the final salutes have been rendered and the last handshakes given, the hearts of good men will then naturally turn toward home, but those hearts will bear a heaviness for a lost brotherhood that will never again be achieved.

And so it is with us as we come to the end of our study of the Image War, for we have been long and far enough together to have knocked upon the gates of Hell and to have peered into the very heart of Darkness. But our ending here is only the ending of a book, for the Image War wages on and is likely to outlive us, and so we must end our time together with thoughts of victory regarding the matter. War must be fought only and always with a clear definition of victory in mind, and with a war as intractable as the Image War this may seem out of reach. But this is fortunately not the case, for victory in it exists for us in two important ways.

The first of these is contained within the idea of the ultimate victory over Evil, which is shown to us in the final two chapters of Scripture, where God sovereignly vanquishes the Enemy for all eternity. This remarkable ending should have the effect of giving us great hope in our current battle against the ungod, for it teaches us that there is an eventual end to the struggle, and that we are fighting for the stronger side (Romans 8:31).

The second way in which we may know victory is through the idea of good stewardship, which for us means leaving this planet a better place for our having been here. Regarding the Image War, this dictates that in each of our lifetimes we are to see Darkness pushed backward and the standard of Light advanced. The Apostle Paul was a great example of this, for as a soldier in the Image War he knew that he would one day stand before his Commanding Officer and give an account for his efforts, and he was confident of the outcome (2 Timothy 4:7,8). The cause of Evil suffered terribly at his hands.

Advancing the cause of Heaven naturally dictates that the Church must be an aggressive, forward-moving entity with an offensive strategy. When Jesus said that the gates of Hades (Hell) would not prevail against the Church (Matthew 16:18), He put the Church squarely on the offensive, for the gates of a city were stationary and *defensive* by design. And so we now turn our gaze toward securing success in pushing the Darkness back to where it belongs.

UNDERSTANDING THE TIMES

The first thing necessary in order to attain the victory of good stewardship against Evil in our lifetime is to have a realistic view of what is actually transpiring upon Earth. When Israel had been wracked by years of civil war between the strengthening House of David and the weakening House of Saul, there came *men of Issachar, who understood the times and knew what Israel should do* (1 Chronicles 12:32). They – and many others like them – willingly left the House of Saul and *made* David king over a united kingdom, for they knew what God had in mind for Israel. They neither ignored reality nor shirked their earthly duties.

Every few years I take the time to read Tolkien's *Lord of the Rings*. Though by now I know the great story only too well, it still never fails to encourage me and to give me strength for continuing my own small part in the war between Light and Darkness that wages upon our very real planet. What often saddens me as I read it, though, is the realization that too many Believers are so much like the little Hobbits tucked away in their comfortable Shire – oblivious to the great struggle between Good and Evil taking place all around them.

What crown is there for such people, and what glory at the foot of the Throne? God has more respect for open enemies than He does for such lukewarm bystanders, for He will one day vomit the lukewarm out of His mouth (Revelation 3:16). At the Cross, Heaven paid the ultimate cost in perfect Blood to establish a beachhead in Hell's territory; as Heaven's soldiers, we are obligated to that Blood and to that beachhead, and so to the spread of Heaven's Truth from it. The men of Issachar are more needed now than ever. Hell knew Paul's name (Acts 19:15). Does it know yours and mine?

CRITICAL MASS

There is no denying that warfare is a game of numbers (Luke 14:31). For Darkness to be pushed back significantly upon Earth therefore requires a large number of Believers working together under unified leadership and purpose, since the ungod has vast numbers to aid him in his campaign. For instance, although it was God's plan to unify and bring Israel to greatness under the Davidic monarchy (Genesis 49:10; 1 Samuel 13:14), this plan never came to fruition until there were a significant number of Israelites willing enough, committed enough, understanding enough and capable enough to forcibly make it so. Such people had to reach critical mass in order to significantly and visibly push back the Darkness of their day.

It is no different for us in our times, and so we must not only see to the salvation of the lost (by which our numbers are increased), but also see to it that the saved are energized by the reality of the Image War and of their need to take part in it – something that requires deep commitment to the principles of Scripture. Evil will fight tooth and nail for every inch of ground that it holds, and it has a vast fighting force that is highly organized and experienced at its trade. We must be equally or more so.

MUSCULAR FAITH

This issue of the establishment of David's strong and unified kingdom illustrates to us yet again that the affairs of Earth are the affairs of humanity (Genesis 1:26,28), and that although God may have a plan for humanity, it is in large part up to humanity to put that plan into action. For instance, once God had delivered Israel from the bondage of Egypt (something they couldn't do for themselves), He then tasked *them* with physically taking the land from its numerically and technologically superior inhabitants (Numbers 13).

Such a thing not only required faith in God, but it also required the application of worldly muscle – a combination I think of as *muscular faith*. David exhibited great faith in God when he faced and slew Goliath, but he also had to pick up sling and stone in order to do so. The Scriptures do not teach us that if the Lord watches over the city it isn't necessary to have watchmen posted, but rather that both are required (Psalm 127:1b). We must therefore love the Lord *and* be deeply and personally involved in the affairs of Earth.

When viewed through such a lens, we are able to see that the affairs of humanity require muscular faith if Evil is to be lessened upon Earth, and this muscular faith dictates that we valiantly defend the image of God and *force Evil back to its home* (Matthew 11:12; 16:18). We must not be cowed by this world into being pacifists against Evil, for Good and Evil by their very natures do unceasing violence to one another. As followers of God, we have a sworn duty to violate Evil at every turn.

THE WORD OF GOD

Warfare requires battle, and battle requires weaponry. In his exile, David fought with a sword that had no equal in its time (1 Samuel 21:9), and God has likewise given to us the finest weapon available: the Word of God. *For the word of God is living and active. Sharper than any double-edged sword, it penetrates even to dividing soul and spirit, joints and marrow; it judges the thoughts and attitudes of the heart* (Hebrews 4:12), and *all Scripture is God-breathed and is useful for teaching, rebuking, correcting and training in righteousness* (2 Timothy 3:16).

Darkness is merely the absence of Light, and not its equal. The weapon of Light is therefore infinitely more powerful than any weapon wielded by Hell or its followers, and is why the ungod is deathly afraid of the Word of God properly used, for the principles of Scripture appropriately applied to the affairs of humanity will literally destroy the cause of Darkness.

We therefore have superior firepower, we serve a superior Commanding Officer (1 John 4:4), we follow a superior cause (Ecclesiastes 2:13), and we know that we will one day stand completely victorious over our foe (Revelation 20:10). There should be nothing that keeps us from being fully engaged in the fight, and we should have Darkness running for its very life.

The first mention of humanity was done in conjunction with the first mention of the image of God (Genesis 1:26), making the Divine Image the defining issue and characteristic of mankind. It is the duty of those who love the One reflected in that Image to see it strong and vibrant upon Earth, and we must swear undying fealty to the principles and application of the Word of God in order to make this so. Let us see to it, then, and may we see the Divine Image's fair standard advanced greatly by the time each of us draws our final breath. But in our fallen world this must be done by force, for Hell will never give ground without a fight. We are veterans now, you and I, and we know our business. Let us put muscle to faith, then, and let fly the arrows of war yet again.

> *I have fought the good fight, I have finished the race, I have kept the faith. Now there is in store for me the crown of righteousness, which the Lord, the righteous Judge, will award to me on that day — and not only to me, but also to all who have longed for his appearing (2 Timothy 4:7,8).*

EPILOGUE: A NOTE ON GRACE

God's kindness leads you toward repentance
Romans 2:4b

If the contents of this book seem martial, stern and accusatory, it is because the Dark Image needs a proper dressing down, and especially as it relates to infiltration and compromise within the lives of Believers and within the Church. But if its contents have offended you, let me now offer you some softer words.

One of the reasons that it has taken me so many years to finish this work is that as its contents have unfolded they have sorely offended me at nearly every turn. Many was the time when I for long laid down pencil and paper in pain for what the Scriptures were showing me – that I and my life and my thinking and my history were all excellent examples of the Dark Image, and that any slight progress that I have made toward the Divine Image I owe solely to the work of God in me (Ephesians 2:8).

Yet despite the fact that Darkness is (and has always been) so natural to me, I have never found myself being degraded by my Heavenly Father, but have instead been shown a series of unending and unbelievable kindnesses that have led me time and time again to repentance (Romans 2:4b). I would have you experience this same wonderful thing.

Though I hope many who do not know Christ will read and learn from this book, it has been written expressly to those who profess faith in Him and who profess allegiance to His Word. To these I would further remind that the Scriptures are a mirror that would show us our warts and would therefore offend us where we are out of compliance with their teachings. To this we may either submit in humble repentance or resist in sinful arrogance. But remember that this wonderful and necessary wounding by the Holy Spirit is ultimately a wounding of love (Proverbs 27:6), for the repentance it brings would see the Son molded in us (2

Corinthians 3:18), which is our highest and noblest calling. As for me, I have learned to welcome the woundings of Scripture, for I long to be like Jesus, but yet find myself so lacking in this regard.

As for those outside of faith in Christ, I thank you for honoring me by granting enough of your precious time to read this book, in which undoubtedly much of what you believe has been bluntly challenged. When I have labeled certain conduct and ideologies as evil, it in no way is meant to imply that those who hold to such conduct and ideologies *are* evil, for in truth we are all a mixture of the Dark and Divine images, since none of us are perfect (and especially me). But Evil is real, and it would own you heart and soul (Genesis 4:7), and so I humbly beg that you lift your gaze upward and know that the Divine Image beats still within the breast of every descendant of Adam. This Image calls you toward eternity (Ecclesiastes 3:11) and toward eternity's Author, who loves you and has offended you with the kindness of Truth toward repentance of sins (Acts 2:37).

As always,

The LORD bless you and keep you;
the LORD make his face shine upon you and be gracious to you;
the LORD turn his face toward you and give you peace
Numbers 6:24-26
